THE PORTABLE

BAKER'S

BIOGRAPHICAL
DICTIONARY OF
MUSICIANS

THE PORTABLE

BAKER'S

BIOGRAPHICAL DICTIONARY OF MUSICIANS

Nicolas Slonimsky

Edited by Richard Kostelanetz

Assistant Editor: Michael Stutzman

SCHIRMER BOOKS
An Imprint of Simon & Schuster Macmillan
New York

Prentice Hall International
London   Mexico City   New Delhi   Singapore   Sydney   Toronto

Copyright © 1995 by Schirmer Books

Schirmer Books
An Imprint of Simon & Schuster Macmillan
866 Third Avenue
New York, NY 10022

Library of Congress Catalog Card Number: 95-376567

Printed in the United States of America

Printing number
1 2 3 4 5 6 7 8 9 10

Library of Congress Cataloging-in-Publication Data

Slonimsky, Nicolas, 1894–
    The portable Baker's biographical dictionary of musicians /
Nicolas Slonimsky : edited by Richard Kostelanetz : assistant
editor, Michael Stutzman.
        p.   cm.
    Includes bibliographical references.
    ISBN 0–02–071225–0
    1. Music—Bio-bibliography—Dictionaries. I. Kostelanetz,
Richard. II. Stutzman, Michael. III. Slonimsky, Nicolas, 1894–.
Baker's biographical dictionary of musicians. IV. Title.
ML105.S62   1995
780'.92.'2—dc20
    [B]   95-376567
                                                                                  CIP
                                                                                  MN

The paper used in this publication meets the minimum requirements of American National Standard for Information Sciences—Permanence of Paper for Printed Library Materials. ANSI Z39.48-1984 ∞ ™

To Karole Peter Benson,
its sole perpetrator

INTRODUCTION

Johnson is engaged in the impersonal task of compiling a dictionary; but he has made that task personal to himself, has rooted himself in the centre of the work that is to be done, partly by the length and arduousness of his labours but even more so by his unreserved acceptance of his own destiny as an English man of letters.

—John Wain, *Samuel Johnson (1974)*

The first *Baker's Biographical Dictionary of Musicians* appeared in 1900. Its editor, Theodore Baker, was an American, born in New York in 1851, who went to Leipzig to do a dissertation on Native American music. Returning to his homeland in 1890, he worked for the New York publishing house of G. Schirmer, producing not only the first edition of *Baker's* but a second in 1905, among other books. Nicolas Slonimsky arrived in the 1940s to produce a Supplement to the fourth edition, which appeared in 1949. Taking charge, he published a completely revised fifth edition in 1958, a sixth in 1978, a seventh in 1984, and an eighth in 1991. Ever larger than its predecessors, the last has 2115 pages with double columns; containing approximately two million words, it weighs eight pounds. As a one-volume compendium, it has no competitors and probably never will.

Some expository writers produce books; others favor essays. A rare few excel at the art of the entry. What Nicolas Slonimsky (1894–) shares with Samuel Johnson (1709–1784) is the production of classic entries—of concise examples so perfect they survive the author's death-in-life. Just as Johnson's *Dictionary* was reprinted decades after his passing, so can one imagine that Slonimsky's will be. The entries in each are so distinguished stylistically they can be read aloud, not only from friend to friend but lover to lover. On a New York City classical music station in 1994, the announcer celebrated Paul McCartney's birthday by declaiming the entire *Baker's* entry. Not only does Slonimsky make every composer distinctive, he draws a fairly full picture. Slonimsky's *Baker's* not only stylistically transcends virtually all comparable one-volume biographical dictionaries in any field; it makes them look amateur and under-worked, as indeed they no doubt are.

Not unlike Samuel Johnson, Slonimsky has supported himself mostly as an independent writer. Among the striking features they share are encyclopedic knowledge (including many languages), intensity and discrimination in their responses to individual works (and people), and a continually surprising breadth of interests. Both men display a commitment to reasoned and thus persuasive critical judgments that are addressed not to specialists but to common readers, and yet ironic authoritativeness that implicitly acknowledges that a skeptical reader might disagree. Both Johnson and Slonimsky infused an impersonal form with individual style; neither was ashamed of citing his own earlier work as appropriate examples. Even in their elaborate, pedantic digressiveness, Johnson and Slonimsky resemble one another.

Both dictionaries were written, to quote Johnson's preface, "with little assistance of the learned and without any patronage of the great." Whereas forty members of the French Academy took forty years to compile a dictionary, Johnson took only six. Slonimsky could echo Johnson in speaking of *Baker's* as "finished, though not completed." Both men wrote more to publishers' orders than upon their own initiative. Slonimsky resembled Johnson in employing assistants, even though only one name graced the title page; both wrote in spurts to overcome congenital indolence (*pigritude* to Slonimsky). Both were essentially self-educated and spoke English with an exotic accent—Slonimsky's reflecting his Russian birth, Johnson's reflecting his native Staffordshire. (His biographer John Wain reminds us that the latter spoke of liquid punch as "poonsh.") Both revised their masterpieces, Slonimsky producing four new editions over a period of more than four decades. Both did distinguished work in areas other than dictionaries. No other English-language writer known to me, in any field, resembles Doctor Johnson as much as Slonimsky.

The truest measure of Slonimsky's genius for writing entries is that others have written books comparable to his autobiographical *Perfect Pitch* (1988) or even his panoramic *Music in Latin America* (1945), but, no one, not even a multiperson committee, can rival the current incarnation of *Baker's*. The only person who could have written it is Samuel Johnson, alas dead for two centuries and not particularly knowledgeable about music. Considering the two exemplars together, it is hard not to conclude that one measure of a major critic is that he or she writes at least one dictionary.

My job in compiling *The Portable Baker's* is simply to put into one volume (small enough to be held comfortably in one hand) those entries that many readers are most likely to want to consult. These are not necessarily the most stylishly written entries, some of which appeared in the "Biographies" section of my other Slonimsky selection, *The First 100 Years* (1994); these are not the most curious or surprising entries (and thus the best evidence of Slonimsky's stupendous research), some of which also appear in that other volume. No, these are the basic entries, so to speak, most of them written with more information and more flair than can be found in any comparable volume.

In addition to selecting entries, I've abridged many of them, seamlessly I hope, usually of the biographical asides for which Slonimsky is noted (or notorious) and bibliographical references; here and there a few facts were corrected or updated. This book doesn't include Slonimsky's spectacular prefaces, some of which are likewise available in *The First 100 Years* (for which this is becoming an advertisement). Nor does this book give the data, such as lists of compositions, for which the source *Baker's* is invaluable. So, if you as reader don't see something here, may I recommend consulting the original. (If your local libraries don't have the eighth edition, badger them.) Michael Stutzman followed me every step of the way, in addition to preparing computer-readable discs, while Richard Carlin of Schirmer Books cleaned up behind us both, to my gratitude.

Richard Kostelanetz
New York, New York
14 May 1995

ANTHEIL, GEORGE (GEORG JOHANN CARL), remarkable American composer who cut a powerful swath in the world of modern music by composing dissonant and loud pieces glorifying the machine age; b. Trenton, N.J., July 8, 1900; d. New York, Feb. 12, 1959. He studied music theory in Philadelphia, and then went to New York to take lessons in composition with **Ernest Bloch**. Defying the norms of flickering musical conservatism, Antheil wrote piano pieces under such provocative titles as *Sonate sauvage*, *Mechanisms*, and *Airplane Sonata*. In 1922, he went to Europe and gave a number of concerts featuring his own compositions as well as some Impressionist music. He spent a year in Berlin and then went to Paris, which was to become his domicile for several years; he was one of the first American students of the legendary Nadia Boulanger, who was to be the *nourrice* of a whole generation of modernistically minded Americans. In Paris he also made contact with such great literary figures as James Joyce and Ezra Pound; in the natural course of events, Antheil became the self-styled *enfant terrible* of modern music. Naively infatuated with the new world of the modern machine, he composed a *Ballet mécanique* with the avowed intention to "épater le bourgeois." The culmination of Antheil's Paris period was marked by the performance of an orchestral suite from his *Ballet mécanique* in 1926, with musical material taken from a score he wrote for a film by Fernand Léger. He then returned to America as a sort of conquering hero of modern music, and staged a spectacular production of the *Ballet mécanique* at Carnegie Hall in New York on April 10, 1927,

1

employing a set of airplane propellers, eight pianos, and a large battery of drums, creating an uproar in the audience and much publicity in the newspapers. Revivals of the *Ballet mécanique* took place in
New York in 1954 and 1992, but the piece was received by the public
and press as merely a curiosity of the past.

Abandoning all attempts to shock the public by extravaganza,
Antheil turned to composition of operas. His first complete opera,
Transatlantic, to his own libretto, portraying the turmoil attendant on
the presidential election, and employing jazz rhythms, was staged in
1930, in Frankfurt, Germany, arousing a modicum of interest.
Another opera, *Mr. Bloom and the Cyclops*, based on James Joyce's
novel *Ulysses*, never progressed beyond fragmentary sketches. A second opera, *Helen Retires*, with a libretto by John Erskine, was produced in New York in 1934. In 1936, Antheil moved to Hollywood,
where he wrote some film music and ran a syndicated column of
advice to perplexed lovers. Another of his whimsical diversions was
working on a torpedo device, in collaboration with the motion picture actress Hedy Lamar; they actually filed a patent in 1941 for an
invention relating to a "secret communication system involving the
use of carrier waves of different frequencies, especially useful in the
remote control of dirigible craft, such as torpedoes." It is not known
whether the Antheil-Lamar device was ever used in naval warfare.
He continued to write symphonies, operas, and other works, but in
the spirit of the times, reduced his musical idiom to accessible masses of sound. These works were rarely performed, and in the light of
musical history, Antheil remains a herald of the avant-garde of
yesterday.

ARMSTRONG, LOUIS, famous black American jazz trumpeter,
singer, bandleader, and entertainer, familiarly known as "Satchmo"
(for "Satchel Mouth," with reference to his spacious and resonant
oral cavity); b. New Orleans, Aug. 4, 1901; d. New York, July 6,
1971. He grew up in Storyville, New Orleans's brothel district, and
in his youth was placed in the Colored Waifs' Home, where he
played cornet in its brass band. After his release, he learned to play
jazz in blues bands in local honky-tonks; and also received pointers
on cornet playing from Joseph "King" Oliver and played in Edward
"Kid" Ory's band (1918–19). In 1922 he went to Chicago to play in

Oliver's Creole Jazz Band, with which he made his first recordings in 1923; then was a member of Fletcher Henderson's band in New York (1924–1925). Returning to Chicago, he organized his own jazz combo, the Hot Five, in 1925, making a series of now historic recordings with it, the Hot Seven, and with other groups he led until 1928. From about 1926 he made the trumpet his principal instrument.

In 1929 he went to New York again, where he became notably successful through appearances on Broadway, in films, and on radio. From 1935 to 1947 he led his own big band, and in 1947 organized his All Stars jazz combo. In succeeding years he made innumerable tours of the U.S., and also toured widely abroad. He became enormously successful as an entertainer, making many television appearances and several hit recordings, including his best-selling versions of "Mack the Knife" and "Hello, Dolly." Although he suffered a severe heart attack in 1959, he continued to make appearances until his death. Armstrong was one of the greatest figures in the history of jazz and one of the most popular entertainers of his time. For many years, Armstrong gave his birthdate as July 4, 1900, to capitalize on the significance of the date. His style of improvisation revolutionized jazz performance in the 1920s. His unique gravelly voiced renditions of jazz and popular songs became as celebrated as his trumpet virtuosity.

AUBER, DANIEL-FRANÇOIS-ESPRIT, prolific French composer of comic operas; b. Caen, Normandy, Jan. 29, 1782; d. Paris, May 12, 1871. His father, an art dealer in Paris, sent him to London to acquire knowledge of business. Auber learned music as well as trade and wrote several songs for social entertainment in London. Political tension between France and England, however, forced him to return to Paris in 1803; there he devoted himself exclusively to music. Auber's first opera to be given publicly in Paris was *Le Séjour militaire* (1813); six years later the Opéra-Comique produced his new work *Le Testament et les billets-doux* (1819). These operas passed without favorable notice, but his next production, *La Bergère châtelaine* (1820), was a definite success. From that time until nearly the end of his life, hardly a year elapsed without the production of a new opera. Not counting amateur performances, 45 operas from Auber's pen were staged in Paris between 1813 and 1869. He was fortunate in having the collaboration of the best librettist of the time, Scribe, who wrote (alone, or with other writers) no fewer than 37 libretti for Auber's operas.

Auber's fame reached its height with *Masaniello, ou La Muette de Portici*, produced at the Opéra in 1828; its success was enormous. Historically, it laid the foundation of French grand opera along with **Meyerbeer**'s *Robert le Diable* and **Rossini**'s *Guillaume Tell*. Its vivid portrayal of popular fury stirred French and Belgian audiences; revolutionary riots followed its performance in Brussels in 1830. Another popular success was achieved by him with his Romantic opera *Fra Diavolo* (1830), which became a standard work. Despite these successes with grand opera, Auber may be rightfully regarded as a founder of the French comic opera. The influence of Rossini was noted by contemporary critics, but on the whole, Auber's music preserves a distinctive quality of its own. Rossini himself remarked that although Auber's music is light, his art is profound.

AURIC, GEORGES, notable French composer; b. Lodève, Hérault, Feb. 15, 1899; d. Paris, July 23, 1983. He first studied music at the Conservatory of Montpellier, and then went to Paris, where he was a student of Georges Caussade at the Conservatoire and of Vincent d'Indy and Albert Roussel at the Schola Cantorum. While still in his early youth (1911–1915), he wrote something like 300 songs and piano pieces; at 18 he composed a ballet, *Les Noces de Gamache*. At 20 he completed a comic opera, *La Reine de coeur*; however, he was dissatisfied with this early effort and destroyed the manuscript. In the aftermath of continental disillusion following World War I, he became a proponent of the anti-Romantic movement in France, with the apostles of this age of disenchantment, **Erik Satie** and Jean Cocteau, preaching the new values of urban culture, with modern America as a model. Satie urged young composers to produce "auditory pleasure without demanding disproportionate attention from the listener," while Cocteau elevated artistic ugliness to an esthetic ideal.

Under Satie's aegis, Auric joined several French composers of his generation in a group described as *Les Nouveaux Jeunes*, which later became known as *Les Six* (the other five were **Darius Milhaud, Arthur Honegger, Francis Poulenc**, Louis Durey, and Germaine

Tailleferre). Auric soon established an important connection with the impresario Serge Diaghilev, who commissioned him to write a number of ballets for his Paris company. Auric's facile yet felicitous manner of composing, with mock-Romantic connotations, fit perfectly into Diaghilev's scheme. Particularly successful were Auric's early ballets, *Les Fâcheux* (1924) and *Les Matelots* (1925). He also wrote music for the movies, of which his score for *A nous la liberté* (1932) achieved popular success as a symphonic suite.

BABBITT, MILTON (BYRON), prominent American composer, teacher, and theorist; b. Philadelphia, May 10, 1916. He received his early musical training in Jackson, Mississippi, while at the same time he revealed an acute flair for mathematical reasoning. This double faculty determined the formulation of his musical theories, in which he promulgated a system of melodic and rhythmic sets ultimately leading to integral serialism. At Princeton and Columbia universities, he inaugurated an experimental program of electronic music, with the aid of a newly constructed synthesizer. He also taught at the Juilliard School in New York (from 1973) and at various other venues in the U.S. and Europe. Taking as the point of departure **Arnold Schoenberg**'s method of composition with 12 different tones, Babbitt extended the serial principle to embrace 12 different note values, 12 different time intervals between instrumental entries, 12 different dynamic levels, and 12 different instrumental timbres. In order to describe the potential combinations of the basic four aspects of the tone-row, he introduced the term "combinatoriality," with symmetric parts of a tone-row designated as "derivations."

Babbitt's scientific-sounding theories have profoundly influenced the musical thinking of young American composers; a considerable literature, both intelligible and unintelligible, arose in special publications to penetrate and, if at all possible, to illuminate Babbitt's mind-boggling speculations. His original music, some of it aurally beguiling, can be fully understood only after a preliminary study of its underlying compositional plan. In 1982 he won a special citation of the Pulitzer Committee for "his life's work as a distinguished and seminal American composer."

BACH is the name of the illustrious German family which, during two centuries, gave to the world a number of musicians and composers of distinction. History possesses few records of such remarkable examples of hereditary art, which culminated in the genius of **Johann Sebastian Bach**. In the Bach genealogy, the primal member was Johannes or Hans Bach, who is mentioned in 1561 as a guardian of the municipality of Wechmar, a town near Gotha. Also residing in Wechmar was his relative Veit Bach; a baker by trade, he was skillful in playing on a small cittern. Another relative, Caspar Bach, who lived from 1570 to 1640, was a Stadtpfeifer (municipal fifer or flutist) in Gotha who later served as a town musician in Arnstadt. His five sons were all town musicians. Another Bach, Johann(es Hans) Bach (1550–1626), was known as "der Spielmann," that is, "minstrel," and thus was definitely described as primarily a musician by vocation. His three sons were also musicians. J.S. Bach took great interest in his family history, and in 1735 prepared a genealogy under the title *Ursprung der musicalisch-Bachischen Familie*. Bach's father, Johann Ambrosius, was a twin brother of Bach's uncle; the twins bore such an extraordinary physical resemblance that, according to the testimony of **Carl Philipp Emanuel Bach**, their own wives had difficulty telling them apart after dark. To avoid confusion, they had them wear vests of different colors.

When the family became numerous and widely dispersed, its members agreed to assemble on a fixed date each year. Erfurt, Eisenach, and Arnstadt were the places chosen for these meetings, which are said to have continued until the middle of the 18th century, as many as 120 persons of the name of Bach then assembling. At these meetings, a cherished pastime was the singing of "quodlibets," comic polyphonic potpourris of popular songs.

BACH, CARL PHILIPP EMANUEL (the "Berlin" or "Hamburg" Bach), third (and second surviving) son of **Johann Sebastian**; b. Weimar, March 8, 1714; d. Hamburg, Dec. 14, 1788. He was educated under his father's tuition at the Thomasschule in Leipzig; then studied jurisprudence at the University of Leipzig and at the University of Frankfurt an der Oder. Turning to music as his chief vocation, he went to Berlin in 1738; in 1740 he was confirmed as chamber musician to Frederick the Great of Prussia. In that capacity he arranged his father's visit to Potsdam. Abandoning his father's strict polyphonic style of composition, he became an adept of the new school of piano writing, a master of "Empfindsamkeit" ("intimate expressiveness"), the North German counterpart of the French Rococo. His *Versuch über die wahre Art das Clavier zu spielen* . . . (two parts, 1753–1762) became a very influential work that has yielded much authentic information about musical practices of the second half of the 18th century.

BACH, JOHANN (JOHN) CHRISTIAN (the "London" Bach), eleventh and youngest surviving son of **Johann Sebastian**; b. Leipzig, Sept. 5, 1735; d. London, Jan. 1, 1782. He received early instruction in music from his father, after whose death in 1750 he went to Berlin to study with his brother **Carl Philipp Emanuel**. In 1754 he went to Italy, where he continued his studies; he also found a patron in Count Agostino Litta of Milan. He converted to the Roman Catholic faith in order to obtain work, and became one of the organists at the Cathedral in Milan (1760–62). In 1762 he went to England; his highly acclaimed opera *Orione* was given its premiere in London in 1763; in 1764 he was appointed music master to the Queen. When **Wolfgang Mozart** was taken to London in 1764, J. C. Bach took great interest in him and improvised with him at the keyboard. Mozart retained a lifelong affection for him; he used three of J. C. Bach's piano sonatas as thematic material for his piano concertos.

    J. C. Bach was a highly prolific composer; he wrote about 90 symphonies, several piano concertos, six quintets, a piano sextet, violin sonatas, and numerous piano sonatas. In his music he adopted the *style galant* of the second half of the 18th century, with an emphasis on expressive "affects" and brilliance of instrumental display. He thus totally departed from the ideals of his father, and became historically a precursor of the Classical era as exemplified by the works of Mozart. Although he was known mainly as an instrumental composer, J. C. Bach also wrote successful operas, most of them to Italian librettos.

BACH, JOHANN SEBASTIAN, supreme arbiter and lawgiver of music, a master comparable in greatness of stature with Aristotle in philosophy and Leonardo da Vinci in art; b. Eisenach, March 21 (baptized, March 23), 1685; d. Leipzig, July 28, 1750. The word "Bach" itself means "stream" in the German language; the rhetorical phrase that Johann Sebastian Bach was not a mere stream but a whole ocean of music ("Nicht Bach aber Meer haben wir hier") epitomizes Bach's encompassing magnitude. Yet despite the grandeur of the phenomenon of Bach, he was not an isolated figure dwelling in the splendor of his genius apart from the *zeitgeist*, the spirit of his time. Just as Aristotle was not only an abstract philosopher but also an educator (Alexander the Great was his pupil), just as Leonardo da Vinci was not only a painter of portraits but also a practical man of useful inventions, so Bach was a mentor to young students, a master organist and instructor who spent his life within the confines of his native Thuringia as a teacher and composer of works designed for immediate performance in church and in the schoolroom.

Bach attended the Latin school in Eisenach and apparently was a good student, as demonstrated by his skill in the Latin language. His mother died in 1694; his father remarried and died soon afterward. Bach's school years were passed at the Lyceum in the town of Ohrdruf; his older brother Johann Christoph lived there, helping Bach in his musical studies. Stories that he treated Bach cruelly must be dismissed as melodramatic inventions. Through the good offices of the cantor of the Ohrdruf school, Bach received an opportunity to move, for further education, to Lüneburg; there he was admitted to the Mettenchor of the Michaeliskirche. In March of 1703 he obtained employment as an attendant to the Duke of Weimar. He was commissioned to make tests on the new organ of the Neukirche in Arnstadt; in 1703, he was appointed organist there. In 1705 he obtained a leave of absence to travel to Lübeck to hear the famous organist Dietrich Buxtehude.

On June 15, 1707, Bach became organist at the Blasiuskirche in Mühlhausen. On Oct. 17, he married his cousin Maria Barbara Bach, who was the daughter of Johann Michael Bach. On Feb. 4, 1708, Bach composed his cantata *Gott ist mein König* ("God Is My King") for the occasion of the installation of a new Mühlhausen town council; this was the first work of Bach's that was published. Although the circumstances of his employment in Mühlhausen were seemingly favorable, Bach resigned his position in 1708, and accepted the post of court organist to Duke Wilhelm Ernst of Weimar. In 1713 Bach visited Halle, the birthplace of **Handel**; despite its proximity to Bach's own place of birth in Eisenach, the two great composers never met. In 1714, the Duke offered Bach the position of Konzertmeister.

In 1717 Bach accepted the position of Kapellmeister and music director to Prince Leopold of Anhalt in Cöthen, but a curious contretemps developed when the Duke of Weimar refused to release Bach from his obligation, and even had him held under arrest for nearly a month, before Bach was finally allowed to proceed to Cöthen. The Cöthen period was one of the most productive in Bach's life; there he wrote his great set of *Brandenburg Concertos*, the *Clavierbüchlein für Wilhelm Friedemann Bach*, and the first book of *Das Wohltemperierte Clavier*. In 1719 Bach was in Halle once more, but again missed meeting Handel, who had already gone to England. In 1720, Bach accompanied Prince Leopold to Karlsbad. A tragedy supervened when Bach's devoted wife was taken ill and died before Bach could be called to her side; she was buried on July 7, 1720, leaving Bach to take care of their seven children. Bach remained a widower for nearly a year and a half before he married his second wife, Anna Magdalena Wilcken, a daughter of a court trumpeter at Weissenfels, in 1721. They had 13 children during their happy marital life.

New avenues were opened to Bach when Johann Kuhnau, the cantor of Leipzig, died, in 1722. Although Bach applied for his post, the Leipzig authorities offered it first to **Georg Philipp Telemann** of Hamburg, and when he declined, to Christoph Graupner of Darmstadt; only when Graupner was unable to obtain a release from his current position was Bach given the post. He traveled to Leipzig on Feb. 7, 1723, for a trial performance, earning a favorable reception. On April 22, Bach was elected to the post of cantor of the city of Leipzig and was officially installed on May 31. As director of church music, Bach's duties included the care of musicians for the Thomaskirche, Nicolaikirche, Matthaeikirche, and Petrikirche, and he was also responsible for the provision of the music to be performed at the Thomaskirche and Nicolaikirche. It was in Leipzig that Bach created his greatest sacred works: the *St. John Passion*, the Mass in B minor, and the *Christmas Oratorio*. In 1729 he organized at the Thomasschule the famous Collegium Musicum, composed of professional musicians and university students with whom he gave regular weekly concerts; he led this group until 1737, and again from 1739 to 1741. He made several visits to Dresden, where his eldest son, Wilhelm Friedemann, served as organist at the Sophienkirche.

Bach's second son, **Carl Philipp Emanuel**, who served as chamber musician to the court of Prussia, arranged for Bach to visit Frederick's palace in Potsdam; Bach arrived there, accompanied by his son Wilhelm Friedemann, in 1747. The ostensible purpose of Bach's visit was to test the Silbermann pianos installed in the palace. The King, who liked to flaunt his love for the arts and sciences, gave Bach a musical theme of his own invention and asked him to compose a fugue upon it. Bach also presented an organ recital at the Heiliggeistkirche in Potsdam and attended a chamber music concert held by the King; on that occasion he improvised a fugue in six parts on a theme of his own. Upon his return to Leipzig, Bach set to work on the King's theme. Gallantly, elegantly, he inscribed the work, in scholastic Latin, "Regis Iussu Cantio et Reliqua Canonica Arte Resoluta" ("At the King's command, the cantus and supplements are in a canonic manner resolved"). The initials of the Latin words form the acronym RICERCAR, a technical term etymologically related to the word "research" and applied to any study that is instructive in nature. The work, known as *Das musikalische Opfer* (The Musical Offering), is subdivided into 13 sections; it includes a puzzle canon in two parts, marked "quaerendo invenietis" ("you will find it by seeking"). Bach had the score engraved, and sent it to the King on July 7, 1747. It was one of Bach's last works.

Bach suffered from a cataract that was gradually darkening his vision. A British optician named John Taylor, who plied his trade in Saxony, operated on Bach's eyes in the spring of 1749; the operation, performed with the crude instruments of the time, left Bach almost totally blind. The same specialist also operated on George Frideric Handel, with no better results. The etiology of Bach's last illness is unclear. It is said that on July 18, 1750, his vision suddenly returned (possibly when the cataract receded spontaneously), but a cerebral hemorrhage supervened, and a few days later Bach was dead. Bach's great contrapuntal work, *Die Kunst der Fuge*, remained unfinished. The final page bears this inscription by C. P. E. Bach:

"Upon this Fugue, in which the name B-A-C-H is applied as a countersubject, the author died." Bach's widow, Anna Magdalena, survived him by nearly 10 years.

Of Bach's 20 children, 10 reached maturity. His sons Wilhelm Friedemann, Carl Philipp Emanuel, Johann Christoph Friedrich, and **Johann (John) Christian** (the "London" Bach) made their mark as independent composers. It is historically incorrect to maintain that Bach was not appreciated by his contemporaries; Bach's sons Carl Philipp Emanuel and the "London" Bach kept his legacy alive for a generation after Bach's death. True, they parted from Bach's art of contrapuntal writing; Carl Philipp Emanuel turned to the fashionable *style galant*, and wrote keyboard works of purely harmonic content.

The term "Baroque" had a humble origin; it was probably derived from *barroco*, the Portuguese word for a deformed pearl. Originally it had a decidedly negative meaning, and was often applied in the 17th century to describe a corrupt style of Renaissance architecture. Through the centuries the word underwent a change of meaning toward lofty excellence. In this elevated sense, "Baroque" came to designate an artistic development between the years 1600 and 1800. The advent of Bach marked the greatest flowering of Baroque music; his name became a synonym for perfection. Although he wrote most of his contrapuntal works as a didactic exercise, there are in his music extraordinary visions into the remote future; consider, for instance, the A minor Fugue of the first book of the *Wohltemperierte Clavier*, in which the inversion of the subject seems to violate all the rules of proper voice-leading in its bold leap from the tonic upward to the seventh of the scale and then up a third. The answer to the subject of the F minor Fugue of the first book suggests the chromatic usages of later centuries.

In the art of variations, Bach was supreme. A superb example is his set of keyboard pieces known as the *Goldberg Variations*, so named because it was commissioned by the Russian diplomat Kayserling through the mediation of Bach's pupil Johann Gottlieb Goldberg, who was in Kayserling's service as a harpsichord player. These variations are listed by Bach as the fourth part of the *Clavier-Übung*; the didactic title of this division is characteristic of Bach's intention to write music for utilitarian purposes, be it for keyboard exercises, church services, or chamber music. A different type of Bach's great musical projections is exemplified by his *Concerts à plusieurs instruments*, known popularly as the *Brandenburg Concertos*, for they were dedicated to Christian Ludwig, Margrave of Brandenburg. They represent the crowning achievement of the Baroque. Nos. 2, 4, and 5 of the *Brandenburg Concertos* are essentially concerti grossi, in which a group of solo instruments—the concertino—is contrasted with the accompanying string orchestra.

Finally, *Die Kunst der Fuge* (The Art of the Fugue), Bach's last composition, which he wrote in 1749, represents an encyclopedia of fugues, canons, and various counterpoints based on the same theme. Here Bach's art of purely technical devices, such as inversion, canon, augmentation, diminution, double fugue, and triple fugue, at times appearing in fantastic optical symmetry so that the written music itself forms a balanced design, is calculated to instruct the musical mind as well as delight the aural sense.

Dramatic accounts of music history are often inflated. It is conventional to say that Bach's music was rescued from oblivion by **Mendelssohn**, who conducted the *St. Matthew Passion* in Berlin in 1829, but **Mozart** and **Beethoven** had practiced Bach's preludes and fugues. Bach's genius was never dimmed; he was never a prophet without a world. In 1850 the centennial of Bach's death was observed by the inception of the Leipzig Bach-Gesellschaft. Concurrently, the publishing firm of Breitkopf & Härtel inaugurated the publication of the complete edition of Bach's works. A Neue Bach-Gesellschaft was founded in 1900; it supervised the publication of the important *Bach-Jahrbuch*, a scholarly journal begun in 1904. The bicentennial of Bach's death, in 1950, brought about a new series of memorials and celebrations. With the development of recordings, Bach's works were made available to large masses of the public. Modern composers, even those who champion the total abandonment of all conventional methods of composition and the abolition of musical notation, are irresistibly drawn to Bach as a precursor. The slogan "Back to Bach," adopted by composers of the early 20th century, seems to hold true for every musical era.

BALAKIREV, MILY (ALEXEIEVICH), greatly significant Russian composer, protagonist of the Russian national school of composition; b. Nizhny-Novgorod, Jan. 2, 1837; d. St. Petersburg, May 29, 1910.

His mother gave him his first piano lessons; he was then sent to Moscow, where he took piano lessons, studied music theory, and met Alexander Oulibishev, author of a book on **Mozart** (who owned an estate in Nizhny-Novgorod). Balakirev often took part in private musical evenings at Oulibishev's estate, playing piano. In 1855 he went to St. Petersburg, where he was introduced to **Mikhail Glinka**, who encouraged him to continue his musical studies. In 1856, Balakirev made his first appearance as a composer in St. Petersburg, playing the solo part in the first movement of his Piano Concerto. In 1859, his *Overture on the Theme of 3 Russian Songs* and his overture *King Lear* premiered. In 1860, he took a boat ride down the Volga River from his birthplace to the delta at the Caspian Sea. During this trip he collected, notated, and harmonized a number of Russian songs; his collection included the universally popular *Song of the Volga Boatmen*, also known as *Song of the Burlaks* (peasants who pulled large boats loaded with grain upstream on the Volga).

In 1863, Balakirev organized in St. Petersburg a musical group that became known as the Balakirev Circle. Its avowed aim was to make national propaganda of Russian music to oppose the passive imitation of classical German compositions, which at the time exercised a commanding influence in Russia. Simultaneously, he founded the Free Music School in St. Petersburg, and gave concerts that included works by Russian musicians as well as those of recognized German masters. These activities coincided with the rise of a Slavophile movement among patriotic Russian writers and artists, based on the realization of a kinship of blood and the similarity of the Slavic languages.

In 1866, he went to Prague with the intention of conducting Glinka's operas there, but the outbreak of the Austro-Prussian War forced the cancellation of these plans. He returned there a year later and conducted *Ruslan and Ludmila* and *A Life for the Czar*. He took this opportunity to invite several Czech musicians to take part in a concert of music by Russian and Czech composers at his Free Music School; the program included, besides the works by the Czech guests, compositions by **Alexander Borodin**, César Cui, **Modest Mussorgsky**, **Nikolai Rimsky-Korsakov**, and Balakirev himself. The occasion moved the critic Vladimir Stasov to write an article in which he proudly declared that Russia, too, had its "mighty little company" (*moguchaya kuchka*) of fine musicians. The phrase became a catchword of Russian musical nationalism; in general music histories, they came to be known as "The Mighty Five."

But the spiritual drive toward the union with the Western Slavic nations was not the only animating force in the music of "The Mighty Five." It combines, somehow, with the historical drive toward the exotic Muslim lands through the Caucasus to Persia in the South and to Central Asia in the East. Balakirev became fascinated with the quasi-oriental melodies and rhythms of the Caucasus during his several trips there. In 1869 he wrote a brilliant oriental fantasy for piano entitled *Islamey*; its technical difficulties rival the transcendental studies of **Franz Liszt**. His associates, especially Rimsky-Korsakov and Borodin, also paid tribute to the colorful glories of the East, the first in his *Scheherazade*, and the second in his symphonic movement *In the Steppes of Central Asia*.

Unaccountably, during the 1870s, Balakirev slackened the tempo of his work as a composer, conductor, and teacher; he seems to have had trouble completing his scores. He took a series of administrative jobs, and even temporarily discontinued his concerts at the Free Music School. In 1881 he returned to musical activities, and a year later, he conducted at the Free Music School the premiere of the first Symphony by the 16-year-old **Alexander Glazunov**. He also began to work on the revision of his early scores. His *Second Overture on Russian Themes*, originally performed in St. Petersburg in 1864, was revised by Balakirev in 1882 and renamed *Russia*. It took Balakirev many years to complete his symphonic poem *Tamara*, which he conducted in 1883; the score, inspired by Lermontov's poem and permeated by Caucasian melodic inflections, was dedicated to Liszt. He spent 33 years (1864–1897) working intermittently on his Symphony in C, which he conducted at a concert at the Free Music School in 1898; this was his last appearance as a conductor. He completed his second Symphony in D minor between 1900 and 1908. He worked on his first Piano Concerto in 1855 and began the composition of his second Piano Concerto in 1861, but laid it aside until 1909; it was completed after his death by Sergei Liapunov.

During his last years, Balakirev was increasingly unsociable and morose; he became estranged from Rimsky-Korsakov who helped sponsor a rival series of Russian Symphony Concerts to the ones held at the Free Music School, which attracted a number of younger Russian composers. Their quarrel reached such lamentable extremes that they did not even greet each other at public places or at concerts. Still, Rimsky-Korsakov continued to perform Balakirev's music at his concerts. Balakirev made a tremendous impact on the destinies of Russian music, particularly because of his patriotic conviction that Russia could rival Germany and other nations in the art of music. But he left fewer works than his long life would have justified, and they are rarely performed.

BARBER, SAMUEL, American composer of superlative gifts; b. West Chester, Pennsylvania, March 9, 1910; d. New York, Jan. 23, 1981. His mother was a good pianist; her sister was the famous opera contralto Louise Homer. At the time when most American composers exerted their ingenuity writing sophisticated music laced with unresolvable dissonances, Barber kept aloof from facile and fashionable modernism. He adopted an idiom, lyrical and romantic in nature, which had a distinct originality in its melodic and harmonic aspects. His *Overture to the School for Scandal*, after Sheridan (1933), attracted favorable attention. It was closely followed by *Music for a Scene from Shelley*, which had numerous performances. In 1938, Arturo Toscanini conducted the NBC Symphony Orchestra in Barber's *Essay for Orchestra No. 1* and *Adagio for Strings* (arranged from Barber's String Quartet); the *Adagio* was destined to become one of the most popular American works of serious music, and through some lurid aberration of circumstance, it also became a favorite selection at state funerals.

Barber served in the air force in World War II, and was discharged in 1945, settling in Mount Kisco, New York, in a house (named "Capricorn") that he had purchased jointly with **Gian Carlo Menotti** in 1943. Barber was always devoted to the art of the theater. He wrote a ballet, *The Serpent Heart*, for Martha Graham (1946), which was later revised and produced by her group under the title *Cave of the Heart*. From it he drew an orchestral suite, *Medea*; a further version of the music was *Medea's Meditation* and *Dance of Vengeance*. In his *Prayers of Kierkegaard* for Soprano, Chorus, and Orchestra (1954), Barber essayed the style of modern oratorio. But it was not until 1957 that he wrote his first opera, *Vanessa*, with a romantic libretto by his lifelong friend Menotti; it was produced by the Metropolitan Opera in New York in 1958.

Barber was gloriously vindicated as an important composer by a succession of fine works of instrumental music. Particularly notable was his Piano Concerto (1962), a striking work in an original modern idiom, spontaneously acclaimed in repeated performances in America and Europe, which won him his second Pulitzer Prize. No less remarkable was his Piano Sonata, introduced by Vladimir Horowitz in 1949; in it, Barber made ample use of modernistic resources, including incidental applications of 12-tone writing. Another example of Barber's brilliant use of pianistic resources was his witty piano suite *Excursions* (1945).

Barber excelled in new American music primarily as a melodist; perhaps the circumstance that he studied singing as a youth had contributed to his sensitive handling of vocally shaped patterns. Although the harmonic structures of his music remained fundamentally tonal, he made free use of chromatic techniques, verging on atonality and polytonality, while his mastery of modern counterpoint enabled him to write canons and fugues in effective neo-Baroque sequences. His orchestration was opulent without being turgid; his treatment of solo instruments was unfailingly congenial to their nature even though requiring a virtuoso technique.

BARTÓK, BÉLA, great Hungarian composer; b. Nagyszentmiklós, March 25, 1881; d. New York, Sept. 26, 1945. His father was a school headmaster; his mother was a proficient pianist, and he received his first piano lessons from her. He began playing the piano in public at the age of 11. In 1894 the family moved to Pressburg, where he took piano lessons with László Erkel, son of the famous Hungarian opera composer; he also studied harmony with Anton Hyrtl. In 1899 he enrolled at the Royal Academy of Music in Budapest, where he studied piano and composition; he graduated in 1903. His earliest compositions reveal the combined influence of **Franz Liszt, Johannes Brahms,** and **Richard Strauss**; however, he soon became interested in exploring the resources of national folk music, which included not only Hungarian melorhythms but also elements of other ethnic strains in his native Transylvania, including Romanian and Slovak. He formed a cultural friendship with **Zoltán Kodály**, and together they traveled through the land collecting folk songs, which they published in 1906. His interest in folk-song research led him to tour

North Africa in 1913. In 1919 he served as a member of the musical directorate of the short-lived Hungarian Democratic Republic with Ernst Dohnányi and Kodály; Bartók was also deputy director of the Academy of Music. Although a brilliant pianist, he limited his concert programs mainly to his own compositions; he also gave concerts playing works for two pianos with his second wife, Ditta Pásztory.

In his own compositions he soon began to feel the fascination of tonal colors and impressionistic harmonies as cultivated by **Claude Debussy** and other modern French composers. The basic texture of his music remained true to tonality, which he expanded to chromatic polymodal structures and unremittingly dissonant chordal combinations. In his piano works he exploited the extreme registers of the keyboard, often in the form of tone clusters to simulate pitchless drumbeats. He made use of strong asymmetrical rhythmic figures suggesting the modalities of Slavic folk music, a usage that imparted a somewhat acrid coloring to his music. The melodic line of his works sometimes veered toward atonality in its chromatic involutions. In some instances he employed melodic figures comprising the 12 different notes of the chromatic scale; however, he never adopted the integral techniques of the 12-tone method.

Bartók toured the U.S. as a pianist from Dec. 1927 to Feb. 1928, and the Soviet Union in 1929. He resigned his position at the Budapest Academy of Music in 1934, but continued his research work in ethnomusicology as a member of the Hungarian Academy of Sciences, where he was engaged in the preparation of the monumental *Corpus Musicae Popularis Hungaricae*. With the outbreak of World War II, Bartók decided to leave Europe; in the fall of 1940 he went to the U.S., where he remained until his death from polycythemia. In 1940 he received an honorary Ph.D. from Columbia University; he also did folk-song research there as a visiting assistant in music (1941–42). His last completed score, the *Concerto for Orchestra*, commissioned by the Boston Symphony's conductor Serge Koussevitzky, proved to be his most popular work. His Third Piano Concerto was virtually completed at the time of his death, except for the last 17 bars, which were arranged and orchestrated by his pupil Tibor Serly.

Far from being a cerebral purveyor of abstract musical designs, Bartók was an ardent student of folkways, seeking the roots of meters, rhythms, and modalities in the spontaneous songs and dances of the people. Indeed, he regarded his analytical studies of popular melodies as his most important contribution to music. Even during the last years of his life, already weakened by illness, he applied himself assiduously to the arrangement of Serbo-Croatian folk melodies of Yugoslavia from recordings placed in his possession. He was similarly interested in the natural musical expression of children; he firmly believed that they are capable of absorbing modalities and asymmetrical rhythmic structures with greater ease than adults trained in the rigid disciplines of established music schools. His remarkable collection of piano pieces entitled, significantly, *Mikrokosmos* was intended as a method to initiate beginners into the world of unfamiliar tonal and rhythmic combinations; in this he provided a parallel means of instruction to the Kodály method of schooling.

BEACH, MRS. H.H.A. (née **Amy Marcy Cheney**), American composer; b. Henniker, New Hampshire, Sept. 5, 1867; d. New York, Dec. 27, 1944. Beach was descended of early New England colonists, and was a scion of a cultural family. She entered a private school in Boston, while also studying piano and harmony. She made her debut as a pianist in Boston on Oct. 24, 1883, playing a concerto by Ignaz Moscheles. On Dec. 3, 1885, at the age of 18, she married Dr. H.H.A. Beach, a Boston surgeon, a quarter of a century older than she was. The marriage was a happy one, and as a token of her loyalty to her husband, she used as her professional name Mrs. H.H.A. Beach. She began to compose modestly, mostly for piano, but soon embarked on an ambitious project, a Mass, which was performed by the Handel and Haydn Society in Boston in 1892; she was the first woman to have a composition performed by that organization. Her *Gaelic Symphony* (1896), based on Irish folk tunes, was performed by the Boston Symphony with exceptional success. In 1897 she played her Violin Sonata with Franz Kneisel. On April 6, 1900, she appeared as the soloist with the Boston Symphony in the first performance of her Piano Concerto. She also wrote a great many songs in an endearing Romantic manner. Her husband died in 1910, and Mrs. Beach decided to go to Europe; she played her works in Berlin, Leipzig, and Hamburg, attracting considerable attention as the first of her sex and national origin to be able to compose music of a European quality of excellence. She returned to the U.S. in 1914 and lived in

New York. Her music, unpretentious in its idiom and epigonic in its historical aspect, retained its importance as the work of a pioneer woman composer in America.

BEETHOVEN, LUDWIG VAN, the great German composer whose unsurpassed genius, expressed with supreme mastery in his symphonies, chamber music, concertos, and piano sonatas, revealing an extraordinary power of invention, marked a historic turn in the art of composition; b. Bonn, Dec. 15 or 16 (baptized, Dec. 17), 1770; d. Vienna, March 26, 1827. His first important teacher of composition was Christian Gottlob Neefe, a thorough musician who seemed to understand his pupil's great potential even in his early youth. He guided Beethoven in the study of **J. S. Bach** and encouraged him in keyboard improvisation. At the age of 12, in 1782, Beethoven composed *Nine Variations for Piano on a March of Dressler*, his first work to be published. In 1783, he played the cembalo in the Court Orchestra in Bonn; in 1784, the Elector Maximilian Franz officially appointed him to the post of deputy court organist, a position he retained until 1792; from 1788 to 1792, Beethoven also served as a violist in theater orchestras. In 1787, the Elector sent him to Vienna, where he stayed for a short time; the report that he played for **Mozart** and that Mozart pronounced him a future great composer seems to be a figment of somebody's eager imagination. After a few weeks in Vienna, Beethoven went to Bonn when he received news that his mother was gravely ill; she died on July 17, 1787. He was obliged to provide sustenance for his two younger brothers; his father, who took to drink in excess, could not meet his obligations.

In 1790 an event of importance took place in Beethoven's life when **Haydn** was honored in Bonn by the Elector on his way to London; it is likely that Beethoven was introduced to him, and that Haydn encouraged him to come to Vienna to study with him. Beethoven went to Vienna in Nov. 1792, and began his studies with Haydn. In the meantime, Haydn had to go to London again, and Beethoven's lessons with him were discontinued. Instead, Beethoven began a formal study of counterpoint with Johann Georg Albrechtsberger, a learned musician and knowledgeable pedagogue; these studies continued for about a year, until 1795. Furthermore, Beethoven took lessons in vocal composition with the illustrious

Italian composer Antonio Salieri, who served as Imperial Kapell-meister at the Austrian court.

Beethoven was fortunate to find a generous benefactor in Prince Karl Lichnowsky, who awarded him, beginning about 1800, an annu-al stipend of 600 florins; he was amply repaid for this bounty by entering the pantheon of music history through Beethoven's dedica-tion to him of the *Sonate pathétique* and other works, as well as his first opus number, a set of three piano trios. Another aristocrat, Prince Razumovsky, the Russian ambassador to Vienna, played an important role in Beethoven's life. From 1808 to 1816 he main-tained in his residence a string quartet in which he himself played the second violin. Beethoven dedicated to him his three string quar-tets, which became known as the Razumovsky quartets, in which Beethoven made use of authentic Russian folk themes.

Beethoven made his first public appearance in Vienna on March 29, 1795, as soloist in one of his piano concertos (probably the B-flat major Concerto, op. 19). In 1796 he played in Prague, Dresden, Leipzig, and Berlin. He also participated in "competitions," fashionable at the time, with other pianists, which were usually held in aristocratic salons. On April 2, 1800, he presented a concert of his works in the Burgtheater in Vienna, at which his First Symphony, in C major, and the Septet in E-flat major were performed for the first time. Other compositions at the threshold of the century were the Piano Sonata in C minor, op. 13, the *Pathétique*; the C-major Piano Concerto, op. 15; "sonata quasi una fantasia" for Piano in C-sharp minor, op. 27, celebrated under the nickname *Moonlight Sonata* (so described by a romantically inclined critic but not specifi-cally accepted by Beethoven); and the D-major Piano Sonata known as *Pastoral*.

Belgian musicologist François-Joseph Fétis was the first to sug-gest the division of Beethoven's compositions into three stylistic peri-ods. It was left to Wilhelm von Lenz to fully elucidate this view in his *Beethoven et ses trois styles* (1852). Despite this arbitrary chronological division, the work became firmly established in Beethoven literature. According to Lenz, the first period embraced Beethoven's works from his early years to the end of the 18th century, marked by a style closely related to the formal methods of Haydn. The second period, cover-ing the years 1801–14, was signaled by a more personal, quasi-Romantic mood, beginning with the *Moonlight Sonata*; the last period, extending from 1814 to Beethoven's death in 1827, comprised the most individual, unconventional, and innovative works, such as his last string quartets and the Ninth Symphony, with its extraordinary choral finale.

Beethoven's early career in Vienna was marked by fine success; he was popular not only as a virtuoso pianist and a composer, but also as a social figure who was welcome in aristocratic circles. But Beethoven's progress was fatefully affected by a mysteriously growing deafness, which reached a crisis in 1802. On Oct. 8 and 10, 1802, he wrote a poignant document known as the "Heiligenstadt Testament," for it was drawn in the village of Heiligenstadt, where he resided at the time. The document, not discovered until after Beethoven's death, voiced his despair at the realization that the most important sense of his being, the sense of hearing, was inexorably failing. He implored his brothers, in case of his early death, to consult his physician, Dr. Schmidt, who knew the secret of his "lasting malady" contracted six years before he wrote the Testament, i.e., in 1796. The etiology of his illness leaves little doubt that the malady was the dreaded "lues," with symptoms including painful intestinal disturbances, enormous enlargement of the pancreas, cirrhosis of the liver, and, most ominously, the porous degeneration of the roof of the cranium. However, the impairment of his hearing may have had an independent cause: an otosclerosis, resulting in the shriveling of the auditory nerves and concomitant dilation of the accompanying arteries. Externally, there were signs of tinnitus, a constant buzzing in the ears, about which Beethoven complained. His reverential biographer A.W. Thayer states plainly that it was known to several friends of Beethoven that the cause of his combined ailments was syphilis.

It is remarkable that under these conditions Beethoven was able to continue his creative work with his usual energy. There were few periods of interruption in the chronology of his list of works, and similarly there is no apparent influence of his moods of depression on the content of his music; tragic and joyful musical passages had equal shares in his inexhaustible flow of varied works. In 1803, Beethoven presented a concert of his compositions in Vienna at which he was soloist in his Third Piano Concerto; the program also contained performances of his Second Symphony and of the oratorio *Christus am Oelberge*. On May 24, he played in Vienna the piano part of his Violin Sonata, op. 47, known as the *Kreutzer Sonata*, although Kreutzer himself did not introduce it; in his place the violin part was taken by the mulatto artist George Bridgetower.

During the years 1803 and 1804 Beethoven composed his great Symphony No. 3, in E-flat major, op. 55, the *Eroica*. It has an interesting history. Beethoven's disciple Ferdinand Ries relates that Beethoven tore off the title page of the manuscript of the score originally dedicated to Napoleon, after learning of his proclamation as Emperor of France in 1804, and supposedly exclaimed, "So he is a tyrant like all the others after all!" Ries reported this story shortly before his death, some 34 years after the composition of the *Eroica*, which throws great doubt on its credibility. Indeed, in a letter to the publishing firm of Breitkopf & Härtel, dated Aug. 26, 1804, long after Napoleon's proclamation of Empire, Beethoven still refers to the title of the work as "really Bonaparte." In Oct. 1806, when the first edition of the orchestral parts was published in Vienna, the symphony received the title "Sinfonia eroica composta per festeggiare il sovvenire d'un grand' uomo" ("heroic symphony, composed to celebrate the memory of a great man"). Napoleon was very much alive and was still leading his Grande Armée to new conquests, so the title would not apply. Yet, the famous funeral march in the score expressed a sense of loss and mourning. The mystery remains.

In 1803 Emanuel Schikaneder, manager of the Theater an der Wien, asked Beethoven to compose an opera to a libretto he had prepared under the title *Vestas Feuer* (The Vestal Flame), but he soon lost interest in the project and instead began work on another opera, based on J.N. Bouilly's *Léonore, ou L'Amour conjugal*. The completed opera was named *Fidelio*, which was the heroine's assumed name in her successful efforts to save her imprisoned husband. The opera was given at the Theater an der Wien on Nov. 20, 1805, under difficult circumstances, a few days after the French army entered Vienna. There were only three performances before the opera was rescheduled for March 29 and April 10, 1806; after another long hiatus a greatly revised version of *Fidelio* was produced on May 23, 1814. Beethoven wrote three versions of the Overture for Léonore; for another performance, on May 26, 1814, he revised the overture once more, and this time it was performed under the title *Fidelio Overture*.

An extraordinary profusion of creative masterpieces marked the years 1802–8 in Beethoven's life. During these years he brought out the three String Quartets, op. 59, dedicated to Count Razumovsky;

the Fourth, Fifth, and Sixth Symphonies; the Violin Concerto; the Fourth Piano Concerto; the Triple Concerto; the *Coriolan Overture*; and a number of piano sonatas, including the D minor, op. 31; No. 2, the *Tempest*; the C major, op. 53, the *Waldstein*; and the F minor, op. 57, the *Appassionata*. On Dec. 22, 1808, his Fifth and Sixth Symphonies were heard for the first time at a concert in Vienna; the concert lasted some four hours. Still, financial difficulties beset Beethoven. The various annuities from patrons were uncertain, and the devaluation of the Austrian currency played havoc with his calculations. In Oct. 1808, King Jerome Bonaparte of Westphalia offered the composer the post of Kapellmeister of Kassel at a substantial salary, but Beethoven decided to remain in Vienna.

Between 1809 and 1812, Beethoven wrote his Fifth Piano Concerto; the String Quartet in E-flat major, op. 74; the incidental music to Goethe's drama *Egmont*; the Seventh and Eighth Symphonies; and his Piano Sonata in E-flat major, op. 81a, whimsically subtitled "Das Lebewohl, Abwesenheit und Wiedersehn," also known by its French subtitle, "Les Adieux, l'absence, et le retour." He also added a specific description to the work, "Sonate caractéristique." This explicit characterization was rare with Beethoven; he usually avoided programmatic descriptions, preferring to have his music stand by itself. Even in his Sixth Symphony, the *Pastoral*, which bore specific subtitles for each movement and had the famous imitations of birds singing and the realistic portrayal of a storm, Beethoven decided to append a cautionary phrase: "More as an expression of one's feelings than a picture."

Beethoven specifically denied that the famous introductory call in the Fifth Symphony represented the knock of Fate at his door, but the symbolic association was too powerful to be removed from the legend; yet the characteristic iambic tetrameter was anticipated in several of Beethoven's works, among them the *Appassionata* and the Fourth Piano Concerto. **Carl Czerny**, who was close to Beethoven in Vienna, claimed that the theme was derived by Beethoven from the cry of the songbird Emberiza, or Emmerling, a species to which the common European goldfinch belongs, which Beethoven may have heard during his walks in the Vienna woods, a cry that is piercing enough to compensate for Beethoven's loss of aural acuity. However that may be, the four-note motif became inexorably connected with the voice of doom for enemies and the exultation of the victor in battle. Another famous nicknamed work by Beethoven was the *Emperor Concerto*, a label attached to the Fifth Piano Concerto, op. 73. He wrote it in 1809, when Napoleon's star was still high in the European firmament, and some publicist decided that the martial strains of the music, with its sonorous fanfares, must have been a tribute to the Emperor of the French.

Beethoven exaggerated his poverty; he possessed some shares and bonds which he kept in a secret drawer. He was untidy in personal habits: he often used preliminary drafts of his compositions to cover the soup and even the chamber pot, leaving telltale circles on the manuscripts. He was strangely naive; he studiously examined the winning numbers of the Austrian government lottery, hoping to find a numerological clue to a fortune for himself. His handwriting was all but indecipherable. The copying of his manuscripts presented difficulties; not only were the notes smudged, but sometimes Beethoven even failed to mark a crucial accidental. A copyist said that he would rather copy 20 pages of Rossini than a single page of Beethoven. On the other hand, Beethoven's sketchbooks, containing many alternative drafts, are extremely valuable, for they introduce a scholar into the inner sanctum of Beethoven's creative process.

Gallons of ink have been unnecessarily expended on the crucial question of Beethoven's relationship with women. That Beethoven dreamed of an ideal life companion is clear from his numerous utterances and candid letters to friends, in some of which he asked them to find a suitable bride for him. But there is no inkling that he kept company with any particular woman in Vienna. Beethoven lacked social graces: he could not dance; he was unable to carry on a light conversation about trivia; and behind it all there was the dreadful reality of his deafness. He could speak, but could not always understand when he was spoken to. With close friends he used an unwieldy ear trumpet; but such contrivances were obviously unsuitable in a social gathering. There were several objects of his secret passions among his pupils or the society ladies to whom he dedicated his works. But somehow he never actually proposed marriage, and they usually married less hesitant suitors.

It was inevitable that Beethoven should seek escape in fantasies. The greatest of these fantasies was the famous letter addressed to an "unsterbliche Geliebte," the "Immortal Beloved," couched in exuberant emotional tones characteristic of the sentimental romances of the time, and strangely reminiscent of Goethe's novel *The Sorrows of Young Werther*. The letter was never mailed; it was discovered in the secret compartment of Beethoven's writing desk after his death. The clues to the identity of the object of his passion were maddeningly few. He voiced his fervid anticipation of an impending meeting at some place indicated only by the initial letter "K."; he dated his letter as Monday, the Sixth of July, without specifying the year. Eager Beethoveniacs readily established that the most likely year was 1812, when July 6 fell on a Monday. A complete inventory of ladies of Beethoven's acquaintance from 14 to 40 years of age was laid out, and the lengthy charade unfolded, lasting one and a half centuries. The most likely "Immortal Beloved" seemed to be Antoine Brentano, the wife of a merchant. But Beethoven was a frequent visitor at their house; his letters to her (sent by ordinary city post) and her replies expressed mutual devotion, but they could not be stylistically reconciled with the torrid protestation of undying love in the unmailed letter. And if indeed Frau Brentano was the "Immortal Beloved," why could not a tryst have been arranged in Vienna when her husband was away on business?

The so-called third style of Beethoven was assigned by biographers to the last 10 or 15 years of his life. It included the composition of his monumental Ninth Symphony, completed in 1824 and first performed in Vienna in 1824; the program also included excerpts from the *Missa Solemnis* and *Die Weihe des Hauses* (The Consecration of the House). It was reported that Caroline Unger, the contralto soloist in the *Missa Solemnis*, had to pull Beethoven by the sleeve at the end of the performance so that he would acknowledge the applause he could not hear. With the Ninth Symphony, Beethoven completed the evolution of the symphonic form as he envisioned it. Its choral finale was his manifesto addressed to the world at large, to the text from Schiller's ode *An die Freude* ("To Joy"). In it, Beethoven, through Schiller, appealed to all humanity to unite in universal love. Here a musical work, for the first time, served a political ideal. Beethoven's last string quartets, opp. 127, 130, 131, and 132, served as counterparts of his last symphony in their striking innovations, dramatic pauses, and novel instrumental tone colors.

In Dec. 1826, on his way back to Vienna from a visit in Gneixendorf, Beethoven was stricken with a fever that developed into a mortal pleurisy. Dropsy and jaundice supervened to this condition;

surgery to relieve the accumulated fluid in his organism was unsuccessful, and he died on the afternoon of March 26, 1827. It was
widely reported that an electric storm struck Vienna as Beethoven
lay dying. Its occurrence was indeed confirmed by the contemporary
records in the Vienna weather bureau, but the story that he raised his
clenched fist aloft as a gesture of defiance to an overbearing Heaven
must be relegated to fantasy. He was far too feeble either to clench
his fist or to raise his arm.

Beethoven's music marks a division between the Classical period of the 18th century, exemplified by the great names of Mozart
and Haydn, and the new spirit of Romantic music that characterized
the entire course of the 19th century. There are certain purely external factors that distinguish these two periods of musical evolution;
one of them pertains to sartorial matters. Music before Beethoven
was *Zopfmusik*, pigtail music. Haydn and Mozart are familiar to us by
portraits in which their heads are crowned by elaborate wigs;
Beethoven's hair was by contrast luxuriant in its unkempt splendor.
The music of the 18th century possessed the magnitude of mass production. The accepted number of Haydn's symphonies, according to
his own count, is 104, but even in his own catalogue Haydn allowed a
duplication of one of his symphonic works. Mozart wrote about 40
symphonies during his short lifetime. Haydn's symphonies were
constructed according to an easily defined formal structure; while
Mozart's last symphonies show greater depth of penetration, they do
not depart from the Classical convention. Besides, both Haydn and
Mozart wrote instrumental works variously entitled cassations, serenades, divertimentos, and suites, which were basically synonymous
with symphonies.

Beethoven's symphonies were few in number and mutually different. The first and second symphonies may still be classified as
Zopfmusik, but with the Third Symphony he entered a new world of
music. No symphony written before had contained a clearly defined
funeral march. Although the Fifth Symphony had no designated
program, it lent itself easily to programmatic interpretation. **Wagner**
attached a bombastic label, "Apotheosis of the Dance," to Beethoven's Seventh Symphony; the Eighth Symphony Beethoven called
his "little symphony," and the Ninth is usually known as the *Choral*
Symphony. With the advent of Beethoven, the manufacture of symphonies en masse had ceased; **Schumann, Brahms, Tchaikovsky**, and

their contemporaries wrote but a few symphonies each, and each had a distinctive physiognomy. Beethoven had forever destroyed *Zopf-musik*, and opened the floodgates of the Romantic era.

Similarly novel were Beethoven's string quartets; a musical abyss separated his last string quartets from his early essays in the same form. Trios, violin sonatas, cello sonatas, and the 32 great piano sonatas also represent evolutionary concepts. Yet Beethoven's melody and harmony did not diverge from the sacrosanct laws of euphony and tonality. The famous dissonant chord introducing the last movement of the Ninth Symphony resolves naturally into the tonic, giving only a moment's pause to the ear. Beethoven's favorite device of pairing the melody in the high treble with triadic chords in close harmony in the deep bass was a peculiarity of his style but not necessarily an infringement of the Classical rules. Yet contemporary critics found some of these practices repugnant and described Beethoven as an eccentric bent on creating unconventional sonorities. Equally strange to the untutored ear were pregnant pauses and sudden modulations in his instrumental works.

Beethoven was not a contrapuntist by taste or skill. With the exception of his monumental *Grosse Fuge*, composed as the finale of the String Quartet, op. 133, his fugal movements were usually free canonic imitations. There is only a single instance in Beethoven's music of the crab movement, a variation achieved by running the theme in reverse. But he was a master of instrumental variation, deriving extraordinary transformations through melodic and rhythmic alterations of a given theme. His op. 120, 33 variations for piano on a waltz theme by the Viennese publisher Diabelli, represents one of the greatest achievements in the art.

BELLINI, VINCENZO, famous Italian opera composer and a master of operatic bel canto; b. Catania, Sicily, Nov. 3, 1801; d. Puteaux, near Paris, Sept. 23, 1835. His first opera, *Adelson e Salvini*, was given in 1825; it was followed by an important production of his second opera, *Bianca e Gernando* (1826), a score later revised as *Bianca e Fernando* (1828). In 1827 Bellini went to Milan, where he was commissioned to write an "opera seria" for the famous Teatro alla Scala, *Il Pirata*, which obtained fine success at its production in 1827; it was also given in Vienna in 1828. *La Straniera* followed in 1829; in the same year, Bellini had the opera *Zaira* produced in Parma. He was then commissioned to write a new opera for the Teatro La Fenice in Venice, on a Shakespearean libretto, *I Capuleti ed i Montecchi*. Produced in 1830, it had a decisive success.

Even more successful was his next opera, *La Sonnambula*, produced in Milan in 1831 with the celebrated prima donna Giuditta Pasta as Amina. Pasta also appeared in the title role of Bellini's most famous opera, *Norma*, also produced in 1831, which at its repeated productions established Bellini's reputation as a young master of the Italian operatic bel canto. His following opera, *Beatrice di Tenda* (1833), failed to sustain his series of successes. He then had an opportunity to go to London and Paris, and it was in Paris that he produced in 1835 his last opera, *I Puritani*, which fully justified the expectations of his admirers. Next to *Norma*, it proved to be one of the greatest masterpieces of Italian operatic art; its Paris production featured a superb cast, which included Grisi, Rubini, Tamburini, and Lablache. Bellini was on his way to fame and universal artistic recognition when he was stricken with a fatal affliction of amebiasis, and died six weeks before his 34th birthday. His remains were reverently removed to his native Catania in 1876.

Bellini's music represents the Italian operatic school at its most glorious melodiousness, truly reflected by the term "bel canto." In his writing, the words, the rhythm, the melody, the harmony, and the instrumental accompaniment unite in mutual perfection. The lyric flow and dramatic expressiveness of his music provide a natural medium for singers in the Italian language, with the result that his greatest masterpieces, *La Sonnambula* and *Norma*, remain in the active repertoire of opera houses of the entire world, repeatedly performed by touring Italian opera companies and by native forces everywhere.

BERBERIAN, CATHY, versatile American mezzo-soprano; b. Attleboro, Massachusetts, July 4, 1925; d. Rome, March 6, 1983. Berberian was of Armenian parentage; she studied singing, dancing, and the art of pantomime. She took courses at Columbia University and New York University, and then went to Italy, where she attracted wide attention in 1958, when she performed the ultrasurrealist *Fontana Mix* by **John Cage**, which demanded a fantastic variety of sound effects. Her vocal range extended to three octaves, causing one bewildered music critic to remark that she could sing both Tristan and Isolde. Thanks to her uncanny ability to produce ultra-human (and subhuman) tones, and her willingness to incorporate into her professional vocalization a variety of animal noises, guttural sounds, grunts and growls, squeals, squeaks and squawks, clicks and clucks, shrieks and screeches, hisses, hoots, and hollers, she instantly became the darling of inventive composers of the avant-garde, who eagerly dedicated to her their otherwise unperformable works. She married one of them, **Luciano Berio**, in 1950, but they were separated in 1966 and divorced in 1968. She could also intone classical music, and made a favorable impression with her recording of works by **Monteverdi**. Shortly before her death, she sang her own version of the *Internationale* for an Italian television program commemorating the centennial of the death of Karl Marx. She was an avant-garde composer in her own right; she wrote multimedia works, such as *Stripsody*, an arresting soliloquy of labial and laryngeal sounds, and an eponymously titled piano piece, *Morsicat(h)y*. She resented being regarded as a "circus freak," and insisted that her objective was merely to meet the challenge of the new art of her time.

BERG, ALBAN (MARIA JOHANNES), greatly significant Austrian composer whose music combined classical clarity of design and highly original melodic and harmonic techniques that became historically associated with the New Viennese School; b. Vienna, Feb. 9, 1885; d. there, Dec. 24, 1935. He played piano as a boy and composed songs without formal training. He worked as a clerk in a government office in Lower Austria. In 1904 he met **Arnold Schoenberg**, who became his teacher, mentor, and close friend; he remained Schoenberg's pupil for six years. A fellow classmate was **Anton von Webern**; together they initiated the radical movement known to history as the Second Vienna School of composition.

Berg's early works reflected the Romantic style of **Richard Wagner**, Hugo Wolf, and **Gustav Mahler**; typical of this period were his *Three Pieces for Orchestra* (1913–1915). As early as 1917 Berg began work on his opera *Wozzeck* (after the romantic play by Büchner), which was to become his masterpiece. The score represents an ingenious synthesis of Classical forms and modern techniques; it is organized as a series of purely symphonic sections in traditional Baroque forms, among them a passacaglia with 21 variations, a dance suite, and a rhapsody, in a setting marked by dissonant counterpoint. Leopold Stokowski, ever eager to defy convention, gave the first American performance of *Wozzeck* in Philadelphia on March 19, 1931; it aroused a great deal of interest and was received with cultured equanimity. Thereafter, performances of *Wozzeck* multiplied in Europe (including Russia), and in due time it became recognized as the modern masterpiece that it is. Shortly after the completion of *Wozzeck*, Berg wrote a *Lyric Suite for String Quartet* in six movements; it was first played in Vienna by the Kolisch Quartet in 1927. In 1928 Berg arranged its second, third, and fourth movements for string orchestra. They were performed in Berlin in 1929.

Berg's second opera, *Lulu* (1928–1935), to a libretto derived from two plays by Wedekind, was left unfinished at Berg's death; two acts and music from the *Symphonische Stücke aus der Oper Lulu* of 1934 were performed posthumously in Zurich on June 2, 1937. As in *Wozzeck*, so in *Lulu*, Berg organized the score in a series of classical forms; but while *Wozzeck* was written before Schoenberg's formulation of the method of composition in 12 tones related solely to one another, *Lulu* was set in full-fledged dodecaphonic techniques. Even so, Berg allowed himself frequent divagations, contrary to the dodecaphonic code, into triadic tonal harmonies.

Berg's last completed work was a Violin Concerto commissioned by the American violinist Louis Krasner, who gave its first performance in Barcelona on April 19, 1936. The score bears the inscription "Dem Andenken eines Engels" ("To the memory of an angel"), the angel being the daughter of Alma Mahler and Walter Gropius who died of consumption at an early age. The work is couched in the 12-tone technique, with free and frequent interludes of passing tonality.

BERIO, LUCIANO, noted Italian composer of extreme musicoscientific tendencies; b. Oneglia, Oct. 24, 1925. He studied music with his father, an organist, then entered the Milan Conservatory, where he took courses in composition and in conducting. In 1951 he went to the U.S., where he married an extraordinary singer named **Cathy**

Berberian, who was willing and able to sing his most excruciating soprano parts; they were divorced in 1968, but magnanimously she continued to sing his music after their separation. Back in Italy, he joined the staff of the Italian Radio; founded the Studio di Fonologia Musicale for experimental work on acoustics; and edited the progressive magazine *Incontri Musicali*. Later on he joined the Institute de Recherche et de Coordination Acoustique/Musique (IRCAM) in Paris, working in close cooperation with its director, **Pierre Boulez**.

Perhaps the most unusual characteristic of his creative philosophy is his impartial eclecticism, by which he permits himself to use the widest variety of resources, from Croatian folk songs to *objets trouvés*. He is equally liberal in his use of graphic notation; some of his scores look like expressionist drawings. He is one of the few contemporary composers who can touch the nerve endings of sensitive listeners and music critics, one of whom described his *Sinfonia* with ultimate brevity: "It stinks." Apart from pure (or impure, depending on perception) music, Berio uses in his works all the artifacts and artifices of popular pageants, including mimodrama, choreodrama, concrete noises, acrobats, clowns, jugglers, and organ grinders.

BERLIN, IRVING (real name, **Israel Balin**), fabulously popular Russian-born American composer of hundreds of songs that became the musical conscience of the U.S.; b. Mogilev, May 11, 1888; d. New York, Sept. 22, 1989, at the incredible age of 101. Fearing anti-Semitic pogroms, his Jewish parents took ship when he was five years old and landed in New York. His father made a scant living as a synagogue cantor, and Izzy, as he was called, earned pennies as a newsboy. He later got jobs as a busboy, in time graduating to the role of a singing waiter in Chinatown. He learned to improvise on the bar piano and, at the age of 19, wrote the lyrics of a song, "Marie from Sunny Italy." Because of a printing error, his name on the song appeared as Berlin instead of Balin. He soon acquired the American vernacular and, throughout his career, never tried to experiment with sophisticated language, thus distancing himself from his younger contemporaries, such as **George Gershwin** and Cole Porter. He was married in 1912, but his young bride died of typhoid fever, contracted during their honeymoon in Havana, Cuba. He wrote a lyric ballad in her memory, "When I Lost You," which sold a million copies.

He never learned to read or write music, and composed most of his songs in F-sharp major for the convenience of fingering the black keys of the scale. To modulate into other keys he had a special hand clutch built at the piano keyboard, so that his later songs acquired an air of technical variety. Victor Herbert specifically discouraged Irving Berlin from learning harmony for fear that he would lose his natural genius for melody, and also encouraged him to join the American Society of Composers, Authors, and Publishers (ASCAP) as a charter member, a position that became the source of his fantastically prosperous commercial success.

Berlin was drafted into the U.S. Army in 1917 but did not have to serve in military action. Instead, he wrote a musical revue, *Yip, Yip, Yaphank*, which contained one of his most famous tunes, "God Bless America"; it was for some reason omitted in the original show, but returned to glory when songster Kate Smith performed it in 1938. The song, patriotic to the core, became an unofficial American anthem. In 1925, when Berlin was 37 years old, he met Ellin Mackay, the daughter of the millionaire head of the Postal Telegaph Cable Co., and proposed to her. She accepted, but her father threatened to disinherit her if she married a Jewish immigrant. Money was not the object, for by that time Berlin was himself a contented millionaire. The yellow press of New York devoted columns upon columns to the romance; the two eventually married in a civil ceremony at the Municipal Building. Ironically, it was the despised groom who helped his rich father-in-law during the financial debacle of the 1920s, for while stocks fell disastrously, Berlin's melodies rose in triumph all over America. The marriage proved to be happy, lasting 62 years, until Ellin's death in July of 1988. Berlin was reclusive in his last years of life; he avoided making a personal appearance when members of ASCAP gathered before his house to serenade him on his 100th birthday.

Berlin was extremely generous with his enormous earnings. According to sales records compiled in 1978, "God Bless America" brought in $673,939.46 in royalties, all of which was donated to the Boy and Girl Scouts of America. Another great song, "White Christmas," which Berlin wrote for the motion picture *Holiday Inn*, became a sentimental hit among American troops stationed in tropical bases in the Pacific during World War II; 113,067,354 records of this song and 5,566,845 copies of sheet music for it were sold in America between 1942 and 1978. The homesick marines altered the first line from "I'm dreaming of a white Christmas" to "I'm dreaming of a white mistress," that particular commodity being scarce in the tropics. In 1954 Berlin received the Congressional Medal of Honor for his patriotic songs.

BERLIOZ, (LOUIS-) HECTOR, great French composer who exercised profound influence on the course of modern music in the direction of sonorous grandiosity, and propagated the Romantic ideal of program music, unifying it with literature; b. La Côte-Saint-André, Isère, Dec. 11, 1803; d. Paris, March 8, 1869. His father was a medical doctor who possessed musical inclinations. Under his guidance Berlioz learned to play the flute, and later took up the guitar; however, he never became an experienced performer on any instrument. His first important work was a *Messe solennelle*, which was performed at a Paris church in 1825; he then wrote an instrumental work entitled *La Révolution grecque*, inspired by the revolutionary uprising in Greece against the Ottoman domination. In 1826, Berlioz wrote an opera, *Les Francs-juges*, which never came to a complete performance. In 1827 he submitted his cantata *La Mort d'Orphée* for the Prix de Rome, but it was rejected. In 1828, he presented a concert of his works at the Paris Conservatoire, including the *Resurrexit* from the *Messe solennelle, La Révolution grecque,* and the overtures *Les Francs-juges* and *Waverley*. Also in 1828 he won the second prize of the Prix de Rome with his cantata *Herminie*. In 1828–1829 he wrote *Huit scènes de Faust*, after Goethe; this was the score that was eventually revised and produced as *La Damnation de Faust*. In 1829, he applied for the Prix de Rome once more with the score of *La Mort de Cléopâtre*, but no awards were given that year. He finally succeeded in winning the Grand Prix de Rome with *La Mort de Sardanapale*; it was performed in Paris a year later.

Romantically absorbed in the ideal of love through music, Berlioz began to write his most ambitious and, as time and history proved, his most enduring work, which he titled *Symphonie fantastique*; it was to be an offering of adoration and devotion to Harriet Smithson. Rather than follow the formal subdivisions of a symphony, Berlioz decided to integrate the music through a recurring unifying theme, which he called an *idée fixe*, appearing in various guises through the movements of the *Symphonie fantastique*. To point out the personal nature of the work he subtitled it "Épisode de la vie d'un artiste." The artist of the title was Berlioz himself, so that in a way the symphony became a musical autobiography. Berlioz supplied a literary program to the music: a "young musician of morbid sensibilities" takes opium to find surcease from amorous madness. In the *Symphonie fantastique* the object of the hero's passion haunts him through the device of the *idée fixe*. She appears first as an entrancing, but unattainable, vision; as an enticing dancer at a ball; then as a deceptive pastoral image. He penetrates her disguise and kills her, a crime for which he is led to the gallows. At the end she reveals herself as a wicked witch at a Sabbath orgy. The fantastic program design does not interfere, however, with an orderly organization of the score, and the wild fervor of the music is astutely subordinated to the symphonic form. The *idée fixe* itself serves merely as a recurring motif, not unlike similar musical reminiscences in Classical symphonies.

Whatever the peripeteias of his personal life, Berlioz never lost the lust for music. During his stay in Italy, following his reception of the Prix de Rome, he produced the overtures *Le Roi Lear* (1831) and *Rob Roy* (1831). His next important work was *Harold en Italie* (1834), for the very unusual setting of a solo viola with orchestra; it was commissioned by **Niccolò Paganini** (although never performed by him), and was inspired by Lord Byron's poem *Childe Harold*. Berlioz followed it with an opera, *Benvenuto Cellini* (1834–1837), which had its first performance at the Paris Opéra in 1838. It was not successful, and Berlioz revised the score; the new version had its first performance in Weimar in 1852, conducted by **Franz Liszt**. About the same time, Berlioz became engaged in writing musical essays: from 1833 to 1863 he served as music critic for the *Journal des Débats*; in 1834 he began to write for the *Gazette Musicale*. In 1835 he entered a career as conductor.

In 1837 he received a government commission to compose the *Grande messe des morts* (*Requiem*), for which he demanded a huge chorus. In 1840, Berlioz received a similar commission to write a *Grande symphonie funèbre et triomphale*. This work gave Berlioz a clear imperative to build a sonorous edifice of what he imagined to be an architecture of sounds. The spirit of grandiosity took possession of Berlioz. At a concert after the Exhibition of Industrial Products in 1844 in Paris, he conducted Beethoven's Fifth Symphony with 36 double basses, Weber's *Freischütz Overture* with 24 French horns, and the *Prayer of Moses* from Rossini's opera with 25 harps. For his grandiose *L'Impériale*, written to celebrate the distribution of prizes by Napoleon III at the Paris Exhibition of Industrial Products in 1855, Berlioz had 1,200 performers, augmented by huge choruses and a military band. As if anticipating the modus operandi of a century thence, Berlioz installed five subconductors and, to keep them in line, activated an "electric metronome" with his left hand while holding the conducting baton in his right.

But whatever obloquy he suffered, he also found satisfaction in the pervading influence he had on his contemporaries, among them **Richard Wagner**, Liszt, and the Russian school of composers. Indeed, his grandiosity had gradually attained true grandeur; he no longer needed huge ensembles to exercise the magic of his music. In 1844 he wrote the overture *Le Carnaval romain*, partially based on music from his unsuccessful opera *Benvenuto Cellini*. There followed the overture *La Tour de Nice* (later revised under the title *Le Corsaire*). In 1845 he undertook the revision of his early score after Goethe, which now assumed the form of a dramatic legend entitled *La Damnation de Faust*. The score included the *Marche hongroise*, in which Berlioz took the liberty of conveying Goethe's Faust to Hungary. The march became extremely popular as a separate concert number. Between 1850 and 1854 he wrote the oratorio *L'Enfance du Christ*.

Although Berlioz was never able to achieve popular success with his operatic productions, he turned to composing stage music once more between 1856 and 1860. For the subject he selected the great epic of Virgil relating to the Trojan War; the title was to be *Les Troyens*. He encountered difficulties in producing this opera in its entirety, and in 1863 divided the score into two sections: *La Prise de Troie* and *Les Troyens à Carthage*. Only the second part was produced in his lifetime, premiering in 1863; the opera had 22 performances, and the financial returns made it possible for Berlioz to abandon his occupation as a newspaper music critic. His next operatic project was *Béatrice et Bénédict* (1862), after Shakespeare's play *Much Ado about Nothing*. Despite frail health and a state of depression generated by his imaginary failure as composer and conductor in France, he achieved a series of successes abroad.

Posthumous recognition came slowly to Berlioz; long after his death some conservative critics still referred to his music as bizarre and willfully dissonant. No cult comparable to the ones around the names of Wagner and Liszt was formed to glorify Berlioz's legacy. Of his works only the overtures and the *Symphonie fantastique* became regular items on symphonic programs. Performances of his operas are still rare events. Since Berlioz never wrote solo works for piano or any other instrument, concert recitals had no opportunity to include his name in the program. However, a whole literature was published about Berlioz in all European languages, securing his rightful place in music history.

BERNSTEIN, LEONARD, prodigiously gifted American conductor and composer, equally successful in writing symphonic music of profound content and strikingly effective Broadway shows, and, in the field of performance, an interpreter of magnetic powers, exercising a charismatic spell on audiences in America and the world; b. Lawrence, Massachusetts, Aug. 25, 1918, of a family of Russian Jewish immigrants; d. New York, Oct. 14, 1990. His original name was Louis, but at the age of 16 he had it legally changed to Leonard to avoid confusion with another Louis Bernstein in the family. He studied piano in Boston with Helen Coates and Heinrich Gebhard. In 1935 he entered Harvard University, where he took courses in music theory, counterpoint and fugue, and orchestration; he graduated with honors in 1939. He then went to Philadelphia, where he studied piano, conducting, and orchestration at the Curtis Institute of Music (diploma, 1941). During the summers of 1940 and 1941, he attended the Berkshire Music Center at Tanglewood, where he received help, instruction, and encouragement from his most important mentor in conducting, Serge Koussevitzky. In his free time, Bernstein did some ancillary work for music publishers under the name Lenny Amber (Bernstein is the German word for "amber"). He also conducted occasional concerts with local groups in Boston.

In 1943 he attained an important position as assistant conductor to Artur Rodzinski, music director of the New York Philharmonic. Bernstein's great chance to show his capacities came on Nov. 14, 1943, when he was called on short notice to conduct a particularly difficult program with the orchestra. He acquitted himself magnificently and was roundly praised in the press for his exemplary achievement. The occasion was the beginning of one of the most extraordinary careers in the annals of American music. In 1958 Bernstein became the first American-born music director of the New York Philharmonic; that year he conducted concerts with it in South America, and in 1959 took the orchestra on a grand tour of Russia and 16 other countries in Europe and the Near East. In 1960 he conducted it in Berlin, and in 1961 in Japan, Alaska, and Canada.

On July 9, 1967, he led a memorable concert with the Israel Philharmonic in Jerusalem, at the conclusion of Israel's victorious Six Day War, in a program of works by two great Jewish composers, **Felix Mendelssohn** and **Gustav Mahler**. In 1953 he became the first American conductor to lead a regular performance (Luigi Cherubini's *Medea*) at La Scala in Milan. In 1964, he made his Metropolitan Opera debut in New York, conducting *Falstaff*, the work he also chose for his debut with the Vienna State Opera in 1966. By that time he was in such great demand as a conductor of opera and orchestras all over the world that he could afford the luxury of selecting occasions to suit his schedule. In 1969 he resigned his position as music director of the New York Philharmonic in order to devote more time to composition and other projects; the orchestra bestowed upon him the unprecedented title of "laureate conductor," enabling him to give special performances with it whenever he could afford the time.

Ebullient with communicative talents, Bernstein initiated in 1958 a televised series of "Young People's Concerts" with the New York Philharmonic in which he served as an astute and self-confident commentator; these concerts became popular with audiences beyond the eponymous youth. He also arranged a series of educational music programs on television. His eagerness to impart his wide knowledge in various fields to willing audiences found its expression in the classes he conducted at Brandeis University (1951–1955), and, concurrently, in the summer sessions at the Berkshire Music Center at Tanglewood. In 1973 he was the prestigious Charles Eliot Norton Professor in Poetry at Harvard University and lectured at M.I.T.

An excellent pianist in his own right, Bernstein often appeared as a soloist in classical or modern concerts, on occasion, conducting the orchestra from the keyboard. An intellectual by nature, and a *litterateur* and modernistically inclined poet by aspiration, he took pride in publishing some excellent sonnets. He also took part in liberal causes, and was once dubbed by a columnist as a member of the

"radical chic." His tremendous overflow of spiritual and purely animal energy impelled him to display certain histrionic mannerisms
on the podium, which elicited on the part of some critics derisive
comments about his "choreography."

Whatever judgment is ultimately to be rendered on Bernstein,
he remains a phenomenon. History knows of a number of composers
who were also excellent conductors, but few professional conductors
who were also significant composers. Bernstein seemed unique in his
protean power to be equally proficient as a symphonic and operatic
conductor as well as a composer of complex musical works and, last
but not least, of original and enormously popular stage productions.
In his *West Side Story* (1957) he created a significant social drama,
abounding in memorable tunes. In his second symphony, *The Age of
Anxiety* (1949; rev. 1965), he reflected the turbulence of modern life.
As an interpreter and program maker, he showed a unique affinity
with the music of Mahler, whose symphonies he repeatedly performed in special cycles. Ever true to his Jewish heritage, Bernstein
wrote a devout choral symphony, *Kaddish* (1963; rev. 1977). As a testimony to his ecumenical religious feelings, he produced a Mass
(1971) on the Roman liturgy.

In 1989, Bernstein conducted celebratory performances of
Beethoven's Ninth Symphony on both sides of the Berlin Wall, the
first at the Kaiser Wilhelm Memorial Church, a World War II memo-
rial in West Berlin, on Dec. 23, and the second at the Schauspielhaus
Theater in East Berlin (telecast live to the world on Dec. 25). The
orchestra was made up of members from the Bavarian Radio
Symphony Orchestra in Munich, augmented by players from New
York, London, Paris, Dresden, and Leningrad.

Bernstein's death (of progressive emphysema, complicated by a
chronic pleurisy, eventuating in a fatal heart attack) shocked the
music world and hundreds of his personal friends, particularly since
he had been so amazingly active as a world-renowned conductor
until his final days.

BILLINGS, WILLIAM, pioneer American composer of hymns and
anthems and popularizer of "fuging tunes"; b. Boston, Oct. 7,
1746; d. there, Sept. 26, 1800. A tanner's apprentice, he acquired

the rudiments of music from treatises by British church organist William Tans'ur; he compensated for his lack of education by a wealth of original ideas and a determination to put them into practice. His first musical collection, *The New England Psalm Singer* (Boston, 1770), contained what he described at a later date as "fuging pieces . . . more than twenty times as powerful as the old slow tunes." The technique of these pieces was canonic, with "each part striving for mastery and victory." He published five other books between 1778 and 1794. In one instance, he harmonized a tune, *Jargon*, entirely in dissonances; this was prefaced by a "Manifesto" to the Goddess of Discord. There was further a choral work, *Modern Music*, in which the proclaimed aim was expressed in the opening lines: "We are met for a concert of modern invention—To tickle the ear is our present intention." Several of his hymns became popular, particularly *Chester* and *The Rose of Sharon*; an interesting historical work was his *Lamentation over Boston*, written in Watertown while Boston was occupied by the British. However, he could not earn a living by his music; appeals made to provide him and his large family with funds bore little fruit, and Billings died in abject poverty. The combination of reverence and solemnity with humor makes the songs of Billings unique in the annals of American music, and aroused the curiosity of many modern American musicians; **Henry Cowell** wrote a series of "fuging tunes" for orchestra.

BIZET, GEORGES (baptismal names, **Alexandre-César-Léopold**), great French opera composer; b. Paris, Oct. 25, 1838; d. Bougival, June 3, 1875. His parents were both professional musicians: his father, a singing teacher and composer; his mother, an excellent pianist. Bizet's talent developed early in childhood; at the age of nine he entered the Paris Conservatoire. He studied piano, organ, and harmony; composition was taught by Fromental Halévy, whose daughter, Geneviève, married Bizet in 1869. In 1852 he won a first prize for piano, in 1855 for organ and for fugue, and in 1857 the Grand Prix de Rome. Also in 1857 he shared (with Charles Lecocq) a prize offered by **Jacques Offenbach** for a setting of a one-act opera, *Le Docteur Miracle*; Bizet's setting was produced at the Bouffes-Parisiens. Instead of the prescribed Mass, he sent from Rome during his first year a two-act Italian opera buffa, *Don*

Procopio (not produced until 1906, when it was given in Monte Carlo in an incongruously edited version); later he sent two movements of a symphony, an overture (*La Chasse d'Ossian*), and a one-act opera (*La Guzla de l'Émir*; accepted by the Paris Opéra-Comique, but withdrawn by Bizet prior to production). Returning to Paris, he produced a grand opera, *Les Pêcheurs de perles* (1863); but this work, like *La Jolie Fille de Perth* (1867), failed to win popular approval. A one-act opera, *Djamileh* (1872), fared no better. Bizet's incidental music for Daudet's play *L'Arlésienne* (1872) was ignored by the audiences and literary critics; it was not fully appreciated until its revival in 1885. But an orchestral suite from *L'Arlésienne* conducted by Jules-Étienne Pasdeloup (1872) was acclaimed; a second suite was made by Ernest Guiraud after Bizet's death.

Bizet's next major work was his masterpiece, *Carmen*, produced, after many difficulties with the management and the cast, at the Opéra-Comique (1875). The reception of the public was not enthusiastic; several critics attacked the opera for its lurid subject, and the music for its supposed adoption of **Richard Wagner**'s methods. Bizet received a generous sum (25,000 francs) for the score from the publisher Choudens and won other honors (he was named a Chevalier of the Légion d'Honneur on the eve of the premiere of *Carmen*); although the attendance was not high, the opera was maintained in the repertoire. There were 37 performances before the end of the season. Bizet was chagrined by the controversial reception of the opera, but it is a melodramatic invention to state (as some biographers have done) that the alleged failure of *Carmen* precipitated the composer's death (he died on the night of the thirty-first performance of the opera).

BLOCH, ERNEST, remarkable Swiss-born American composer of Jewish ancestry, b. Geneva, July 24, 1880; d. Portland, Oregon, July 15, 1959. In 1900 he went to Germany, where he studied music theory in Frankfurt and took private lessons with Ludwig Thuille in Munich; there he began the composition of his first full-fledged symphony, in C-sharp minor, with its 4 movements originally bearing titles expressive of changing moods. He then spent a year in Paris, where he met **Debussy**; Bloch's first published work, *Historiettes au crépuscule* (1903), shows Debussy's influence. In 1904 he returned to

Geneva, where he began the composition of his only opera, *Macbeth*. As a tribute to his homeland, he outlined the orchestral work *Helvetia*, based on Swiss motifs, as early as 1900, but the full score was not completed until 1928.

In 1917 he received an offer to teach at the Mannes School of Music in New York, and once more he sailed for America; he became an American citizen in 1924. This was also the period when Bloch began to express himself in music as an inheritor of Jewish culture. His *Israel Symphony, Trois poèmes juifs,* and *Schelomo*, a "Hebrew Rhapsody" for Cello and Orchestra, mark the height of Bloch's greatness as a Jewish composer; long after his death, *Schelomo* still retains its popularity at symphonic concerts. In America, he found sincere admirers and formed a group of greatly talented students, among them **Roger Sessions**, Ernst Bacon, **George Antheil**, and Leon Kirchner. From 1920 to 1925 he was director of the Institute of Music in Cleveland, and from 1925 to 1930, director of the San Francisco Conservatory. When the magazine *Musical America* announced in 1927 a contest for a symphonic work, Bloch won first prize for his "epic rhapsody" entitled simply *America*; he fondly hoped that the choral ending extolling America as the ideal of humanity would become a national hymn. The work was performed with a great outpouring of publicity, but as happens often with prize-winning works, it failed to strike the critics and the audiences as truly great, and in the end remained a mere byproduct of Bloch's genius. From 1930 to 1939 Bloch lived mostly in Switzerland; and then returned to the U.S. and taught classes at the University of California, Berkeley (1940–1952). He finally retired and lived at his newly purchased house at Agate Beach, Oregon.

In his harmonic idiom Bloch favored sonorities formed by the bitonal relationship of two major triads with the tonics standing at the distance of a tritone, but even the dissonances he employed were euphonious. In his last works of chamber music he experimented for the first time with thematic statements of 12 different notes, but he never adopted the strict Schoenbergian technique of deriving the entire contents of a composition from the basic tone row. In his early Piano Quintet, Bloch made expressive use of quarter-tones in the string parts. In his Jewish works, he emphasized the interval of the augmented second, without a literal imitation of Hebrew chants.

BOCCHERINI, (RIDOLFO) LUIGI, famous Italian composer and cellist; b. Lucca, Feb. 19, 1743; d. Madrid, May 28, 1805. He grew up in a musical environment and became a cello player. In 1757 he was engaged as a member of the orchestra of the Court Theater in Vienna. From 1761 to 1763 he was in Lucca; after a year in Vienna he returned to Lucca and played cello at the theater orchestra there. He then undertook a concert tour with the violinist Filippo Manfredi in 1766. Then he went to Paris, where he appeared at the Concert Spirituel in 1768. He became exceedingly popular as a performer, and his own compositions were published in Paris; his first publications were six string quartets and two books of string trios. In 1769 he received a flattering invitation to the Madrid court, and became chamber composer to the Infante Luis; after the latter's death he served as court composer to Friedrich Wilhelm II of Prussia, and was appointed to the German court in 1786. After the death of the King in 1797, he returned to Madrid. In 1800 he enjoyed the patronage of Napoleon's brother, Lucien Bonaparte, who served as French ambassador to Madrid. Despite his successes at various European courts, Boccherini lost his appeal to his patrons and to the public. He died in poverty. Boccherini had profound admiration for **Haydn**; indeed, so close was Boccherini's style to Haydn's that this affinity gave rise to the saying, "Boccherini is the wife of Haydn." He was an exceptionally fecund composer, specializing almost exclusively in chamber music. He also wrote much guitar music, a Christmas cantata, and some sacred works.

BORODIN, ALEXANDER (PORFIRIEVICH), celebrated Russian composer; b. St. Petersburg, Nov. 12, 1833; d. there, Feb. 27, 1887. He was the illegitimate son of a Georgian prince, Gedianov; his mother was the wife of an army doctor. In accordance with customary procedure in such cases, the child was registered as the lawful son of one of Gedianov's serfs, Porfiry Borodin; hence, the patronymic, Alexander Porfirievich. He was given an excellent education, learning several foreign languages, and was taught to play the flute. He played four-hand arrangements of **Haydn**'s and **Beethoven**'s symphonies with his musical friend M. Shchiglev. At the age of 14 he tried his hand at composition, writing a piece for flute and piano and a String Trio on themes from *Robert le Diable*. In 1850 he became a student of the Academy of Medicine in St. Petersburg, and developed a great interest in chemistry; he graduated in 1856 with honors, and joined the staff as assistant professor; in 1858 received his doctorate in chemistry. Borodin contributed several important scientific papers to the bulletin of the Russian Academy of Sciences, and traveled in Europe on a scientific mission (1859–1862).

Although mainly preoccupied with his scientific pursuits, Borodin continued to compose. In 1863 he married Catherine Protopopova, who was an accomplished pianist; she remained his faithful companion and musical partner. Together they attended concerts and operas in Russia and abroad; his letters to her from Germany (1877), describing his visit to **Franz Liszt** in Weimar, are of great interest. Of a decisive influence on Borodin's progress as a composer was his meeting with **Mily Balakirev** in 1862; later he formed friendships with the critic Vladimir Stasov, who named Borodin as one of the "Mighty Five" (actually, Stasov used the expression "mighty handful"), with **Modest Mussorgsky** and other musicians of the Russian national school. He adopted a style of composition in conformity with their new ideas; he particularly excelled in a type of Russian Orientalism that had a great attraction for Russian musicians at the time. He never became a consummate craftsman, like **Nikolai Rimsky-Korsakov**. Although quite proficient in counterpoint, he avoided purely contrapuntal writing. His feeling for rhythm and orchestral color was extraordinary, and his evocation of exotic scenes in his orchestral works and in his opera *Prince Igor* is superb. Composition was a very slow process for Borodin; several of his works remained incomplete, and were edited after his death by Rimsky-Korsakov and Glazunov.

BOULEZ, PIERRE, celebrated French composer and conductor; b. Montbrison, March 26, 1925. He studied composition with **Olivier Messiaen** at the Paris Conservatiore, graduating in 1945; he later took lessons with René Leibowitz, who initiated him into the procedures of serial music. In 1948 he became a theater conductor in Paris, and made a tour of the U.S. with a French ballet troupe in 1952. In 1954 he organized in Paris a series of concerts called "Domaine Musical," devoted mainly to avant-garde music. In 1963 he delivered a course of lectures on music at Harvard University, and in 1964, made his American debut as conductor in New York. In 1958 he went to Germany, where he gave courses at the International Festivals for New Music in Darmstadt. It was in Germany that he gained experience as conductor of opera. He was one of the few Frenchmen to conduct Wagner's *Parsifal* in Germany; in 1976 he was engaged to conduct the *Ring* cycle in Bayreuth. The precision of his leadership and his knowledge of the score produced a profound impression on both the audience and the critics.

Boulez was engaged to conduct guest appearances with the Cleveland Orchestra, and in 1971 he was engaged as music director of the New York Philharmonic, a choice that surprised many and delighted many more. From the outset he asserted complete independence from public and managerial tastes, and proceeded to feature on his programs works by **Arnold Schoenberg, Alban Berg, Anton Webern, Edgard Varèse**, and other modernists who were reformers of music, giving a relatively small place to Romantic composers. The musicians themselves voiced their full appreciation of his remarkable qualities as a professional of high caliber, but they described him derisively as a "French correction," with reference to his extraordinary sense of rhythm, perfect pitch, and memory, but a signal lack of emotional participation in the music. His departure in 1977 and the accession of the worldly Zubin Mehta as his successor were greeted with a sigh of relief, as an antidote to the stern regimen imposed by Boulez. While attending to his duties at the helm of the New York Philharmonic, he accepted outside obligations. From 1971 to 1975 he served as chief conductor of the London BBC Symphonic Orchestra; as a perfect Wagnerite he gave exemplary performances of Wagner's operas both in Germany and elsewhere.

Boulez established his residence in Paris in the early '70s, where he had founded, in 1974, the Institute de Recherche et Coordination Acoustique/Musique (IRCAM), a futuristic establishment generously subsidized by the French government. In this post he could freely carry out his experimental programs of electronic techniques with the aid of digital synthesizers and a complex set of computers capable of acoustical feedback. In 1989 he was awarded the Praemium Imperiale prize of Japan for his various contributions to contemporary music. His own music is an embodiment of such futuristic techniques; it is fiendishly difficult to perform and even more difficult to describe in the familiar terms of dissonant counterpoint, free serialism, or indeterminism. He specifically disassociated himself from any particular modern school of music.

BRAHMS, JOHANNES, great German composer; b. Hamburg, May 7, 1833; d. Vienna, April 3, 1897. His father, who played the double bass in the orchestra of the Philharmonic Society in Hamburg, taught Brahms the rudiments of music; later he began to study piano with Otto F.W. Cossel, and made his first public appearance as a pianist with a chamber music group at the age of 10. Impressed with his progress, Cossel sent Brahms to his own former teacher, the noted pedagogue Eduard Marxsen, who accepted him as a scholarship student, without charging a fee. Soon Brahms was on his own, and had to eke out his meager subsistence by playing piano in taverns, restaurants, and other establishments (but not in brothels, as insinuated by some popular biographers). In 1848, at the age of 15, Brahms played a solo concert in Hamburg under an assumed name. In 1853 he met the Hungarian violinist Eduard Reményi, with whom he embarked on a successful concert tour. While in Hannover, Brahms formed a friendship with the famous violin virtuoso Joseph Joachim, who gave him an introduction to **Liszt** in Weimar.

Of great significance was his meeting with **Robert Schumann** in Düsseldorf. In his diary of the time, Schumann noted: "Johannes Brahms, a genius." He reiterated his appraisal of Brahms in his famous article "Neue Bahnen" (New Paths), which appeared in the *Neue Zeitschrift für Musik* in 1853; in a characteristic display of metaphor, he described young Brahms as having come into life as Minerva sprang in full armor from the brow of Jupiter. Schumann's death in 1856, after years of agonizing mental illness, deeply affected Brahms. He remained a devoted friend of Schumann's family; his correspondence with Schumann's widow **Clara Schumann** reveals a deep affection and spiritual intimacy, but the speculation about their friendship growing into a romance exists only in the fevered imaginations of psychologizing biographers.

Objectively judged, the private life of Brahms was that of a middle-class bourgeois who worked systematically and diligently on his current tasks while maintaining a fairly active social life. He was always ready and willing to help young composers (his earnest efforts on behalf of **Dvořák** were notable). Brahms was entirely free of professional jealousy; his differences with **Wagner** were those of style. Wagner was an opera composer, whereas Brahms never wrote for the stage. True, some ardent admirers of Wagner (such as Hugo Wolf) found little of value in the music of Brahms, while admirers of Brahms (such as Eduard Hanslick) were sharp critics of Wagner, but Brahms held aloof from such partisan wranglings.

From 1857 to 1859 Brahms was employed in Detmold as court pianist, chamber musician, and choir director. In the meantime, he began work on his first piano concerto. He played it on Jan. 22, 1859, in Hannover, with Joachim as conductor. He expected to be named conductor of the Hamburg Philharmonic Society, but the directoriat preferred to engage, in 1863, the singer Julius Stockhausen in that capacity. Instead, Brahms accepted the post of conductor of the Singakademie in Vienna, which he led from 1863 to 1864. In 1869 he decided to make Vienna his permanent home. As early as 1857 he began work on his choral masterpiece, *Ein deutsches Requiem*; he completed the score in 1868, and conducted its first performance in this version in the Bremen Cathedral on April 10. In May, he added another movement to the work (the fifth, "Ihr habt nun Traurigkeit") in memory of his mother, who died in 1865; the first performance of the final version was given in Leipzig in 1869. Its title had no nationalistic connotations; it simply stated that the text was in German rather than Latin. His other important vocal scores include *Rinaldo*, a cantata; the *Liebeslieder* waltzes for Vocal Quartet and Piano, four-hands; the *Alto Rhapsody*; the *Schicksalslied*; and many songs.

In 1869, he published two volumes of *Hungarian Dances* for Piano Duet; these were extremely successful. Among his chamber music works, the Piano Quintet in F minor; the String Sextet No. 2, in G major; the Trio for French Horn, Violin, and Piano; the two String Quartets, op. 51; and the String Quartet op. 67 are exemplary works of their kind. In 1872 Brahms was named artistic director of the concerts of Vienna's famed Gesellschaft der Musikfreunde; he held this post until 1875. During this time, he composed the *Variations on a Theme by Joseph Haydn*, op. 56a. The title was a misnomer; the theme occurs in a Feld-partita for Military Band by **Haydn**, but it was not Haydn's own. It was originally known as the St. Anthony

Chorale, and in pedantic scholarly editions of Brahms it is called St. Anthony Variations. Otto Dessoff conducted the first performance of the work with the Vienna Philharmonic in 1873.

For many years friends and admirers of Brahms urged him to write a symphony. He clearly had a symphonic mind; his piano concertos were symphonic in outline and thematic development. As early as 1855 he began work on a full-fledged symphony; in 1862 he nearly completed the first movement of what was to be his First Symphony. The famous horn solo in the finale of the First Symphony was jotted down by Brahms on a picture postcard to Clara Schumann dated Sept. 12, 1868, from his summer place in the Tyrol. In it Brahms said that he heard the tune played by a shepherd on an Alpine horn; and he set it to a rhymed quatrain of salutation. The great C minor Symphony, his first, was completed in 1876; Hans von Bülow, the German master of the telling phrase, called it "The 10th," thus placing Brahms on a direct line from **Beethoven**.

Brahms composed his Second Symphony in 1877; it was performed for the first time by the Vienna Philharmonic, under the direction of Hans Richter. Also in 1878 Brahms wrote his Violin Concerto; the score was dedicated to Joachim, who gave its premiere on Jan. 1, 1879. Brahms then composed his Second Piano Concerto, in B-flat major, and was soloist in its first performance in Budapest in 1881. There followed the Third Symphony, in F major, first performed by the Vienna Philharmonic in 1883; and the Fourth Symphony, in E minor, followed in quick succession, premiering in 1885.

The symphonic cycle was completed in less than a decade; it has been conjectured, without foundation, that the tonalities of the four symphonies of Brahms—C, D, F, and E—correspond to the fugal subject of **Mozart**'s *Jupiter Symphony*, and that some symbolic meaning was attached to it. All speculations aside, there is an inner symmetry uniting these works. The four symphonies contain four movements each, with a slow movement and a scherzo-like Allegretto in the middle of the corpus. There are fewer departures from the formal scheme than in Beethoven, and there are no extraneous episodes interfering with the grand general line. Brahms wrote music pure in design and eloquent in sonorous projection; he was a true classicist, a quality that endeared him to the critics who were repelled by Wagnerian streams of sound, and by the same token alienated those who sought something more than mere geometry of thematic configurations from a musical composition.

The chamber music of Brahms possesses similar symphonic qualities; when **Arnold Schoenberg** undertook to make an orchestral arrangement of the Piano Quartet of Brahms, all he had to do was to expand the sonorities and enhance instrumental tone colors already present in the original. The string quartets of Brahms are edifices of Gothic perfection; his three violin sonatas; his Second Piano Trio (the first was a student work and yet it had a fine quality of harmonious construction), all contribute to a permanent treasure of musical classicism. The piano writing of Brahms is severe in its contrapuntal texture, but pianists for a hundred years included his rhapsodies and intermezzos in their repertoire; and Brahms was able to impart sheer delight in his Hungarian rhapsodies and waltzes, representing the Viennese side of his character, as contrasted with the profound Germanic quality of his symphonies. The song cycles of Brahms continued the evolution of the art of the lieder, a natural continuation of the song cycles of **Schubert** and Schumann.

In 1879 the University of Breslau proffered him an honorary degree of Doctor of Philosophy, citing him as "Artis musicae severioris in Germania nunc princeps." As a gesture of appreciation and gratitude he wrote an *Akademische Festouverture* for Breslau, and he accepted the invitation to conduct its premiere in Breslau in 1881; its rousing finale using the German student song "Gaudeamus igitur" pleased the academic assembly. From the perspective of a century, Brahms appears as the greatest master of counterpoint after Bach; one can learn polyphony from a studious analysis of the chamber music and piano works of Brahms. He excelled in variation forms; his piano variations on a theme of **Niccolò Paganini** are exemplars of contrapuntal learning, and they are also among the most difficult piano works of the 19th century. Posterity gave him a full measure of recognition; Hamburg celebrated his sesquicentennial in 1983 with great pomp. Brahms had lived a good life, but died a bad death, stricken with cancer of the liver.

BRITTEN, (EDWARD) BENJAMIN, LORD BRITTEN OF ALDEBURGH, one of the most remarkable composers of England; b.

Lowestoft, Suffolk, Nov. 22, 1913; d. Aldeburgh, Dec. 4, 1976. He grew up in moderately prosperous circumstances; his father was an orthodontist, his mother an amateur singer. He played the piano and improvised facile tunes; many years later he used these youthful inspirations in a symphonic work that he named *Simple Symphony*. In addition to piano, he began taking viola lessons. At the age of 13 he was accepted as a pupil in composition by Frank Bridge, whose influence was decisive on Britten's development as a composer. In 1930 he entered the Royal College of Music in London, where he studied piano and composition. He progressed rapidly; even his earliest works showed a mature mastery of technique and a fine lyrical talent of expression. His *Fantasy Quartet* for Oboe and Strings was performed in Florence in 1934. He became associated with the theater and the cinema and began composing background music for films. He was in the U.S. at the outbreak of World War II, and returned to England in the spring of 1942; but was exempted from military service as a conscientious objector.

After the war, Britten organized the English Opera Group (1947), and in 1948 founded the Aldeburgh Festival, in collaboration with Eric Crozier and the singer Peter Pears. This festival, devoted mainly to production of short operas by English composers, became an important cultural institution in England. Many of Britten's own works were performed for the first time there, often under his own direction; he also had productions at the Glyndebourne Festival. In his operas he observed the economic necessity of reducing the orchestral contingent to 12 performers, with the piano part serving as a modern version of the Baroque ripieno. This economy of means made it possible for small opera groups and university workshops to perform Britten's works; yet he succeeded in creating a rich spectrum of instrumental colors, in an idiom ranging from simple triadic progressions, often in parallel motions, to ultrachromatic dissonant harmonies. Upon occasion he applied dodecaphonic procedures, with thematic materials based on 12 different notes; however, he never employed the formal design of the 12-tone method of composition. A *sui generis* dodecaphonic device is illustrated by the modulatory scheme in Britten's opera *The Turn of the Screw*, in which each successive scene begins in a different key, with the totality of tonics aggregating to a series of 12 different notes.

A characteristic feature in Britten's operas is the inclusion of orchestral interludes, which become independent symphonic poems in an impressionistic vein related to the dramatic action of the work. Britten was equally successful in treating tragic subjects, as in *Peter Grimes* and *Billy Budd*; comic subjects, exemplified by his *Albert Herring*; and mystical evocation, as in *The Turn of the Screw*. He was also successful in depicting patriotic subjects, as in *Gloriana*, composed for the coronation of Queen Elizabeth II. He possessed a flair for writing music for children, in which he managed to present a degree of sophistication and artistic simplicity without condescension. Britten was an adaptable composer who could perform a given task according to the specific requirements of the occasion. He composed a "realization" of Gay's *Beggar's Opera*. He also wrote modern "parables" for church performance, and produced a contemporary counterpart of the medieval English miracle play *Noye's Fludde*. Among his other works, perhaps the most remarkable is *War Requiem*, a profound tribute to the dead of many wars.

BROWN, EARLE (APPLETON, JR.), American composer of the avant-garde; b. Lunenburg, Massachusetts, Dec. 26, 1926. He played trumpet in school bands, then enrolled in Northeastern University in Boston to study engineering. Later, he played trumpet in the U.S. Army Air Force Band, and also served as a substitute trumpet player with the San Antonio Symphony in Texas. Returning to Boston, he began to study the Schillinger system of composition. He soon adopted the most advanced types of techniques in composition, experimenting in serial methods as well as in aleatory improvisation. He was fascinated by the parallelism existing in abstract expressionism in painting, mobile sculptures, and free musical forms; to draw these contiguities together he initiated the idea of open forms, using graphic notation with visual signs in musical terms.

The titles of his works give clues to their contents: *Folio* (1952–1953) is a group of six compositions in which the performer is free to vary the duration, pitch, and rhythm; *25 Pages* (1953) is to be played by any number of pianists up to 25, reading the actual pages in any desired order, and playing the notes upside down or right side up. Further development is represented by *Available Forms I* for

18 Instruments, consisting of musical "events" happening in accordance with guiding marginal arrows. Brown made much use of magnetic tape in his works, both in open and closed forms. He professes no *parti pris* in his approach to techniques and idioms of composition, whether dissonantly contrapuntal or serenely triadic; rather, his music represents a mobile assembly of plastic elements, in open-ended or closed forms. As a result, his usages range from astute asceticism and constrained constructivism to soaring sonorism and lush lyricism.

BRUCKNER, (JOSEF) ANTON, inspired Austrian composer; b. Ansfelden, Sept. 4, 1824; d. Vienna, Oct. 11, 1896. While in his early youth, Bruckner held teaching positions in elementary public schools in Windhaag (1841–1843) and Kronstorf (1843–1845); later he occupied a responsible position as a schoolteacher at St. Florian (1845–1855), and also served as provisional organist there (1848–1851). Despite his professional advance, he felt a lack of basic techniques in musical composition, and at the age of 31 went to Vienna to study harmony and counterpoint with the renowned pedagogue Simon Sechter. He continued his studies with him off and on until 1861. Determined to acquire still more technical knowledge, he sought further instruction and began taking lessons in orchestration with the first cellist of the Linz municipal theater (1861–1863). In the meantime he undertook an assiduous study of the Italian polyphonic school, and of masters of German polyphony, especially **J. S. Bach**.

These tasks preoccupied him so completely that Bruckner did not engage in free composition until he was nearly 40 years old. Then he fell under the powerful influence of **Richard Wagner**'s music, an infatuation that diverted him from his study of classical polyphony. His adulation of Wagner was extreme; the dedication of his Third Symphony to Wagner reads: "To the eminent Excellency Richard Wagner the Unattainable, World-Famous, and Exalted Master of Poetry and Music, in Deepest Reverence Dedicated by Anton Bruckner." Strangely enough, in his own music Bruckner never embraced the tenets and practices of Wagner, but followed the sanctified tradition of Germanic polyphony. Whereas Wagner strove toward the ideal union of drama, text, and music in a new type of operatic production, Bruckner kept away from the musical theater,

confining himself to symphonic and choral music. Even in his harmonic techniques, Bruckner seldom followed Wagner's chromatic
style of writing, and he never tried to emulate the passionate rise
and fall of Wagnerian "endless" melodies depicting the characters of
his operatic creations.

To Bruckner, music was an apotheosis of symmetry; his symphonies were cathedrals of Gothic grandeur. He never hesitated to
repeat a musical phrase several times in succession so as to establish
the thematic foundation of a work. The personal differences between
Wagner and Bruckner could not be more striking: Wagner was a man
of the world who devoted his whole life to the promotion of his artistic and human affairs, while Bruckner was unsure of his abilities and
desperately sought recognition. Devoid of social graces, being a person of humble peasant origin, Bruckner was unable to secure the
position of respect and honor that he craved. A signal testimony to
this lack of self-confidence was Bruckner's willingness to revise his
works repeatedly, not always to their betterment, taking advice from
conductors and ostensible well-wishers. He suffered from periodic
attacks of depression; his entire life seems to have been a study of
unhappiness.

A commanding trait of Bruckner's personality was his devout
religiosity. To him the faith and the sacraments of the Roman
Catholic Church were not mere rituals but profound psychological
experiences. Following the practice of **Haydn**, he signed most of his
works with the words *Omnia ad majorem Dei gloriam*; indeed, he must
have felt that every piece of music he composed redounded to the
greater glory of God. His original dedication of his *Te Deum* was
actually inscribed "an dem lieben Gott." From reports of his friends
and contemporaries, it appears that he regarded each happy event
of his life as a gift of God, and each disaster as an act of divine
wrath. His yearning for secular honors was none the less acute for
that. He was tremendously gratified upon receiving an honorary
doctorate from the University of Vienna in 1891; he was the first
musician to be so honored there.

Bruckner's symphonies constitute a monumental achievement;
they are characterized by a striking display of originality and a profound spiritual quality. His sacred works are similarly expressive of
his latent genius. Bruckner is usually paired with **Gustav Mahler**,
who was a generation younger, but whose music embodied qualities

of grandeur akin to those that permeated the symphonic and choral works of Bruckner. Accordingly, Bruckner and Mahler societies sprouted in several countries, with the express purpose of elucidating, analyzing, and promoting their music. The textual problems concerning Bruckner's works are numerous and complex. He made many revisions of his scores, and dejectedly acquiesced in alterations suggested by conductors who expressed interest in his music. As a result, conflicting versions of his symphonies appeared in circulation.

BUSONI, FERRUCCIO (DANTE MICHELANGIOLO BENVE-NUTO), greatly admired pianist and composer of Italian-German parentage; b. Empoli, near Florence, April 1, 1866; d. Berlin, July 27, 1924. His father played the clarinet; his mother, Anna Weiss, was an amateur pianist. Busoni grew up in an artistic atmosphere, and learned to play the piano as a child; at the age of eight he played in public in Trieste. He gave a piano recital in Vienna when he was 10, and included in his program some of his own compositions. He conducted his *Stabat Mater* in Graz at the age of 12. At 15 he was accepted as a member of the Accademia Filarmonica in Bologna; he performed there his oratorio *Il sabato del villaggio* in 1883. In 1886 he went to Leipzig; there he undertook a profound study of **J. S. Bach**'s music. In 1889 he was appointed a professor of piano at the Helsingfors Conservatory, where among his students was **Jean Sibelius** (who was actually a few months older than his teacher).

In 1890 Busoni participated in the Rubinstein Competition in St. Petersburg, and won first prize with his *Konzertstück* for Piano and Orchestra. On the strength of this achievement, he was engaged to teach piano at the Moscow Conservatory (1890–1891). He then accepted the post of professor at the New England Conservatory of Music in Boston (1891–1894); however, he had enough leisure to make several tours, maintaining his principal residence in Berlin. During the season of 1912–1913, he made a triumphant tour of Russia. In 1913 he was appointed director of the Liceo Musicale in Bologna. The outbreak of the war in 1914 forced him to move to neutral Switzerland; he stayed in Zurich until 1923; went to Paris, and then returned to Berlin, remaining there until his death in 1924. In various cities, at various times, he taught piano in music schools, as well as composition. He exercised great influence on

Edgard Varèse, who was living in Berlin when Busoni was there; Varèse greatly prized Busoni's advanced theories of composition.

Busoni was a philosopher of music who tried to formulate a universe of related arts. He issued grandiloquent manifestos urging a return to classical ideals in modern forms. He sought to establish a unifying link between architecture and composition; in his editions of Bach's works he included drawings illustrating the architectonic plan of Bach's fugues. He incorporated his innovations in his grandiose piano work *Fantasia contrappuntistica*, which opens with a prelude based on a Bach chorale, and closes with a set of variations on Bach's acronym, B-A-C-H (i.e., B-flat, A, C, B-natural). In his theoretical writings, Busoni proposed a system of 113 different heptatonic modes, and also suggested the possibility of writing music in exotic scales and subchromatic intervals; he expounded those ideas in his influential essay *Entwurf einer neuen Aesthetik der Tonkunst* (1907). Busoni's other publications of significance were *Von der Einheit der Musik* (1923) and *Über die Möglichkeiten der Oper* (1926).

Despite Busoni's great innovations in his own compositions and his theoretical writing, the Busoni legend is kept alive not through his music but mainly through his sovereign virtuosity as a pianist. In his performances he introduced a concept of piano sonority as an orchestral medium; indeed, some listeners reported having heard simulations of trumpets and French horns sounded at Busoni's hands. The few extant recordings of his playing transmit a measure of the grandeur of his style, but they also betray a tendency, common to Busoni's era, toward a free treatment of the musical text, surprisingly so, since Busoni preached an absolute fidelity to the written notes. On concert programs Busoni's name appears most often as the author of magisterial and eloquent transcriptions of Bach's works. His gothic transfiguration for piano of Bach's *Chaconne* for Unaccompanied Violin became a perennial favorite of pianists all over the world.

BYRD (or **Byrde**, **Bird**), **WILLIAM**, great English composer; b. probably in Lincoln, 1543; d. Stondon Massey, Essex, July 4, 1623. There are indications that Byrd studied music with **Tallis**. On March 25, 1563, Byrd was appointed organist of Lincoln Cathedral; in 1568 he married Juliana Birley. In 1570 he was sworn in as a Gentleman of the Chapel Royal, while retaining his post at Lincoln Cathedral until 1572; he then assumed his duties, together with Tallis, as organist of the Chapel Royal. In 1575 Byrd and Tallis were granted a patent by Queen Elizabeth I for the exclusive privilege of printing music and selling music paper for a term of 21 years; however, the license proved unprofitable and they successfully petitioned the Queen in 1577 to give them an annuity in the form of a lease. In 1585, after the death of Tallis, the license passed wholly into Byrd's hands. The earliest publication of the printing press of Byrd and Tallis was the first set of *Cantiones sacrae* for five to eight voices (1575), dedicated to the Queen; works issued by Byrd alone under his exclusive license were *Psalmes, Sonets and Songs* (1588), *Songs of Sundrie Natures* (1589), and two further volumes of *Cantiones sacrae* (1589, 1591). Many of his keyboard pieces appeared in the manuscript collection *My Ladye Nevells Booke* (1591) and in Francis Tregian's *Fitzwilliam Virginal Book* (c. 1612–1619), among others. During the winter of 1592–1593, he moved to Stondon Massey, Essex. He subsequently was involved in various litigations and disputes concerning the ownership of the property. Between 1592 and 1595 he published three Masses, and between 1605 and 1607 he brought out two volumes of Gradualia. His last collection, *Psalmes, Songs and Sonnets*, was published in 1611. Byrd was unsurpassed in his time in compositional versatility. His masterly technique is revealed in his ecclesiastical works, instrumental music, madrigals, and solo songs.

CAGE, JOHN (MILTON, JR.), highly inventive American composer, writer, philosopher, and artist of ultramodern tendencies; b. Los
Angeles, Sept. 5, 1912; d. New York, Aug. 12, 1992. His father, John
Milton, Sr., was an inventor, his mother active as a clubwoman in
California. He studied piano with Fannie Dillon and Richard Buhlig
in Los Angeles and with Lazare Lévy in Paris; returning to the U.S.,
he studied composition in California with Adolph Weiss and **Arnold
Schoenberg**, and with **Henry Cowell** in New York. In 1938–1939 he
was employed as a dance accompanist at the Cornish School in
Seattle, where he also organized a percussion group. He developed
Cowell's piano technique, making use of tone clusters and playing
directly on the strings, and initiated a type of procedure to be called
"prepared piano," which consists of placing on the piano strings a
variety of objects, such as screws, copper coins, and rubber bands,
which alter the tone color of individual keys. Eventually the term
and procedure gained acceptance among avant-garde composers
and was listed as a legitimate method in several music dictionaries.
In 1949 Cage was awarded a Guggenheim fellowship and an award
from the National Academy of Arts and Letters for having "extended
the boundaries of music."

Cage taught for a season at the School of Design in Chicago
(1941–1942); he then moved to New York, where he began a fruitful
association with the dancer Merce Cunningham, with whom he collaborated on a number of works that introduced radical innovations
in musical and choreographic composition. He served as musical

adviser to the Merce Cunningham Dance Company until 1987. Another important association was his collaboration with the pianist David Tudor, who was able to reify Cage's exotic inspirations, works in which the performer shares the composer's creative role. In 1952, at Black Mountain College, he presented a theatrical event historically marked as the earliest musical Happening.

With the passing years, Cage departed from the pragmatism of precise musical notation and definite ways of performance, electing instead to mark his creative intentions in graphic symbols and pictorial representations. He established the principle of indeterminacy in musical composition, producing works any two performances of which can never be identical. In the meantime, he became immersed in an earnest study of mushrooms, acquiring formidable expertise and winning a prize in Italy in competition with professional mycologists. He also became interested in chess, and played demonstration games with Marcel Duchamp, the famous painter turned chessmaster, on a chessboard designed by Lowell Cross to operate on aleatory principles with the aid of a computer and a system of laser beams. In his endeavor to achieve ultimate freedom in musical expression, he produced a piece entitled *4'33"*, in three movements, during which no sounds are intentionally produced. It was performed in Woodstock, New York, in 1952, by David Tudor, who sat at the piano playing nothing for the length of time stipulated in the title. This was followed by another "silent" piece, *0'00"*, an idempotent "to be played in any way by anyone," presented for the first time in Tokyo in 1962. Any sounds, noises, coughs, chuckles, groans, and growls produced by the listeners are automatically regarded as integral to the piece itself, so that the wisecrack about the impossibility of arriving at a fair judgment of a silent piece, since one cannot tell what music is not being played, is invalidated by the uniqueness of Cage's art.

Cage was a consummate showman, and his exhibitions invariably attracted music-lovers and music-haters alike, expecting to be exhilarated or outraged, as the case may be. In many such public Happenings he departed from musical, unmusical, or even antimusical programs in favor of a free exercise of surrealist imagination, often instructing the audience to participate actively, as for instance going out into the street and bringing in garbage pails needed for percussion effects, with or without garbage.

In order to eliminate the subjective element in composition, Cage resorted to a method of selecting the components of his pieces by dice throwing, suggested by the Confucian classic *I Ching*, an ancient Chinese oracle book; the result is a system of total serialism, in which all elements pertaining to acoustical pulses, pitch, noise, duration, relative loudness, tempi, combinatory superpositions, etc., are determined by previously drawn charts. His stage work *Europeras 1 & 2* (1987), which he wrote, designed, staged, and directed, is a sophisticated example, a collage comprised of excerpts from extant operas selected and manipulated by a computer software program, *IC* (short for *I Ching*), designed by Cage's assistant, Andrew Culver.

Cage was also a brilliant writer, much influenced by the manner, grammar, syntax, and glorified illogic of Gertrude Stein. Among his works are *Silence* (1961), *A Year from Monday* (1967), *M* (1973), *Empty Words* (1979), and *X* (1983). He developed a style of poetry called "mesostic," which uses an anchoring string of letters down the center of the page that spell a name, a word, or even a line of text relating to the subject matter of the poem. Mesostic poems are composed by computer, the "source material" pulverized and later enhanced by Cage into a semi-coherent, highly evocative poetic text. He has also collaborated on a number of other projects, including *The First Meeting of the Satie Society*, with illustrations by Jasper Johns, Cy Twombly, Robert Rauschenberg, Sol LeWitt, Mell Daniel, Henry David Thoreau, and Cage himself. Since Cage's works are multigenetic, his scores have been exhibited in galleries and museums; he almost always made an annual trip to Crown Point Press in San Francisco to make etchings. A series of 52 paintings, the *New River Watercolors*, executed in 1987 at the Miles C. Horton Center at the Virginia Polytechnic Institute and State University, has been shown at the Phillips Collection in Washington, D.C. (1990).

CARTER, ELLIOTT (COOK, JR.), outstanding American composer; b. New York, Dec. 11, 1908. After graduating from the Horace Mann High School in 1926, Carter entered Harvard University, majoring in literature and languages, at the same time studying piano at the Longy School of Music in Cambridge, Massachusetts. In 1930 he devoted himself exclusively to music, taking up harmony and counterpoint with Walter Piston, and orchestration with Edward

Burlingame Hill; he also attended in 1932 a course given at Harvard University by **Gustav Holst**. The evolution of Carter's style of composition is marked by his constant preoccupation with taxonomic considerations. His early works are set in a neo-Classical style. He later absorbed the Schoenbergian method of composition with 12 tones; finally he developed a system of serial organization in which all parameters, including intervals, metric divisions, rhythm, counterpoint, harmony, and instrumental timbres become parts of the total conception of each individual work. In this connection he introduced the term "metric modulation," in which secondary rhythms in a polyrhythmic section assume dominance expressed in constantly changing meters, often in such unusual time signatures as 10/16, 21/8, etc. Furthermore, he assigns to each participating instrument in a polyphonic work a special interval, a distinctive rhythmic figure, and a selective register, so that the individuality of each part is clearly outlined, a distribution that is often reinforced by placing the players at a specified distance from one another.

CARUSO, ENRICO (ERRICO), celebrated Italian tenor; b. Naples, Feb. 25, 1873; d. there, Aug. 2, 1921. He sang Neapolitan ballads by ear; as a youth he applied for a part in *Mignon* at the Teatro Fondo in Naples, but was unable to follow the orchestra at the rehearsal and had to be replaced by another singer. His operatic debut took place at the Teatro Nuovo in Naples on Nov. 16, 1894, in *L'Amico Francesco*, by an amateur composer, Mario Morelli. In 1895 he appeared at the Teatro Fondo in *La Traviata*, *La Favorita*, and *Rigoletto*; during the following few seasons he added *Aida*, *Faust*, *Carmen*, *La Bohème*, and *Tosca* to his repertoire. The decisive turn in his career came when he was chosen to appear as leading tenor in the first performance of Giordano's *Fedora* (1898), in which he made a great impression. Several important engagements followed. In 1899 and 1900 he sang in St. Petersburg and Moscow; between 1899 and 1903 he appeared in four summer seasons in Buenos Aires. The culmination of these successes was the coveted opportunity to sing at La Scala; he sang there in *La Bohème* (1900), and in the first performance of Mascagni's *Le Maschere* (1901). He made his London debut in 1902 as the Duke in *Rigoletto* and was immediately successful with the

British public and press. He gave 25 performances in London in that year, appearing with Melba, Nordica, and Calvé. In the season of 1902-3, Caruso sang in Rome and Lisbon; during the summer of 1903 he was in South America.

Finally, in 1903, he made his American debut at the Metropolitan Opera, in *Rigoletto*. After that memorable occasion, Caruso was connected with the Metropolitan to the end of his life. He traveled with various American opera companies from coast to coast; he happened to be performing in San Francisco when the 1906 earthquake nearly destroyed the city. He achieved his most spectacular successes in America, attended by enormous publicity. In 1907 Caruso sang in Germany (Leipzig, Hamburg, Berlin) and in Vienna; he was acclaimed there as enthusiastically as in the Anglo-Saxon and Latin countries. Caruso's fees soared from $2 as a boy in Italy in 1891 to the fabulous sum of $15,000 for a single performance in Mexico City in 1920. He made recordings in the U.S. as early as 1902; his annual income from this source alone netted him $115,000 at the peak of his career. He excelled in realistic Italian operas; his Cavaradossi in *Tosca* and Canio in *Pagliacci* became models that every singer emulated. He sang several French operas, however, the German repertoire remained completely alien to him; his only appearances in Wagnerian roles were three performances of *Lohengrin* in Buenos Aires (1901).

His voice possessed such natural warmth and great strength in the middle register that as a youth he was believed to be a baritone. The sustained quality of his bel canto was exceptional and enabled him to give superb interpretations of lyrical parts. For dramatic effect, he often resorted to the "coup de glotte" (which became known as the "Caruso sob"); here the singing gave way to intermittent vocalization without tonal precision. While Caruso was criticized for such usages from the musical standpoint, his characterizations on the stage were overwhelmingly impressive. Although of robust health, he abused it by unceasing activity. He was stricken with a throat hemorrhage during a performance at the Brooklyn Academy of Music (1920), but was able to sing in New York one last time, on Dec. 24. Several surgical operations were performed in an effort to arrest a pleurisy; Caruso was taken to Italy, but succumbed to the illness after several months of remission.

CHALIAPIN, FEODOR (IVANOVICH), celebrated Russian bass; b. Kazan, Feb. 13, 1873; d. Paris, April 12, 1938. He was of humble origin; at the age of 10 he was apprenticed to a cobbler. At 14 he got a job singing in a chorus in a traveling opera company; his companion was the famous writer Maxim Gorky, who also sang in a chorus. Together they made their way through the Russian provinces, often forced to walk the railroad tracks when they could not afford the fare. Chaliapin's wanderings brought him to Tiflis, in the Caucasus, where he was introduced to the singing teacher Dimitri Usatov, who immediately recognized Chaliapin's extraordinary gifts and taught him free of charge, helping him besides with board and lodgings. In 1894 Chaliapin received employment in a summer opera company in St. Petersburg, and shortly afterward he was accepted at the Imperial Opera during the regular season. In 1896 he sang in Moscow with a private opera company and produced a great impression by his dramatic interpretation of the bass parts in Russian operas. He also gave numerous solo concerts, which were sold out almost immediately; young music-lovers were willing to stand in line all night long to obtain tickets.

Chaliapin's first engagement outside Russia was in 1901, at La Scala in Milan, where he sang the role of Mefistofele in Boito's opera; he returned to La Scala in 1904 and again in 1908. On Nov. 20, 1907, he made his American debut at the Metropolitan Opera as Mefistofele, and then sang Méphistophélès in **Gounod**'s *Faust* and Leporello in **Mozart**'s *Don Giovanni* in Jan. 1908. He did not return to America until 1921, when he sang one of his greatest roles, that of the Czar Boris in *Boris Godunov*; he continued to appear at the Metropolitan between 1921 and 1929. He sang in Russian opera roles at Covent Garden in London in 1913; returned to Russia in 1914, and remained there during World War I and the Revolution. He was given the rank of People's Artist by the Soviet government, but this title was withdrawn after Chaliapin emigrated in 1922 to Paris, where he remained until his death, except for appearances in England and America. He was indeed one of the greatest singing actors of all time; he dominated every scene in which he appeared, and to the last he never failed in his ability to move audiences, even though his vocal powers declined considerably during his last years.

CHOPIN, FRÉDÉRIC(-FRANÇOIS) (FRYDERYK FRANCISZEK),
greatly renowned Polish composer, incomparable genius of the piano
who created a unique romantic style of keyboard music; b. Zelazowa
Wola, near Warsaw, in all probability on March 1, 1810; d. Paris, Oct.
17, 1849. His father was a native of Marainville, France, who went to
Warsaw as a teacher of French; his mother was Polish. Chopin's talent was manifested in early childhood; at the age of eight he played
in public a piano concerto by Adalbart Gyrowetz, and he had already
begun to compose polonaises, mazurkas, and waltzes. Chopin was 15
years old when his Rondo for Piano was published in Warsaw as op.
1. In the summer of 1829 he set out for Vienna, where he gave highly successful concerts on Aug. 11 and Aug. 18. While in Vienna he
made arrangements to have his variations on **Mozart**'s aria *Là ci
darem la mano*, for piano and orchestra, published by Haslinger as
op. 2. It was this work that attracted the attention of **Robert
Schumann**, who saluted Chopin in his famous article published in
the *Allgemeine Musikalische Zeitung* in 1831, in which Schumann's
alter ego, Eusebius, is represented as exclaiming, "Hats off, gentle-
men! A genius!" The common assumption in many biographies that
Schumann "launched" Chopin on his career is deceptive; actually
Schumann was some months younger than Chopin, and was referred
to editorially merely as a "student."

Returning to Warsaw, Chopin gave the first public performance
of his Piano Concerto in F minor, op. 21, on March 17, 1830. On Oct.
11, 1830, he was soloist in his Piano Concerto in E minor, op. 11. A
confusion resulted in the usual listing of the E minor Concerto as first,
and the F minor Concerto as his second; chronologically, the composition of the F minor Concerto preceded the E minor. He spent the
winter of 1830-31 in Vienna. The Polish rebellion against Russian
domination, which ended in defeat, determined Chopin's further
course of action, and he proceeded to Paris, visiting Linz, Salzburg,
Dresden, and Stuttgart on the way. He arrived in Paris in Sept. 1831.
Paris was then the center of Polish emigration, and Chopin maintained his contacts with the Polish circle there. He presented his first
Paris concert on Feb. 26, 1832. The Paris critics found an apt Shakespearean epithet for him, calling him "the Ariel of the piano."

In 1836 he met the famous novelist Aurore Dupin (Mme.
Dudevant), who published her works under the affected masculine

English name George Sand. They became intimate, even though quite incompatible in character and interests. They parted in 1847; by that time he was quite ill with tuberculosis; a daguerreotype taken of him represents a prematurely aged man with facial features showing sickness and exhaustion, with locks of black hair partly covering his forehead. Yet he continued his concert career. He undertook a tour as pianist in England and Scotland in 1848; he gave his last concert in Paris on Feb. 16, 1848. He died the following year; Mozart's Requiem was performed at Chopin's funeral at the Madeleine, with the orchestra and chorus of the Paris Conservatoire. He was buried between the graves of Luigi Cherubini and **Vincenzo Bellini**; however, at his own request, his heart was sent to Warsaw for entombment in his homeland.

Chopin represents the full liberation of the piano from traditional orchestral and choral influences, the authoritative assumption of its role as a solo instrument. Not seeking "orchestral" sonorities, he may have paled as a virtuoso beside the titanic **Franz Liszt**, but the poesy of his pianism, its fervor of expression, the pervading melancholy in his nocturnes and ballades, and the bounding exultation of his scherzos and études were never equaled. And, from a purely technical standpoint, Chopin's figurations and bold modulatory transitions seem to presage the elaborate transtonal developments of modern music.

CLEMENTI, MUZIO, (baptized **Mutius Philippus Vincentius Franciscus Xaverius**), celebrated Italian pianist and composer; b. Rome, Jan. 23, 1752; d. Evesham, Worcestershire, England, March 10, 1832. He began to study music as a child, and at the age of seven commenced studying the organ, and later voice. By 1766 he was organist of the parish San Lorenzo in Damaso. About this time Peter Beckford, cousin of the English novelist William Beckford, visited Rome; he was struck by Clementi's youthful talent and, with the permission of Clementi's father, took the boy to England. For the next seven years Clementi lived, performed, and studied at his patron's estate of Stepleton Iwerne in Dorset. During the winter of 1774–1775, Clementi settled in London, making his first appearance as a harpsichordist in a benefit concert on April 3, 1775. For the next several years he appears to have spent most of his time as harpsichordist at the King's Theatre, where he conducted operatic performances. In 1779 his six sonatas, op. 2, were published, which brought him his first public success, both in England and on the Continent.

In 1780 he embarked on a tour of the Continent, giving a series of piano concerts in Paris; in 1781 he continued his tour with appearances in Strasbourg, Munich, and Vienna. It was during his stay in Vienna that the famous piano contest with **Mozart** took place at court before Emperor Joseph II on Dec. 24, 1781. In 1786 several of his symphonies were performed in London, only to be eclipsed by the great symphonies of **Haydn**. In 1790 he retired from public performances as a pianist, but he continued to conduct orchestra concerts from the keyboard.

After 1796 he appears to have withdrawn from all public performances, devoting himself to teaching, collecting large fees. He lost part of his fortune through the bankruptcy of Longman and Broderip in 1798; however, with John Longman, he formed a partnership on the ruins of the old company and became highly successful as a music publisher and piano manufacturer. His business acumen was keen, and he remained successful with subsequent partners during the next three decades. From 1802 to 1810 he traveled extensively on the Continent, pursuing business interests, teaching, composing, and giving private concerts. While in Vienna in 1807, he met **Beethoven** and arranged to become his major English publisher.

He returned to England in 1810, and in 1813 helped organize the Philharmonic Society of London, with which he appeared as a conductor. In 1816–1817 he conducted his symphonies in Paris, followed by engagements in Frankfurt in 1817–1818. He again visited Paris in 1821, and was in Munich in 1821–1822. In 1822 he conducted his works with the Gewandhaus Orchestra in Leipzig. Returning to England, he made several more conducting appearances with the Philharmonic Society until 1824; however, his symphonies were soon dropped from the repertoire as Beethoven's masterpieces eclipsed his own efforts. In 1830 he retired from his mercantile ventures, and eventually made his home at Evesham, Worcestershire.

COPLAND, AARON, greatly distinguished and exceptionally gifted American composer; b. New York, Nov. 14, 1900; d. North Tarrytown, New York, Dec. 2, 1990. He was educated at the Boys'

High School in Brooklyn, and began to study piano as a young child. In 1917 he took lessons in harmony and counterpoint, and soon began to compose. His first published piece, *The Cat and the Mouse for Piano* (1920), subtitled "Scherzo humoristique," shows the influence of **Claude Debussy**. In 1920 he entered the American Conservatory in Fontainebleau, near Paris, where he studied composition and orchestration with Nadia Boulanger. Returning to America in 1924, he lived mostly in New York, becoming active in many musical activities, not only as a composer but also as a lecturer, pianist, and organizer in various musical societies.

Copland attracted the attention of noted conductor Serge Koussevitzky, who gave the first performance of his early score *Music for the Theater* with the Boston Symphony Orchestra in 1925; he then engaged Copland as soloist in his Concerto for Piano and Orchestra in 1927. The work produced a considerable sensation because of the jazz elements incorporated in the score, and there was some subterranean grumbling among the staid subscribers to the Boston Symphony concerts. Koussevitzky remained Copland's steadfast supporter throughout his tenure as conductor of the Boston Symphony, and later as the founder of the Koussevitzky Music Foundation. In the meantime in New York, Walter Damrosch conducted Copland's Symphony for Organ and Orchestra, with Nadia Boulanger as soloist. Other orchestras and their conductors also performed his music, which gained increasing recognition. Particularly popular were Copland's works based on folk motifs; of these the most remarkable are *El Salón México* (1933–1936) and the American ballets *Billy the Kid* (1938), *Rodeo* (1942), and *Appalachian Spring* (1944). A place apart is occupied by Copland's *Lincoln Portrait* for Narrator and Orchestra (1942), with the texts arranged by the composer from speeches and letters of Abraham Lincoln; this work has had a great many performances, with the role of the narrator performed by such notables as Adlai Stevenson and Eleanor Roosevelt. His patriotic *Fanfare for the Common Man* (1942) achieved tremendous popularity and continued to be played on various occasions for decades; Copland incorporated it *in toto* into the score of his Third Symphony.

About 1955 Copland developed a successful career as a conductor, and led major symphony orchestras in Europe, the U.S., South America, and Mexico; he also traveled to Russia under the auspices of the State Department. In 1982 the Aaron Copland School of

Music was created at Queens College of the City University of New York. In 1983 he made his last appearance as a conductor in New York. He was awarded the National Medal of Arts in 1986. As a composer, Copland made use of a broad variety of idioms and techniques, tempering dissonant textures by a strong sense of tonality. He enlivened his musical textures by ingenious applications of syncopation and polyrhythmic combinations; but in such works as his Piano Variations he adopted an austere method of musical constructivism. He used a modified 12-tone technique in his Piano Quartet (1950) and an integral dodecaphonic idiom in the score of *Connotations* (1962).

CORELLI, ARCANGELO, famous Italian violinist and composer; b. Fusignano, near Imola, Feb. 17, 1653; d. Rome, Jan. 8, 1713. Little is known of his early life; about 1671 he went to Rome, where he was a violinist at the French Church (1675). In the beginning of 1679, he played in the orchestra of the Teatro Capranica; Rome remained his chief residence to the end of his life. Corelli was famous as a virtuoso on the violin and may be regarded as the founder of modern violin technique; he systematized the art of proper bowing, and was one of the first to use double stops and chords on the violin. His role in music history is very great despite the fact that he wrote but few works; only six opus numbers can be definitely attributed to him. His greatest achievement was the creation of the concerto grosso. **Handel**, who as a young man met Corelli in Rome, was undoubtedly influenced by Corelli's instrumental writing. Corelli was buried in the Pantheon in Rome.

COWELL, HENRY (DIXON), remarkable, innovative American composer; b. Menlo Park, California, March 11, 1897; d. Shady, New York, Dec. 10, 1965. His father, of Irish birth, was a member of a clergyman's family in Kildare; his mother was an American of progressive persuasion. Cowell studied violin with Henry Holmes in San Francisco; after the earthquake of 1906, his mother took him to New York, where they were compelled to seek support from the Society for the Improvement of the Condition of the Poor. They returned to Menlo Park, where Cowell was able to save enough money, earned from menial jobs, to buy a piano. He began to experiment with the keyboard by striking the keys with fists and forearms; he named such chords "tone clusters," and at the age of 13 composed a piece called *Adventures in Harmony*, containing such chords. Later he began experimenting in altering the sound of the piano by placing various objects on the strings, and also by playing directly under the lid of the piano pizzicato and glissando. He first exhibited these startling innovations in 1914, at the San Francisco Musical Society at the St. Francis Hotel, much to the consternation of its members, no doubt.

The tone clusters *per se* were not new; they were used for special sound effects by composers in the 18th century to imitate thunder or cannon fire. The Russian composer Vladimir Rebikov applied them in his piano piece *Hymn to Inca*, and **Charles Ives** used them in his *Concord Sonata* to be sounded by covering a set of white or black keys with a wooden board. However, Cowell had a priority by systematizing tone clusters as harmonic amplifications of tonal chords, and he devised logical notation for them. The tone clusters eventually acquired legitimacy in the works of many European and American composers. Cowell also extended the sonorities of tone clusters to instrumental combinations and applied them in several of his symphonic works.

In the meantime Cowell began taking lessons in composition at the University of California in Berkeley, and later at the Institute of Musical Art in New York, and, privately, with Charles Seeger (1914–1916). After brief service in the U.S. Army in 1918, where he was employed first as a cook and later as arranger for the U.S. Army Band, he became engaged professionally to give a series of lectures on new music, illustrated by his playing his own works on the piano. In 1927 Cowell founded the *New Music Quarterly* for publication of ultramodern music, mainly by American composers. In 1928 he went to Russia, where he attracted considerable attention as the first American composer to visit there; some of his pieces were published in a Russian edition, the first such publications by an American. Upon return to the U.S., he was appointed lecturer on music at The New School in New York.

In 1931 he received a Guggenheim fellowship grant, and went to Berlin to study ethnomusicology with Erich von Hornbostel. This was the beginning of his serious study of ethnic musical materials. He had already experimented with some Indian and Chinese devices in some of his works; in his *Ensemble* for Strings (1924) he included Indian thundersticks; the piece naturally aroused considerable curiosity. In 1931 he formed a collaboration with the Russian electrical engineer **Leon Theremin**, then visiting the U.S.; with his aid he constructed an ingenious instrument which he called the Rhythmicon, making possible the simultaneous production of 16 different rhythms on 16 different pitch levels of the harmonic series. He demonstrated it at a lecture-concert in San Francisco in 1932.

Cowell's career was brutally interrupted in 1936, when he was arrested in California on charges of homosexuality (then a heinous offense in California) involving the impairment of the morals of a minor. Lulled by the deceptive promises of a wily district attorney of a brief confinement in a sanatorium, Cowell pleaded guilty to a limited offense, but he was vengefully given a maximum sentence of imprisonment, up to 15 years. Incarcerated at San Quentin, he was assigned to work in a jute mill, but indomitably continued to write music in prison. Thanks to interventions in his behalf by a number of eminent musicians, he was paroled in 1940 to Percy Grainger as a guarantor of his good conduct; he obtained a full pardon in 1942, from the governor of California, after it was discovered that the evidence against him was largely contrived.

On Sept. 27, 1941, he married Sidney Robertson, a noted ethnomusicologist. He was then able to resume his full activities as an editor and instructor; he held teaching positions at The New School for Social Research in New York (1940–1962), the University of Southern California, Mills College, and the Peabody Conservatory of Music in Baltimore (1951–1956), and was also appointed adjunct professor at summer classes at Columbia University (1951–1965). In 1951 Cowell was elected a member of the National Academy of Arts and Letters; he received an honorary Mus.D. from Wilmington College (1953) and from Monmouth (Ill.) College (1963). In 1956–1957 he undertook a world tour with his wife through the Near East, India, and Japan, collecting rich prime materials for his compositions, which by now had acquired a decisive turn toward the use of ethnomusicological melodic and rhythmic materials, without abandoning, however, the experimental devices which were the signposts of most of his works. In addition to his symphonic and chamber music, Cowell published in 1930 an important book, *New Musical Resources*. He also edited a symposium, *American Composers on American*

Music; in collaboration with his wife he wrote the first, basic biography of Charles Ives (1955).

CRAWFORD, RUTH PORTER, remarkable American composer; b. East Liverpool, Ohio, July 3, 1901; d. Chevy Chase, Maryland, Nov. 18, 1953. She studied composition with Charles Seeger, whom she later married; her principal piano teacher was Heniot Lévy. She dedicated herself to teaching and to collecting American folk songs. When still very young, she taught at the School of Musical Arts in Jacksonville, Fla. (1918–1921); then gave courses at the American Conservatory in Chicago (1925–1929) and at the Elmhurst College of Music in Illinois (1926–1929). In 1930 she received a Guggenheim fellowship. She became known mainly as a compiler of American folk songs, compiling *American Folk Songs for Children* (1948), *Animal Folk Songs for Children* (1950), and *American Folk Songs for Christmas* (1953). Her own compositions, astonishingly bold in their experimental aperçus and insights, often anticipated many techniques of the future avant-garde; while rarely performed during her lifetime, they had a remarkable revival in subsequent decades.

After her marriage, she took husband's surname, and so is sometimes catalogued under the name Seeger, R. C.

CRUMB, GEORGE (HENRY, JR.), distinguished and innovative American composer; b. Charleston, W. Va., Oct. 24, 1929. He was brought up in a musical environment; his father played the clarinet and his mother was a cellist. He studied music at home, began composing while in school, and had some of his pieces performed by the Charleston Symphony Orchestra. He then took courses in composition at Mason College in Charleston (B.M., 1950), later enrolling at the University of Illinois (M.M., 1952), and continuing his studies in composition at the University of Michigan (D.M.A., 1959). In 1955 he received a Fulbright fellowship for travel to Germany, where he studied at the Berlin Hochschule für Musik. Parallel to working on his compositions, he was active as a music teacher.

In his music, Crumb is a universalist. Nothing in the realm of sound is alien to him; no method of composition is unsuited to his artistic purposes. Accordingly, his music can sing as sweetly as the proverbial nightingale, and it can be as rough, rude, and crude as a primitive man of the mountains. The vocal parts especially demand extraordinary skills of lungs, lips, tongue, and larynx to produce such sound effects as percussive tongue clicks, explosive shrieks, hissing, whistling, whispering, and sudden shouting of verbal irrelevancies, interspersed with portentous syllabification, disparate phonemes, and rhetorical logorrhea. In startling contrast, Crumb injects into his sonorous kaleidoscope citations from popular works, such as the middle section of **Chopin**'s *Fantaisie-Impromptu*, **Ravel**'s *Bolero*, or some other *objet trouvé*, a procedure first introduced facetiously by **Erik Satie**. In his instrumentation, Crumb is no less unconventional. Among the unusual effects in his scores is instructing the percussion player to immerse the loudly sounding gong into a tub of water, having an electric guitar played with glass rods over the frets, or telling wind instrumentalists to blow soundlessly through their tubes. Spatial distribution also plays a role: instrumentalists and singers are assigned their reciprocal locations on the podium or in the hall.

All this is, of course, but an illustrative decor; the music is of the essence. Like most composers who began their work around the middle of the 20th century, Crumb adopted the Schoenbergian idiom, seasoned with pointillistic devices. After these preliminaries, he wrote his unmistakably individual *Madrigals*, to words by the martyred poet Federico García Lorca, scored for voice and instrumental groups. There followed the most extraordinary work, *Ancient Voices of Children*, performed for the first time at a chamber music festival in Washington, D.C., in 1970; the text is again by Lorca. A female singer intones into the space under the lid of an amplified grand piano; a boy's voice responds in anguish. The accompaniment is supplied by an orchestral group and an assortment of exotic percussion instruments, such as Tibetan prayer stones, Japanese temple bells, a musical saw, and a toy piano. A remarkable group of four pieces, entitled *Makrokosmos*, calls for unusual effects; in one of these, the pianist is ordered to shout at specified points of time. Crumb's most grandiose creation is *Star-Child*, representing, in his imaginative scheme, a progression from tenebrous despair to the exaltation of luminous joy. The score calls for a huge orchestra, which includes two children's choruses and eight percussion players performing on all kinds of utensils, such as pot lids, and also iron chains and metal sheets, as well as ordinary drums. It had its first performance under the direction of **Pierre Boulez** with the New York Philharmonic in 1977.

CZERNY, CARL, celebrated Austrian pianist, composer, and pedagogue; b. Vienna, Feb. 20, 1791; d. there, July 15, 1857. He was of Czech extraction (*czerny* means "black" in Czech), and his first language was Czech. He received his early training from his father, a stern disciplinarian who never let his son play with other children and insisted on concentrated work. Czerny had the privilege of studying for three years with **Beethoven**, and their association in subsequent years became a close one. Very early in life he demonstrated great ability as a patient piano teacher; Beethoven entrusted to him the musical education of his favorite nephew. When Czerny himself became a renowned pedagogue, many future piano virtuosos flocked to him for lessons, among them **Liszt** (whom he taught without a fee). Despite the heavy teaching schedule, Czerny found time to compose a fantastic amount of music, 861 opus numbers in all, each containing many individual items. These included not only piano studies and exercises, for which he became celebrated, but also sonatas, concertos, string quartets, masses, and hymns. In addition, he made numerous piano arrangements of classical symphonies, including all of Beethoven's, and wrote fantasies for piano on the themes from famous operas of the time.

DEBUSSY, (ACHILLE-)CLAUDE, great French composer whose music created new poetry of mutating tonalities and became a perfect counterpart of Impressionist painting in France; b. St-Germain-en-Laye, Aug. 22, 1862; d. Paris, March 25, 1918. Mme. Mauté de Fleurville, the mother-in-law of the poet Verlaine, prepared him for the Paris Conservatoire; he was admitted at the age of 10, and remained until 1882. In 1880 Marmontel recommended him to Mme. Nadezhda von Meck, **Tchaikovsky**'s patroness. She summoned him to Interlaken, and they subsequently visited Rome, Naples, and Fiesole. During the summers of 1881 and 1882, Debussy stayed with Mme. von Meck's family in Moscow, where he became acquainted with the symphonies of Tchaikovsky; however, he failed to appreciate Tchaikovsky's music and became more interested in the idiosyncratic compositions of **Modest Mussorgsky**. Back in France, he became friendly with Mme. Vasnier, wife of a Paris architect and an amateur singer.

Debussy made his earliest professional appearance as a composer in Paris in 1882, at a concert given by the violinist Maurice Thieberg. In Dec. 1880 he enrolled in the composition class of Ernest Guiraud at the Paris Conservatoire with the ambition of winning the Grand Prix de Rome; after completing his courses, he won the second Prix de Rome in 1883. Finally, in 1884, he succeeded in obtaining the Grand Prix de Rome with his cantata *L'Enfant prodigue*, written in a poetic but conservative manner reflecting the trends of French romanticism. During his stay in Rome he wrote a choral work, *Zuleima* (1885–1886), and began work on another cantata, *Diane au bois*. Neither of these two incunabulae was preserved. His choral suite with orchestra, *Printemps* (1887), failed to win formal recognition. He then set to work on another cantata, *La Damoiselle élue* (1887–1889), which gained immediate favor among French musicians.

In 1888 Debussy visited Bayreuth, where he heard *Parsifal* and *Die Meistersinger von Nürnberg* for the first time, but Wagner's grandiloquence never gained his full devotion. What thoroughly engaged his interest was the Oriental music that he heard at the Paris World Exposition in 1889. He was fascinated by the asymmetric rhythms of the thematic content and the new instrumental colors achieved by native players; he also found an inner valence between these Oriental modalities and the verses of certain French Impressionist poets, including Mallarmé, Verlaine, Baudelaire, and Pierre Louÿs. The combined impressions of exotic music and symbolist French verses were rendered in Debussy's vocal works, such as *Cinq poèmes de Baudelaire* (1887–1889), *Ariettes oubliées* (1888), *Trois mélodies* (1891), and *Fêtes galantes* (1892). He also wrote *Proses lyriques* (1892–1893) to his own texts. For the piano, he composed *Suite bergamasque* (1890–1905), which includes the famous *Clair de lune*.

In 1892 he began work on his instrumental *Prélude à l'après-midi d'un faune*, after Mallarmé, which comprises the quintessence of tonal painting with its free modal sequences under a subtle umbrage of oscillating instrumentation. The work was first heard in Paris in 1894; a program book cautioned the audience that the text contained sensuous elements that might be distracting to young females. It was about that time that Debussy attended a performance of Maeterlinck's drama *Pelléas et Mélisande*, which inspired him to begin work on an opera on that subject. In 1893 there followed *Trois chansons de Bilitis*, after prose poems by Louÿs, marked by exceptional sensuality of the text in a musical context of free modality; a later work, *Les Chansons de Bilitis* for two harps, two flutes, and celesta, was heard in Paris in 1901 as incidental music to accompany recited and mimed neo-Grecian poetry of Louÿs. Between 1892 and 1899 Debussy worked on three Nocturnes for orchestra: *Nuages*, *Fêtes*, and *Sirènes*.

With his opera *Pelléas et Mélisande*, Debussy assumed a leading place among French composers. It was premiered at the Opéra-

Comique in 1902, after many difficulties, including the open opposition of Maeterlinck, who objected to having the role of Mélisande sung by the American soprano Mary Garden, whose accent jarred Maeterlinck's sensibilities; he wanted his mistress, Georgette Leblanc, to be the first Mélisande. The production of the opera aroused a violent controversy among French musicians and *litterateurs*. The press was vicious in the extreme: "Rhythm, melody, tonality, these are three things unknown to Monsieur Debussy," wrote the doyen of the Paris music critics, Arthur Pougin, "What a pretty series of false relations! What adorable progressions of triads in parallel motion and fifths and octaves which result from it! What a collection of dissonances, sevenths and ninths, ascending with energy! . . . No, decidedly I will never agree with these anarchists of music!"

Debussy's next important work was *La Mer*, completed during a sojourn in England in 1905, which premiered in Paris in the same year. Like his String Quartet, it was conceived monothematically; a single musical idea permeated the entire work despite a great variety of instrumentation. It consists of three symphonic sketches: *De l'aube à midi sur la mer* (From Sunrise to Moon); *Jeux de vagues* (Play of the Waves); and *Dialogue du vent et de la mer* (Dialogue of Wind and the Sea). *La Mer* was attacked by critics with even greater displeasure than *Pelléas et Mélisande*. The American critic Louis Elson went so far as to suggest that the original title was actually "Le Mal de mer," and that the last movement represented a violent seizure of vomiting. To summarize the judgment on Debussy, a volume entitled *Le Cas Debussy* was published in Paris in 1910. It contained a final assessment of Debussy as a "déformateur musical," suffering from a modern nervous disease that affects one's power of discernment.

Meanwhile, Debussy continued to work. To be mentioned is the remarkable orchestral triptych, *Images* (1906–1912), comprising *Gigues*, *Ibéria*, and *Rondes de printemps*. In 1908 he conducted a concert of his works in London; he also accepted engagements as conductor in Vienna (1910), Turin (1911), Moscow and St. Petersburg (1913), and Rome, Amsterdam, and The Hague (1914). Among other works of the period are the piano suites, *Douze préludes* (two books, 1909–1910; 1910–1913) and *Douze études* (two books, 1915). *En blanc et noir*, for two pianos, dates from 1915. In 1913, Diaghilev produced Debussy's ballet *Jeux* in Paris. In 1917, Debussy played the piano part of his Violin Sonata at its premiere in Paris with violinist Gaston

Poulet. But his projected tour of the U.S. with the violinist Arthur Hartmann had to be abandoned when it was discovered that Debussy had irreversible cancer of the colon. Surgery was performed in Dec. 1915, but there was little hope of recovery. The protracted First World War depressed him; his hatred of the Germans became intense as the military threat to Paris increased. He wrote the lyrics and the accompaniment to a song, *Noël des enfants*, in which he begged Santa Claus not to bring presents to German children whose parents were destroying the French children's Christmas. To underline his national sentiments, he emphatically signed his last works "musicien français." Debussy died on the evening of March 25, 1918, as the great German gun, "Big Bertha," made the last attempt to subdue the city of Paris by long-distance bombardment.

Debussy emphatically rejected the term "Impressionism" as applied to his music. But it cannot alter the essential truth that, like Mallarmé in poetry, he created a style peculiarly sensitive to musical mezzotint, a palette of half-lit delicate colors. He systematically applied the Oriental pentatonic scale for exotic evocations, as well as the whole-tone scale (which he did not invent, however; earlier samples of its use are found in works by **Glinka** and **Liszt**). His piece for piano solo, *Voiles*, is written in a whole-tone scale, while its middle section is set entirely in the pentatonic scale. In his music Debussy emancipated discords; he also revived the archaic practice of consecutive perfect intervals (particularly fifths and fourths). In his formal constructions, the themes are shortened and rhythmically sharpened, while in the instrumental treatment the role of individual solo passages is enhanced and the dynamic range made more subtle.

DELIBES, (CLÉMENT-PHILIBERT-)LÉO, famous French composer; b. St-Germain-du-Val, Sarthe, Feb. 21, 1836; d. Paris, Jan. 16, 1891. In 1856 his first work for the stage, *Deux sous de charbon*, a one-act operetta, humorously designated an "asphyxie lyrique," was produced at the Folies-Nouvelles. His second work, the opérette bouffe *Deux vieilles gardes* (1856), won considerable acclaim at its premiere at the Bouffes-Parisiens. Several more operettas were to follow, as well as his first substantial work for the stage, *Le Jardinier et son seigneur*, given at the Théâtre-Lyrique in 1863. It was with his ballet, *Coppélia, ou La Fille aux yeux d'émail*, that Delibes achieved lasting fame after its premiere at the Paris Opéra in 1870. Another ballet, *Sylvia, ou La Nymphe de Diane* (1876), was equally successful. He then wrote a grand opera, *Jean de Nivelle* (1880), which was moderately successful; it was followed by his triumphant masterpiece, the opera *Lakmé* (1883), in which he created a most effective lyric evocation of India; the "Bell Song" from *Lakmé* became a perennial favorite in recitals. His last opera, *Kassya*, was completed but not orchestrated at the time of his death; **Jules Massenet** orchestrated the score, and it was premiered at the Opéra-Comique in 1893. Delibes was a master of melodious elegance and harmonious charm; his music possessed an autonomous flow in colorful timbres, and a finality of excellence that seemed effortless while subtly revealing a mastery of the Romantic technique of composition.

DELIUS, FREDERICK (baptized, **Fritz Theodor Albert**), significant English composer of German parentage; b. Bradford, Jan. 29, 1862; d. Grez-sur-Loing, France, June 10, 1934. His father was a successful merchant, owner of a wool company; he naturally hoped to have his son follow a career in industry, but did not object to his study of art and music. Delius learned to play the piano and violin. At the age of 22 he went to Solano, Florida, to work on an orange plantation owned by his father; a musical souvenir of his sojourn there was his symphonic suite *Florida*. There he met an American organist who gave him a thorough instruction in music theory. In 1885 he went to Danville, Virginia, as a teacher.

In 1886, he returned to Europe to enroll at the Leipzig Conservatory, where he took courses in harmony and counterpoint. It was there that he met **Edvard Grieg**, becoming his friend and admirer. Indeed Grieg's music found a deep resonance in his own compositions. An even more powerful influence was **Wagner**, whose principles of continuous melodic line and thematic development Delius adopted in his own works. Euphonious serenity reigns on the symphonic surface of his music, diversified by occasional resolvable dissonances. In some works he made congenial use of English folk motifs, often in elaborate variation forms. Particularly successful are his evocative symphonic sketches *On Hearing the First Cuckoo in Spring, North Country Sketches, Brigg Fair,* and *A Song of the High Hills.* His orchestral nocturne *Paris: The Song of a Great City* is a tribute to a city in which he spent many years of his life. Much more ambitious in scope is his choral work *A Mass of Life*, in which he draws on passages from Nietzsche's *Also sprach Zarathustra*.

Delius settled in Paris in 1888; in 1897 he moved to Grez-sur-Loing, near Paris, where he remained for the rest of his life, except for a few short trips abroad. In 1903 he married the painter Jelka Rosen. His music began to win recognition in England and Germany; he became a favorite composer of conductor Sir Thomas Beecham, who gave numerous performances of his music in London. But these successes came too late for Delius; a syphilitic infection which he had contracted early in life eventually grew into an incurable illness accompanied by paralysis and blindness. Still eager to compose, he engaged as his amanuensis the English musician Eric Fenby, who wrote down music at the dictation of Delius, including complete orchestral scores. In 1929, Beecham organized a Delius Festival in London, and the composer was brought from France to hear it. However, he remains a solitary figure in modern music. Affectionately appreciated in England, in America, and to some extent in Germany, his works are rarely performed elsewhere.

DES PREZ, JOSQUIN, great Franco-Flemish composer; b. probably in Hainaut, c. 1440; d. Condé-sur-Escaut, near Valenciennes, Aug. 27, 1521. Few details of Josquin's early life are known. He may have been a boy chorister of the Collegiate Church at St-Quentin, later becoming canon and choirmaster there; he possibly was a pupil of Ockeghem, whom he greatly admired (after Ockeghem's death, in 1497, he wrote *La Déploration de Johan Okeghem*). From 1459 to 1472 he sang at the Milan Cathedral; by July 1474, he was at the Court of Duke Galeazzo Maria Sforza, Milan, as chorister. After the Duke's assassination he entered the service of the Duke's brother, Cardinal Ascanio Sforza, and, from 1486 to 1494, was a singer in the papal choir under the Popes Innocent VIII and Alexander VI. He was also active, for various periods, in Florence, where he met the famous theorist Pietro Aron; in Modena; and in Ferrara (where Flemish composer Heinrich Isaac was also) as maestro di cappella in 1503–1504. Later Josquin returned to Burgundy, settling in Conde-sur-Escaut (1504), where he became provost of Notre Dame.

As a composer, he was considered by contemporary musicians and theorists to be the greatest of his period, and he had a strong influence on all those who came into contact with his music or with him personally, as a teacher; Adriaan Petit Coclicus, who may have been one of Josquin's pupils, published a method in 1552 entitled *Compendium musices*, based on Josquin's teaching. He described Josquin as "princeps musicorum." His works were sung everywhere, and universally admired. In them he achieves a complete union between word and tone, thereby fusing the intricate Netherlandish contrapuntal devices into expressive and beautiful art forms. Two contrasting styles are present in his compositions: some are intricately contrapuntal, displaying the technical ingenuity characteristic of the Netherlands style; others, probably as a result of Italian influence, are homophonic.

DONIZETTI, (DOMENICO) GAETANO (MARIA), famous Italian composer; b. Bergamo, Nov. 29, 1797; d. there, April 1, 1848. His first opera, *Il Pigmalione* (1816), appears never to have been performed in his lifetime. He composed two more operas in quick succession, but they were not performed. His next work, *Enrico di Borgogna*, was performed in Venice in 1818, but it evoked little interest. He finally achieved popular success with his opera buffa *Il Falegname di Livonia, o Pietro il grande, czar delle Russie* (1819). In Dec. 1820 he was exempted from military service when a woman of means paid the sum necessary to secure his uninterrupted work at composition. His opera seria *Zoraide de Granata* (1822) proved a major success. During the next nine years, Donizetti composed 25 operas, none of which remain in the active repertoire today; however, the great success of his *L'Ajo nell'imbarazzo* (1824) brought him renown at the time.

With *Anna Bolena* (Milan, Dec. 26, 1830), Donizetti established himself as a master of the Italian operatic theater. The opera was an overwhelming success. His next enduring work was the charming comic opera *L'elisir d'amore* (1832). Two more operas followed, one produced in Italy, one in France, and then Donizetti returned to Italy, producing his tragic masterpiece *Lucia di Lammermoor* (1835), followed by *Roberto Devereux* (1837).

When the censor's veto prevented the production of *Poliuto* due to its sacred subject, he decided to return to Paris. He produced the highly successful *La Fille du régiment* there in 1840. It was followed by *Les Martyrs* (1840), a revision of the censored *Poliuto*, which proved successful. His *La Favorite* (1840) made little impression at its first performance, but it soon became one of his most popular operas. In 1843 he brought out his great comic masterpiece *Don Pasquale*. With such famous singers as Grisi, Mario, Tamburini, and Lablache in the cast, its premiere was a triumph. In that same year, he returned to Vienna, where he conducted the successful premiere of *Maria di Rohan*, and then came back again in Paris, where he produced *Dom Sebastien*. The audience approved the work enthusiastically, but the critics were not pleased. Considering the opera to be his masterpiece, Donizetti had to wait until the Vienna premiere (in German) of 1845 before the work was universally acclaimed. The last opera produced in his lifetime was *Caterina Cornaro* (1844). His finest works serve as the major link in the development of Italian opera between the period of **Rossini** and that of **Verdi**.

DUFAY, GUILLAUME, great French composer; b. probably in or near Cambrai, c. 1400; d. there, Nov. 27, 1474. His last name is pronounced "du-fah-ee," in three syllables, as indicated by the way he set his name to music in *Ave regina caelorum*. He was held in the highest esteem in his lifetime by the church authorities and his fellow musicians; contemporary composer Loyset Compère described him as "the moon of all music, and the light of all singers." He was the foremost representative of the Burgundian school of composition. He proved himself a master of both sacred and secular music, producing masses, motets, and chansons of extraordinary beauty and distinction. His contributions to the development of fauxbourdon and the cyclic mass are particularly noteworthy.

DVOŘÁK, ANTONÍN (LEOPOLD), famous Czech composer; b. Mühlhausen, Sept. 8, 1841; d. Prague, May 1, 1904. His father ran a village inn and butcher shop and intended Antonín to learn his trade. However, when he showed his musical inclinations, his father let him study piano and violin with a local musician. Later, Dvořák went to Prague, where he studied with the director of a church music school. He also began to compose so assiduously that in a short time he completed two symphonies, two operas, and some chamber music. His first public appearance as a composer took place in Prague on March 9, 1873, with a performance of his cantata *The Heirs of the White Mountain (Hymnus)*. An important event in his career occurred in Prague on March 29, 1874, when Bohemian composer Bedřich Smetana conducted his Symphony in E-flat major, op. 10. Dvořák then entered several of his works in a competition for the Austrian State Prize, adjudicated by a distinguished committee that included **Johannes Brahms**; he won the prize in 1875 and twice in 1877. Brahms appreciated Dvořák's talent and recommended him to his publisher, who issued Dvořák's *Moravian Duets* and the highly popular *Slavonic Dances*. His *Stabat Mater* (1880) and Symphony in D major, op. 60 (1881), followed in close succession, securing for him a leading position among Czech composers.

At the invitation of the Philharmonic Society of London, Dvořák visited England in 1884 and conducted several of his works. They commissioned his new symphony, the Symphony in D minor, op. 70, which he conducted there in 1885. His cantata *The Spectre's Bride*, composed for the Birmingham Festival, was accorded an excellent reception in the same year. On his third visit to England, he conducted the premiere of his oratorio *St. Ludmila* (1886), at the Leeds Festival. In 1890 he appeared as a conductor of his own works in Russia. On Feb. 2, 1890, he conducted in Prague the first performance of his Symphony in G major, op. 88, which became one of his most popular works. In 1891 Dvořák was appointed professor of composition at the Prague Conservatory; his brilliant *Carnival Overture* came later that year.

In 1892 Dvořák accepted the position of director of the National Conservatory of Music of America in New York. He composed his *Te Deum* for his first U.S. appearance as a conductor (New York, Oct. 21, 1892); he also conducted a concert of his music at the 1892 World Columbian Exposition in Chicago. It was in the U.S. that he composed his most celebrated work, the Symphony in E minor, op. 95, *From the New World*, which received its premiere performance on Dec. 15, 1893, with Anton Seidl conducting the New York Philharmonic. The melodies seemed to reflect actual African-American and Native American music, but Dvořák's insisted upon their absolute originality. The symphony is essentially a Czech work from the old world; nevertheless, by appearing as a proponent of the use of African-American-influenced themes in symphonic music, Dvořák had a significant impact on American musical nationalism. Dvořák also composed his great Cello Concerto during his American sojourn, and conducted its first performance in London on March 19, 1896.

Resigning his New York position in 1895, he returned home to resume his duties at the Prague Conservatory; he became its director in 1901. During the last years of his life, Dvořák devoted much of his creative efforts to opera; *Rusalka* (1900) remains best known outside Czechoslovakia. He made his last appearance as a conductor on April 4, 1900, leading a concert of the Czech Philharmonic in Prague. Dvořák was made a member of the Austrian House of Lords in 1901, the first Czech musician to be so honored. Czechs celebrated his 60th birthday with special performances of his music in Prague.

Dvořák's musical style was eclectic. His earliest works reflect the influence of **Beethoven** and **Schubert**, then **Wagner**, culminating in the Classicism of Brahms. After mastering his art, he proved himself to be a composer of great versatility and fecundity. A diligent and meticulous craftsman, he brought to his finest works a seemingly inexhaustible and spontaneous melodic invention, rhythmic variety, judicious employment of national folk tunes, and contrapuntal and harmonic skill. His last five symphonies, the Cello Concerto, *Stabat Mater*, his *Slavonic Dances*, the *Carnival Overture*, and many of his chamber works have become staples of the repertoire.

DYLAN, BOB (real name, **Robert Allen Zimmerman**), American folksinger and songwriter; b. Duluth, Minnesota, May 24, 1941. He adopted the name Dylan out of admiration for the poet Dylan Thomas. Possessed by wanderlust, he rode across the country, and then played guitar and crooned in the coffeehouses of New York. He also improvised songs to his own lyrics. His nasalized voice and his self-haunted guitar strumming captured the imagination not only of untutored adolescents but also of certified cognoscenti in search of convincing authenticity. His original songs were in a social-protest mode, commenting on current events (including the classic "Blowin'

in the Wind" and "The Times They Are a-Changin'"). Around 1964–1965, coming under the influence of poet Allen Ginsberg and The Beatles, Dylan began writing more personal and free-flowing material; he also adopted electric instrumentation. Songs from this period include mini-epics like "Just Like A Woman" and "Like A Rollin' Stone." In 1966 he broke his neck in a motorcycle accident, which forced him to interrupt his charismatic career for two years. He semi-retired to rural Woodstock, New York, home of his manager, Albert Grossman, where he hooked up with a group of Canadian rock musicians known as The Band; they would perform together sporadically over the coming decades. Upon his return from retirement, he recorded music in a country style, surprising his fans with his sweet-voiced crooning on his *Nashville Skyline* album. In 1970 he was awarded an honorary doctorate from Princeton University, the first such honor given to a popular singer innocent of all academic training.

Through the '70s, '80s, and '90s Dylan has undergone a number of personal transformations. Performing as a singer/songwriter in the '70s, he documented the dissolution of his marriage on the classic *Blood on the Tracks* album. Becoming a "born-again" Christian in the late '70s, he recorded a series of gospel-influenced albums, most notably *Slow Train Coming*. He soon abandoned his Christian preaching to return to his usual style. Many of his albums of the mid-'80s had a dashed-off quality, and Dylan began to sound like a parody of his former self. In the late '80s, he teamed with ex-Beatle George Harrison, Tom Petty, Roy Orbison, and Jeff Lynne to form the mock-group, The Traveling Wilburys, cutting two albums with them (Orbison died before the second was recorded). Dylan then recorded more on his own, including two all-acoustic albums featuring just his vocals, guitar, and harmonica on a series of classic folksongs. At the time of the second Woodstock festival, Dylan seemed rejuvenated, performing with a new backup band, with a level of conviction that had not been heard in years.

ELGAR, SIR EDWARD (WILLIAM), great English composer; b. Broadheath, near Worcester, June 2, 1857; d. Worcester, Feb. 23, 1934. He received his earliest music education from his father, who owned a music shop and was organist for the St. George's Roman Catholic Church in Worcester; he also took violin lessons from a local musician. He rapidly acquired the fundamentals of music theory and served as arranger with the Worcester Glee Club, becoming its conductor at the age of 22; simultaneously he accepted a rather unusual position for a young aspiring musician with the County of Worcester Lunatic Asylum at Powick, where he was for several years in charge of the institution's concert band.

Elgar's first signal success was with the concert overture *Froissart* (1890). His cantata *The Black Knight* was produced at the Worcester Festival (1893) and was also heard in London at the Crystal Palace (1897). The production of his cantata *Scenes from the Saga of King Olaf* at the North Staffordshire Music Festival (1896) attracted considerable attention. He gained further recognition with his *Imperial March* (1897), composed for the Diamond Jubilee of Queen Victoria; from then on, Elgar's name became familiar to the musical public. There followed the cantata *Caractacus* (1898) and Elgar's great masterpiece, the oratorio *The Dream of Gerontius* (1900).

From about the turn of the century, Elgar turned his attention increasingly to orchestral music. On June 19, 1899, Hans Richter presented the first performance of Elgar's *Variations on an Original Theme* (generally known as *Enigma Variations*) in London. This work consists of 14 sections, each marked by initials of fancied names of Elgar's friends; in later years, Elgar issued cryptic hints as to the identities of these persons, which were finally revealed. The success of the *Enigma Variations* was followed (1901–1903) by the production of Elgar's *Pomp and Circumstance* marches, the first of which became his most famous piece through a setting to words by Arthur Christopher Benson, used by Elgar in the *Coronation Ode* (1902) as *Land of Hope and Glory*; another successful orchestral work was the *Cockaigne Overture* (1901). Elgar's two symphonies, written between 1903 and 1910, became staples in the English orchestral repertoire. His Violin Concerto, first performed by Fritz Kreisler (1910), won notable success; there was also a remarkable Cello Concerto (1919).

The emergence of Elgar as a major composer about 1900 was all the more remarkable since he had no formal academic training. Yet he developed a masterly technique of instrumental and vocal writing. His style of composition may be described as functional Romanticism. His harmonic procedures remain firmly within the 19th-century tradition; the formal element is always strong, and the thematic development logical and precise. Elgar had a melodic gift, which asserted itself in his earliest works, such as the popular *Salut d'amour*. His oratorios, particularly *The Apostles*, were the product of his fervent religious faith (he was a Roman Catholic). He avoided archaic usages of Gregorian chant; rather, he presented the sacred subjects in a communicative style of secular drama. His link with America was secured when the hymnlike section from his first *Pomp and Circumstance* march became a popular recessional for American high school graduation exercises.

ELLINGTON, "DUKE" (EDWARD KENNEDY), famous black American pianist, bandleader, and composer; b. Washington, D.C., April 29, 1899; d. New York, May 24, 1974. He played ragtime as a boy, and worked with various jazz bands in Washington, D.C., during the 1910s and early 1920s. In 1923, Ellington went to New York, where he organized a "big band" (originally 10 pieces) that he was to lead for the next half-century, a band that revolutionized the concept of jazz: no longer was jazz restricted to small combos of four to six "unlettered" improvisers. With the Ellington band, complex arrangements were introduced, requiring both improvising skill and the ability to read scores; eventually these scores were to take on the dimensions and scope of classical compositions while retaining an underlying jazz feeling. In the early days his chief collaborator in composition and arrangements was trumpeter James "Bubber" Miley. Baritone saxophonist Harry Carney, another arranger, was with the band from its inception until Ellington's death. From 1939, Ellington's main collaborator was pianist-composer Billy Strayhorn, who wrote the band's well-known theme song, "Take the A Train." Ellington possessed a social elegance and gift of articulate verbal expression that inspired respect: he became known as "Duke" Ellington. He was the first jazz musician to receive an honorary degree from Columbia University (1973). Although Ellington wrote a number of classical suites in a jazz style, he is best remembered for his well-loved songs that remain in the jazz repertoire, including "It Don't Mean A Thing (If It Ain't Got that Swing)."

FALLA (Y MATHEU), MANUEL (MARÍA) DE, great Spanish composer; b. Cádiz, Nov. 23, 1876; d. Alta Gracia, Córdoba province, Argentina, Nov. 14, 1946. He studied piano with his mother; after further instruction from Eloisa Galluzo, he studied harmony, counterpoint, and composition. He then went to Madrid, to study piano and composition at the conservatory. He wrote several zarzuelas, but only *Los amores de la Inés* was performed (1902). His opera *La vida breve* won the prize of the Real Academia de Bellas Artes in Madrid in 1905, but it was not premiered until eight years later. In 1905 he also won the Ortiz y Cussó Prize for pianists. In 1907 he went to Paris, where he became friendly with **Claude Debussy**, Paul Dukas, and **Maurice Ravel**, who aided and encouraged him as a composer. Under their influence, he adopted the principles of Impressionism without, however, giving up his personal and national style. He returned to Spain in 1914 and produced his tremendously effective ballet *El amor brujo* (1915). It was followed by the evocative *Noches en los jardines de España* for Piano and Orchestra (1916). In 1919 he made his home in Granada, where he completed work on his celebrated ballet *El sombrero de tres picos* (1919).

Falla's art was rooted in both the folk songs of Spain and the purest historical traditions of Spanish music. Until 1919 his works were cast chiefly in the Andalusian idiom, and his instrumental technique was often conditioned by effects peculiar to Spain's national instrument, the guitar. In his puppet opera *El retablo de maese Pedro* (1919–1922), he turned to the classical tradition of

87

Spanish (especially Castilian) music. The keyboard style of his Harp-sichord Concerto (1923–1926) reveals in the classical lucidity of its writing a certain kinship with **Domenico Scarlatti**, who lived in Spain for many years. When the Spanish Civil War broke out, and General Franco overcame the Loyalist government with the aid of Hitler and Mussolini, Falla left Spain and went to South America, never to return to his homeland. He went to Buenos Aires, where he conducted concerts of his music. He then withdrew to the small locality of Alta Gracia, where he lived the last years of his life in seclusion, working on his large scenic cantata *Atlántida*. It remained unfinished at his death and was later completed by his former pupil Ernesto Halffter.

FAURÉ, GABRIEL (-URBAIN), great French composer and peda-gogue; b. Pamiers, Ariège, May 12, 1845; d. Paris, Nov. 4, 1924. His father was a provincial inspector of primary schools; noticing the musical instinct of his son, he took him to Paris to study with noted Swiss composer Louis Niedermeyer. After Niedermeyer's death in 1861, Fauré studied with **Camille Saint-Saëns**, from whom he received thorough training in composition. He developed a musical idiom all his own. By subtle application of old modes he evoked the aura of eternally fresh art; by using unresolved mild discords and special coloristic effects, he anticipated procedures of Impressionism. In his piano works, he shunned virtuosity in favor of the Classical lucidity of the French masters of the clavecin. The precisely articulat-ed melodic line of his songs is in the finest tradition of French vocal music. His great Requiem and his *Élégie* for Cello and Piano have entered the general repertoire.

FRANCK, CÉSAR (-AUGUSTE-JEAN-GUILLAUME-HUBERT), great Belgian composer and organist; b. Liège, Dec. 10, 1822; d. Paris, Nov. 8, 1890. As a child prodigy, he gave concerts in Belgium. In 1835 his family moved to Paris, where he studied privately with theorist/composer Anton Reicha; in 1837 he entered the Paris Con-servatoire, studying piano, organ, and theory. On Jan. 4, 1846, his first major work, the oratorio *Ruth*, was given there. In 1872 he suc-ceeded his former teacher François Benoist as professor of organ at the Conservatoire. Franck's organ classes became the training school for a whole generation of French composers. Until the appearance of Franck in Paris, operatic art dominated the entire musical life of the nation, and the course of instruction at the Conservatoire was influenced by this tendency. By his emphasis on organ music, based on the contrapuntal art of **J. S. Bach**, Franck swayed the new generation of French musicians toward the ideal of absolute music.

Franck was not a prolific composer, but his creative powers rose rather than diminished with advancing age. His only symphony was completed when he was 66; his remarkable Violin Sonata was written at the age of 63; his String Quartet was composed in the last year of his life. Lucidity of contrapuntal design and fullness of harmony are the distinguishing traits of Franck's music; in melodic writing he balanced the diatonic and chromatic elements in fine equilibrium. Although he did not pursue innovation for its own sake, he was not averse to using unorthodox procedures. The novelty of introducing an english horn into the score of his symphony aroused some criticism among academic musicians of the time. Franck was quite alien to the **Wagner-Liszt** school of composition, which attracted many of his own pupils; the chromatic procedures in Franck's music derive from Bach rather than from Wagner.

FRESCOBALDI, GIROLAMO, great Italian organist and composer; b. Ferrara (baptized), Sept. 9, 1583; d. Rome, March 1, 1643. He studied with Luzzasco Luzzaschi in Ferrara. By the age of 14, he was organist at the Accademia della Morte in Ferrara, and in early 1607 became organist of S. Maria in Trastevere. Then, in June 1607, he traveled to Brussels in the retinue of the Papal Nuncio, publishing his first work, a collection of five-part madrigals, in Antwerp in 1608. Returning to Rome in the same year, he was appointed organist at St. Peter's; he retained this all-important post until his death, with the exception of the years 1628 to 1634, when he was court organist in Florence. A significant indication of Frescobaldi's importance among musicians of his time was that Johann Jakob Froberger, who was court organist in Vienna, came to Rome especially to study with him (1637–1641).

Frescobaldi's place in music history is very great; particularly as a keyboard composer, he exercised a decisive influence on the style of the early Baroque. He enlarged the expressive resources of keyboard music so as to include daring chromatic progressions and acrid passing dissonances, which he called "durezze" (literally, "harshnesses"); in Frescobaldi's terminology "toccata di durezza" signified a work using dissonances. He used similar procedures in organ variations on chorale themes, which he called "fiori musicali" ("musical flowers"). His ingenious employment of variations greatly influenced the entire development of Baroque music.

GABRIELI, GIOVANNI, celebrated Italian organist, composer, and teacher; b. Venice, between 1554 and 1557; d. there, Aug. 12, 1612. He lived in Munich from 1575 to 1579. In 1584, he was engaged to substitute for Claudio Merulo as first organist at San Marco in Venice; a year later, he was permanently appointed as second organist, and retained this post until his death. As a composer, he stands at the head of the Venetian school. He was probably the first to write vocal works with parts for instrumental groups in various combinations, partly specified, partly left to the conductor, used as accompaniment as well as interspersed instrumental *sinfonie* (*Sacrae symphoniae*). His role as a composer and teacher is epoch-making; through his innovations and his development of procedures and devices invented by others (free handling of several choirs in the many-voiced vocal works, "concerted" solo parts and duets in the few- voiced vocal works, trio-sonata texture, novel dissonance treatment, speech rhythm, root progressions in fifths, use of tonal and range levels for structural purposes, coloristic effects) and through his numerous German pupils (particularly Heinrich Schütz) and other transalpine followers, he gave a new direction to the development of music. His instrumental music helped to spark the composition of German instrumental ensemble music, which reached its apex in the symphonic and chamber music works of the Classical masters. Of interest also is the fact that one of his ricercari, a four-part work in the 10th tone (1595), is an early example of the "fugue with episodes."

GERSHWIN, GEORGE, immensely gifted American composer, brother of lyricist Ira Gershwin; b. New York, Sept. 26, 1898; d. Los Angeles, July 11, 1937. His real name was Jacob Gershvin, according to the birth registry; his father was an immigrant from Russia whose original name was Gershovitz. Gershwin's extraordinary career began when he was 16, playing the piano in music stores to demonstrate new popular songs. His studies were desultory; he took private piano lessons and studied harmony. Later on, when he was already a famous composer of popular music, he studied counterpoint with **Henry Cowell** and Wallingford Riegger. During the last years of his life, he applied himself with great earnestness to studying with Joseph Schillinger in an attempt to organize his technique in a scientific manner; some of Schillinger's methods he applied in *Porgy and Bess*. But it was his melodic talent and a genius for rhythmic invention, rather than any studies, that made him a genuinely important American composer.

As far as worldly success was concerned, there was no period of struggle in Gershwin's life; one of his earliest songs, "Swanee," written at the age of 19, became enormously popular (more than a million sheet-music copies sold; 2,250,000 phonograph records). He also took time to write a lyrical *Lullaby* for String Quartet (1920). Possessing phenomenal energy, he produced musical comedies in close succession, using fashionable jazz formulas in original and ingenious ways. A milestone in his career was *Rhapsody in Blue* for Piano and Jazz Orchestra, in which he applied the jazz idiom to an essentially classical form. He played the solo part at a special concert conducted by Paul Whiteman at Aeolian Hall in New York on Feb. 12, 1924. The orchestration was by Ferde Grofé, a circumstance that generated rumors of Gershwin's inability to score for instruments; these rumors, however, were quickly refuted by his production of several orchestral works, scored by himself in a brilliant fashion. He played the solo part of his Piano Concerto in F with Walter Damrosch and the New York Symphony Orchestra (1925); this work had a certain vogue, but its popularity never equaled that of the *Rhapsody in Blue*. Reverting again to a more popular idiom, Gershwin wrote a symphonic work, *An American in Paris* (1928). His Rhapsody No. 2 was performed by Serge Koussevitzky and the Boston Symphony in 1932, but was unsuccessful; there followed a

Cuban Overture (1932) and Variations for Piano and Orchestra on his song "I Got Rhythm" (1934), with Gershwin playing the solo part in its Boston premiere.

In the meantime, Gershwin became engaged in his most ambitious undertaking: the composition of *Porgy and Bess*, an American opera in a folk manner, for black singers, after the book by Dubose Heyward. It was first staged in Boston in 1935, and then in New York. Its reception by the press was not uniformly favorable, but its songs rapidly attained great popularity ("Summertime"; "I Got Plenty o' Nuthin'"; "It Ain't Necessarily So"; "Bess, You Is My Woman Now"); the opera has been successfully revived in New York and elsewhere. Gershwin's death (of a gliomatous cyst in the right temporal lobe of the brain) at the age of 38 was mourned as a great loss to American music. His musical comedies include *Lady, Be Good!* (1924); *Oh Kay!* (1926); *Strike Up the Band* (1927); *Funny Face* (1927); *Girl Crazy* (1930); *Of Thee I Sing* (1931; a political satire that was the first musical to win a Pulitzer Prize); and *Let 'Em Eat Cake* (1933); for motion pictures: *Shall We Dance*, *A Damsel in Distress*, and *The Goldwyn Follies* (left unfinished at his death; completed by Vernon Duke).

GESUALDO, CARLO, PRINCE OF VENOSA AND COUNT OF CONZA, Italian lutenist and composer; b. probably in Naples, c. 1560; d. there, Sept. 8, 1613. In 1590, his unfaithful wife and first cousin, Maria d'Avalos, and her lover were murdered at Gesualdo's orders. In 1594, he was at the court of the Estensi in Ferrara, where he married his second wife, Leonora d'Este. Sometime after the death of the Duke of Ferrara, in 1597, Carlo returned to Naples, where he remained till death. Living in the epoch when the "new music" (the homophonic style) made its appearance, he was one of the most original musicians of the time. Like Flemish composer Cipriano de Rore and Italian Adriano Banchieri, he was a so-called chromaticist; his later madrigals reveal a distinctly individual style of expression and are characterized by strong contrasts, new (for their time) harmonic progressions, and a skillful use of dissonance. He was a master in producing tone color through the use of different voice registers and in expressing the poetic contents of his texts.

GIBBONS, ORLANDO, celebrated English composer and organist; b. Oxford (baptized), Dec. 25, 1583; d. Canterbury, June 5, 1625. He was taken to Cambridge as a small child; in 1596 he became chorister at King's College there; matriculated in 1598; and composed music for various occasions for King's College (1602–1603). In 1605 he was appointed organist of the Chapel Royal, retaining this position until his death. He received the degree of B. Mus. from Cambridge University in 1606, and that of D. Mus. from Oxford in 1622. In 1619 he became chamber musician to the King; in 1623, organist at Westminster Abbey. He conducted the music for the funeral of James I in 1625, and died of apoplexy two months later. His fame as a composer rests chiefly on his church music. He employed the novel technique of the "verse anthem" (a work for chorus and solo voices, the solo passages having independent instrumental accompaniment, for either organ or strings). His other works followed the traditional polyphonic style, of which he became a master. He was also one of the greatest English organists of the time.

GLASS, PHILIP, remarkable American composer; b. Baltimore, Jan. 31, 1937. He entered the Peabody Conservatory of Music in Baltimore as a flute student when he was eight, and then took courses in piano, mathematics, and philosophy at the University of Chicago (1952–1956). Glass subsequently studied composition with Vincent Persichetti at the Juilliard School of Music in New York, earning his M.S. in 1962. He received a Fulbright fellowship in 1964 and went to Paris to study with Nadia Boulanger; much more important to his future development was his meeting with Indian sitarist **Ravi Shankar**, who introduced him to Hindu ragas. During a visit to Morocco, Glass absorbed the modalities of North African melorhythms, which taught him the art of melodic repetition.

When he returned to New York in 1967, his style of composition became an alternately concave and convex mirror image of Eastern modes, undergoing melodic phases of stationary harmonies in lieu of modulations. He formed associations with modern painters and sculptors who strove to obtain maximum effects with a minimum of means. He began to practice a similar method in music, which soon acquired the factitious sobriquet of Minimalism. He also organized an ensemble of electrically amplified instruments, which became the chief medium of his compositions. On April 13, 1968, he presented the first concert of the Philip Glass Ensemble at Queens College in New York. He subsequently toured widely with it, making visits abroad as well as traveling throughout the U.S. His productions, both in America and in Europe, became extremely successful among young audiences, who were mesmerized by his mixture of rock realism and alluring mysticism; undeterred by the indeterminability and interminability of his productions, some lasting several hours, these young people accepted him as a true representative of earthly and unearthly art. The mind-boggling titles of his works added to the tantalizing incomprehensibility of the subjects that he selected for his inspiration.

The high point of his productions was the opera *Einstein on the Beach* (in collaboration with playwright/director Robert Wilson), which involved a surrealistic comminution of thematic ingredients and hypnotic repetition of harmonic subjects. It was premiered at the Avignon Festival on July 25, 1976, and at the Metropolitan Opera in New York that November, where it proved something of a sensation of the season. In Rotterdam on Sept. 5, 1980, he produced his opera *Satyagraha*, a work based on Gandhi's years in South Africa. "Satyagraha" was Gandhi's slogan, composed of two Hindu words: *satya* (truth) and *agraha* (firmness). Another significant production was a film, *Koyaanisqatsi*, a Hopi word meaning "life out of balance." The music represented the ultimate condensation of the basic elements of Glass's compositional style; here the ritualistic repetition of chords arranged in symmetrical sequences becomes hypnotic, particularly since the screen action is devoid of narrative; the effect is enhanced by the deep bass notes of a Native American chant.

GLINKA, MIKHAIL (IVANOVICH), great Russian composer, often called "the father of Russian music" for his pioneering cultivation of Russian folk modalities; b. Novospasskoye, Smolensk district, June 1, 1804; d. Berlin, Feb. 15, 1857. A scion of a fairly rich family of landowners, he was educated at an exclusive school in St. Petersburg (1817–1822). He also took private lessons in piano and violin; when the pianist John Field was in St. Petersburg, Glinka had an opportunity to study with him, but he had only three lessons before Field departed. He began to compose even before acquiring adequate training in theory. As a boy he traveled in the Caucasus; then stayed for a while at his father's estate. At 20 he entered the Ministry of Communications in St. Petersburg; he remained in government employ until 1828. At the same time, he constantly improved his general education by reading; he had friends among the best Russian writers of the time, including the poets Zhukovsky and Pushkin. He also took singing lessons with an Italian teacher. In 1830 he went to Italy; he continued irregular studies in Milan (where he spent most of his Italian years), while also visiting Naples, Rome, and Venice. He met **Donizetti** and **Bellini**. He became enamored of Italian music, and his early vocal and instrumental compositions are thoroughly Italian in melodic and harmonic structure. In 1833 he went to Berlin, where he took a course in counterpoint and general composition; thus he was nearly 30 when he completed his theoretical education.

In 1834 his father died, and Glinka went back to Russia to take care of family affairs. The return to his native land led him to consider the composition of a truly national opera on a subject depicting a historical episode in Russian history: the saving of the first Czar of the Romanov dynasty by a simple peasant, Ivan Susanin. Glinka's opera was produced in St. Petersburg on Dec. 9, 1836, under the title *A Life for the Czar*. The event was hailed by the literary and artistic circles of Russia as a milestone of Russian culture, and indeed the entire development of Russian national music received its decisive creative impulse from Glinka's patriotic opera. It remained in the repertoire of Russian theaters until the Revolution made it unacceptable, but it was revived, under the original title, *Ivan Susanin*, in 1939, in Moscow, without alterations in the music, but with the references to the Czar eliminated from the libretto, the idea of saving the country being substituted for that of saving the Czar.

Glinka's next opera, *Ruslan and Ludmila*, after Pushkin's fairy tale, was produced in St. Petersburg in 1842; this opera, too, became extremely popular in Russia. Glinka introduced into the score many elements of Oriental music; one episode contains the earliest use of the whole-tone scale in an opera. Both operas retain the traditional Italian form, with arias, choruses, and orchestral episodes clearly separated. In 1844 Glinka was in Paris, where he met **Hector Berlioz**. He also traveled in Spain, where he collected folk songs; the fruits of his Spanish tour were two orchestral works, *Jota Aragonesa* and *Night in Madrid*. On his way back to Russia, he stayed in Warsaw for three years; the remaining years of his life he spent in St. Petersburg, Paris, and Berlin.

GLUCK, CHRISTOPH WILLIBALD, RITTER VON, renowned German composer; b. Erasbach, near Weidenwang, in the Upper Palatinate, July 2, 1714; d. Vienna, Nov. 15, 1787. His father was a forester at Erasbach until his appointment as forester to Prince Lobkowitz of Eisenberg about 1729. Gluck received his elementary instruction in the village schools at Kamnitz and Albersdorf near Komotau, where he also was taught singing and instrumental playing. In 1732 he went to Prague to complete his education, but it is doubtful that he took any courses at the university. He earned his living by playing violin and cello at rural dances in the area, and also sang at various churches. He met Bohuslav Čzernohorsky, and it is probable that Gluck learned the methods of church music from him. He went to Vienna in 1736, and was chamber musician to young Prince Lobkowitz, son of the patron of Gluck's father. In 1737 he was taken to Milan by Prince Melzi; this Italian sojourn was of the greatest importance to Gluck's musical development. There he became a student of G.B. Sammartini and acquired a solid technique of composition in the Italian style. After four years of study, he brought out his first opera, *Artaserse*; it was produced in Milan in 1741 with such success that he was immediately commissioned to write more operas. He wrote seven more operas between 1742 and 1745 in Italian. He also contributed separate numbers to several other operas produced in Italy.

In 1745 he received an invitation to go to London; on his way, he visited Paris and met **Jean-Philippe Rameau**. He was commissioned by the Italian Opera of London to write two operas for the Haymarket Theatre, as a competitive endeavor to **Handel**'s enterprise. He produced two works in 1746, the second a pastiche drawing on his previous operas. Gluck also gave a demonstration in London, playing on the "glass harmonica." He left London late in 1746 when he received an engagement as conductor with Pietro Mingotti's traveling Italian opera company.

In 1750 Gluck married Marianna Pergin, daughter of a Viennese merchant; for several years afterward he conducted operatic performances in Vienna. As French influence increased there, he wrote several entertainments to French texts, containing spoken dialogue, in the style of opéra comique. His greatest work of the Vienna period was *Orfeo ed Euridice*, to a libretto by Calzabigi (1762). Gluck revised it for a Paris performance, produced in French in 1774, with Orfeo sung by a tenor. There followed another masterpiece, *Alceste* (1767), also to Calzabigi's text. In the preface to *Alceste*, Gluck formulated his esthetic credo, which elevated the dramatic meaning of musical stage plays above a mere striving for vocal effects: "I sought to reduce music to its true function, that of seconding poetry in order to strengthen the emotional expression and the impact of the dramatic situations without interrupting the action and without weakening it by superfluous ornaments."

The success of his French operas in Vienna led Gluck to the decision to try his fortunes in Paris, yielding to the persuasion of François du Roullet, an attaché at the French embassy in Vienna, who also supplied him with his first libretto for a serious French opera, an adaptation of Racine's *Iphigénie en Aulide* (1774). He set out for Paris early in 1773, preceded by declarations in the Paris press by du Roullet and Gluck himself, explaining in detail his ideas of dramatic music. These statements set off an intellectual battle in the Paris press and among musicians in general between the adherents of traditional Italian opera and Gluck's novel French opera. It reached an unprecedented degree of acrimony when the Italian composer Nicola Piccinni was engaged by the French court to write operas to French texts, in open competition with Gluck; intrigues multiplied, even though Marie Antoinette never wavered in her admiration for Gluck, who taught her singing and harpsichord playing. The sensational successes of the French version of Gluck's *Orfeo* and of *Alceste* were followed by the production of *Armide* (1777), which aroused great admiration. Then followed his masterpiece, *Iphigénie en Tauride* (1779), which established Gluck's superiority to Piccinni, who was commissioned to write an opera on the same subject but failed to complete it in time.

Gluck's last opera, *Echo et Narcisse* (Paris, 1779), did not measure up to the excellence of his previous operas. By that time, his health had failed; he had several attacks of apoplexy, which resulted in partial paralysis. In the autumn of 1779 he returned to Vienna, where he lived as an invalid. His last work was a *De profundis* for Chorus and Orchestra, written five years before his death.

Besides his operas, he wrote several ballets, of which *Don Juan* (1761) was the most successful; he also wrote a cycle of seven songs, seven trio sonatas, several overtures, etc. **Wagner** made a complete revision of the score of *Iphigénie en Aulide*; this arrangement was so extensively used that a Wagnerized version of Gluck's music became the chief text for performances during the 19th century.

GOULD, GLENN (HERBERT), remarkably individualistic Canadian pianist; b. Toronto, Sept. 25, 1932; d. there, Oct. 4, 1982. His parents were musically gifted and gladly fostered his precocious development; he began to play piano, and even compose, in his single-digit years. At the age of 10, he entered the Royal Conservatory of Music in Toronto, where he studied piano, organ and music theory; he received his diploma as a graduate at 13, in 1945. He made his debut in Toronto in 1946. As he began practicing with total concentration on the mechanism of the keyboard, he developed mannerisms that were to become his artistic signature. He reduced the use of the pedal to a minimum in order to avoid a harmonic haze; he cultivated "horizontality" in his piano posture, bringing his head down almost to the level of the keys. He regarded music as a linear art; this naturally led him to an intense examination of Baroque structures. **J. S. Bach** was the subject of his close study rather than **Chopin**; he also cultivated performances of the early polyphonists Sweelinck, **Gibbons**, and others. He played **Mozart** with emphasis on the early pianoforte techniques; he peremptorily omitted the Romantic composers Chopin, **Schumann**, and **Liszt** from his repertoire. He found the late sonatas of **Beethoven** more congenial to his temperament, and, remarkably enough, he played the piano works of the modern Vienna school—**Schoenberg, Berg,** and **Webern**—perhaps because of their classical avoidance of purely decorative tonal formations.

Following his U.S. debut in Washington, D.C. in 1955, he evoked unequivocal praise at his concerts, but in 1964 he abruptly terminated his stage career and devoted himself exclusively to recording, which he regarded as a superior art to concertizing. This enabled him to select the best portions of the music he played in the studio, forming a mosaic unblemished by accidental mishaps. A great part of the interest he aroused with the public at large was due to mannerisms that marked his behavior on the stage. He used a 14-inch-high chair that placed his eyes almost at the level of the keyboard; he affected informal dress; he had a rug put under the piano and a glass of distilled water within reach. He was in constant fear of bodily injury; he avoided shaking hands with the conductor after playing a concerto; and he sued the Steinway piano company for a large sum of money when an enthusiastic representative shook his hand too vigorously. But what even his most ardent admirers could not palliate was his unshakable habit of singing along with his performance; he even allowed his voice to be audible on his carefully wrought, lapidary phonograph recordings. Socially, he was a recluse; he found a release from his self-imposed isolation in editing a series of radio documentaries for the Canadian Broadcasting Company (CBC). He called three of them a "solitude trilogy." Symbolically, they were devoted to the natural isolation of the Canadian Arctic, the insular life of Newfoundland, and the religious hermetism of the Mennonite sect. He also produced a radio documentary on Schoenberg, treating him as a musical hermit. Other activities included conducting a chamber orchestra without an audience.

GOUNOD, CHARLES (FRANÇOIS), famous French composer; b. St-Cloud, June 17, 1818; d. Paris, Oct. 18, 1893. In 1836 he entered the Paris Conservatoire, studying with Fromental Halévy, Jean-François Le Sueur, and Ferdinando Paër. In 1837 he won the second Prix de Rome with his cantata *Marie Stuart et Rizzio*; in 1839 he won the Grand Prix with his cantata *Fernand*. In Rome, he studied church music, particularly the works of **Palestrina**, and composed a Mass for Three Voices and Orchestra. In 1842, during a visit to Vienna, he conducted a Requiem of his own. Upon his return to Paris, he became precentor and organist of the Missions Étrangères, and studied theology for two years but decided against taking Holy Orders, yet he was often referred to as l'Abbé Gounod.

Soon he tried his hand at stage music. In 1851, his first opera, *Sapho*, was produced at the Paris Opéra, with only moderate success; he revised it much later, extending it to four acts from the original three, and it was performed again in 1884, but it was unsuccessful. His second opera, *La Nonne sanglante*, in five acts, was staged in 1854; there followed a comic opera, *Le Médecin malgré lui*, after Molière (1858), which also failed to realize his expectations. In the meantime, he was active in other musical ways in Paris; he conducted the choral society Orphéon (1852–60) and composed for it several choruses.

Gounod's great success came with the production of *Faust*, after Goethe (1859; performed ten years later with additional recitatives and ballet). *Faust* remained Gounod's greatest masterpiece, and indeed the most successful French opera of the 19th century, triumphant all over the world without any sign of diminishing effect through a century of changes in musical tastes. However, it was widely criticized for the melodramatic treatment of Goethe's poem by the librettists, Barbier and Carré, and for the somewhat sentimental style of Gounod's music. The succeeding operas *Philémon et Baucis* (1860), *La Colombe* (1860), *La Reine de Saba* (1862), and *Mireille* (1864) were only partially successful, but with *Roméo et Juliette* (1867), Gounod recaptured universal acclaim. In 1870, during the Franco-Prussian War, he went to London; when Paris fell, he wrote an elegiac cantata, *Gallia*, to words from the Lamentations of Jeremiah, which he conducted in London in 1871. The last years of his life were devoted mainly to sacred works, of which the most important was *La Rédemption*, a trilogy, first performed in 1882. One of his most popular settings to religious words is *Ave Maria*, adapted to the first prelude of Bach's *Well-tempered Clavier*, but its original version was *Méditation sur le premier prélude de piano de J.S. Bach* for Violin and Piano (1853); the words were added later (1859).

GRAINGER, (GEORGE) PERCY (ALDRIDGE), celebrated Australian-born American pianist and composer; b. Melbourne, July 8, 1882; d. White Plains, New York, Feb. 20, 1961. He received his early musical training from his mother. At the age of 10, he appeared as pianist at several public concerts, and then had lessons with Louis Pabst. In 1894, he went to Germany, where he studied with James Kwast in Frankfurt, and also took a few lessons with **Ferruccio Busoni**. In 1901 he began his concert career in England; then toured South Africa and Australia. In 1906 he met **Edvard Grieg**, who became enthusiastic about his talent; Grainger's performances of Grieg's Piano Concerto were famous. In 1914 Grainger settled in the U.S. He married Ella Viola Ström in 1928 in a spectacular ceremony staged at the Hollywood Bowl, at which he conducted his work *To a Nordic Princess*, written for his bride.

Grainger's philosophy of life and art calls for the widest communion of peoples and opinions; his profound study of folk music underlies the melodic and rhythmic structure of his own music. He made a determined effort to recreate in art music the free flow of instinctive songs of the people; he experimented with "gliding" intervals within the traditional scales and polyrhythmic combinations with independent strong beats in the component parts. In a modest way he was a pioneer of electronic music; as early as 1937 he wrote a quartet for electronic instruments, notating the pitch by zigzags and curves. He introduced individual forms of notation and orchestral scoring, rejecting the common Italian designations of tempi and dynamics in favor of colloquial English expressions.

GRIEG, EDVARD (HAGERUP), celebrated Norwegian composer; b. Bergen, June 15, 1843; d. there, Sept. 4, 1907. His great-grandfather, Alexander Greig, of Scotland, emigrated to Norway about 1765. Edvard Grieg received his first instruction in music from his mother, an amateur pianist. At the suggestion of the Norwegian violinist Ole Bull, young Grieg was sent to the Leipzig Conservatory in 1858, where he studied piano and theory. He became immersed in the atmosphere of German Romanticism, with the esthetic legacy of **Mendelssohn** and **Schumann**; Grieg's early works are permeated with lyric moods related to these influences.

In 1863 he went to Copenhagen, where he met the young Norwegian composer Rikard Nordraak, with whom he organized the Euterpe Society for the promotion of national Scandinavian music, in opposition to the German influences dominating Scandinavian music. The premature death of Nordraak at the age of 23 in 1866 left Grieg alone to carry on the project. After traveling in Italy, he returned to Norway, where he opened a Norwegian Academy of Music (1867), and gave concerts of Norwegian music; he was also engaged as conductor of the Harmonic Society in Christiania. In

1867 he married his cousin, the singer Nina Hagerup. At that time he had already composed his two violin sonatas and the first set of his *Lyric Pieces* for Piano, which used Norwegian motifs. In 1869, Grieg played the solo part in the world premiere of his Piano Concerto, which took place in Copenhagen. Thus, at the age of 25, he established himself as a major composer of his time.

In 1874–1875 he wrote incidental music to Ibsen's *Peer Gynt*; the two orchestral suites arranged from this music became extremely popular. The Norwegian government granted him an annuity of 1,600 crowns, which enabled him to devote most of his time to composition. Performances of his works were given in Germany with increasing frequency; soon his fame spread all over Europe. In 1888, he gave a concert of his works in London; he also prepared recitals of his songs with his wife. He revisited England frequently, and received the honorary degrees of Mus.D. from Cambridge (1894) and Oxford (1906), along with other honors. Despite his successes, Grieg was of a retiring disposition, and spent most of his later years in his house at Troldhaugen, near Bergen, avoiding visitors and shunning public acclaim. However, he continued to compose at a steady rate. His death, of heart disease, was mourned by all Norway; he was given a state funeral and his remains were cremated, at his own request, and sealed in the side of a cliff projecting over the fjord at Troldhaugen.

Grieg's importance as a composer lies in the strongly pronounced nationalism of his music; without resorting to literal quotation from Norwegian folk songs, he succeeded in recreating their melodic and rhythmic flavor. In his harmony, he remained well within the bounds of tradition; the lyric expressiveness of his best works and the contagious rhythm of his dancelike pieces imparted a charm and individuality that contributed to the lasting success of his art. His unassuming personality made friends for him among his colleagues; he was admired by **Brahms** and **Tchaikovsky**. The combination of lyricism and nationalism in Grieg's music led some critics to describe him as "the **Chopin** of the North." He excelled in miniatures, in which the perfection of form and the clarity of the musical line are remarkable. The unifying purpose of Grieg's entire creative life is exemplified by his lyric pieces for piano. He composed 10 sets of these pieces in 34 years, between 1867 and 1901. His songs are distinguished by the same blend of Romantic and characteristically national inflections. In orchestral composition, Grieg limited himself almost exclusively to symphonic suites, and arrangements of his piano pieces. In chamber music, his three violin sonatas, a Cello Sonata, and a String Quartet are examples of fine instrumental writing.

GRIFFES, CHARLES T(OMLINSON), outstanding American composer; b. Elmira, New York, Sept. 17, 1884; d. New York, April 8, 1920. He studied piano with a local teacher and also took organ lessons. In 1903 he went to Berlin, where he studied piano and composition. To eke out his living, he gave private lessons, and also played his own compositions in public recitals. In 1907 he returned to the U.S., and took a music teacher's job at the Hackley School for Boys at Tarrytown, New York; at the same time he continued to study music by himself. He was fascinated by the exotic art of the French Impressionists, and investigated the potentialities of Oriental scales. He also was strongly influenced by the Russian school, particularly **Modest Mussorgsky** and **Alexander Scriabin**. A combination of natural talent and determination to acquire a high degree of craftsmanship elevated Griffes to the position of a foremost American composer in the Impressionist genre; despite changes of taste, his works retain an enduring place in American music.

GUIDO D'AREZZO or **Guido Aretinus**, famous Italian reformer of musical notation and vocal instruction; b. c. 991; d. after 1033. He received his education at the Benedictine abbey at Pomposa, near Ferrara. He left the monastery in 1025, as a result of disagreements with his fellow monks, who were envious of his superiority in vocal teaching. He was then summoned by Bishop Theobald of Arezzo to the cathedral school there; it was because of this association that he became known as Guido d'Arezzo. His fame spread and reached the ears of Pope John XIX, who called him to Rome to demonstrate his system of teaching (1028). In his last years, he was a prior of the Camaldolite fraternity at Avellano.

Guido's fame rests on his system of solmization, by which he established the nomenclature of the major hexachord Ut, Re, Mi, Fa, Sol, La, from syllables in the initial lines of the Hymn of St. John: *Ut* queant laxis *Re*sonare fibris/*Mi*ra gestorum *Fa*muli tuorum,/*Sol*ve polluti *La*bii reatum,/Sancte Joannes.

No less epoch-making was Guido's introduction of the music staff of four lines, retaining the red *f*-line and the yellow *c*-line of his predecessors, and drawing between them a black *a*-line, above them a black *e*-line, and writing the plainsong notes (which he did not invent) in regular order on these lines and in the spaces. He also added new lines above or below these, as occasion required; thus, Guido's system did away with all uncertainty of pitch. Another invention credited to Guido is the so-called Guidonian hand, relating the degrees of the overlapping hexachords to various places on the palm of the left hand, a device helpful in directing a chorus by indicating manually the corresponding positions of the notes. Opinions differ widely as to the attribution to Guido of all these innovations; some scholars maintain that he merely popularized the already-established ideas, and that solmization, in particular, was introduced by a German abbot, Poncius Teutonicus, at the abbey of Saint-Maur des Fossés.

HANDEL, GEORGE FRIDERIC (originally **Georg Friedrich Händel**), great German-born English composer; b. Halle, Feb. 23, 1685; d. London, April 14, 1759. His father was a barber-surgeon and valet to the Prince of Saxe-Magdeburg. At the age of 61, he took a second wife, Dorothea Taust, daughter of the pastor of Giebichenstein, near Halle; Handel was the second son of this marriage. As a child, Handel was taken by his father on a visit to Saxe-Weissenfels, where he had a chance to try out the organ of the court chapel. The Duke, Johann Adolf, noticing his interest in music, advised that he be sent to Halle for organ lessons with Friedrich Wilhelm Zachau, the organist of the Liebfrauenkirche there. Zachau gave him instruction in harpsichord and organ playing and also introduced him to the rudiments of composition. Handel proved to be an apt student, and was able to substitute for Zachau as organist whenever necessary; he also composed trio sonatas and motets for church services on Sundays. After the death of his father in 1697, he entered the University of Halle in 1702, and was named probationary organist at the Domkirche there. In 1703 he went to Hamburg, where he was engaged as "violino di ripieno" by Reinhard Keiser, the famous composer and director of the Hamburg Opera.

Handel's first opera, *Almira*, was produced at the Hamburg Opera on Jan. 8, 1705; his next opera, *Nero*, was staged there on Feb. 25, 1705. He was then commissioned to write two other operas, *Florindo* and *Daphne*, originally planned as a single opera combining both subjects. In 1706 he undertook a long voyage to Italy, where he visited Florence, Rome, Naples, and Venice. The first opera he wrote in Italy was *Rodrigo*, presented in Florence in 1707. Then followed *Agrippina*, produced in Venice in 1709; it obtained an excellent success, being given 27 performances. In Rome, he composed the serenata *Il trionfo del Tempo e del Disinganno*, which was performed there in the spring of 1707. Handel's oratorio *La Resurrezione* was given in Rome on April 8, 1708. In July, he brought out in Naples his serenata *Aci, Galatea, e Polifemo*; its score was remarkable for a bass solo that required a compass of two octaves and a fifth. During his Italian sojourn he met Alessandro and **Domenico Scarlatti**.

In 1710 he returned to Germany and was named Kapellmeister to the Elector of Hannover, as successor to Agostino Steffani. Later that year he visited England, where he produced his opera *Rinaldo* at the Queen's Theatre in London on Feb. 24, 1711; it received 15 performances in all. After a brief return to Hannover in June 1711, he made another visit to London, where he produced his operas *Il Pastor fido* (1712) and *Teseo* (1713). He also wrote an ode for Queen Anne's birthday, which was presented at Windsor Palace on Feb. 6, 1713; it was followed by two sacred works, his *Te Deum* and *Jubilate*, performed on July 7, 1713, to celebrate the Peace of Utrecht. These performances won him royal favor and an annuity of 200 pounds sterling.

An extraordinary concurrence of events persuaded Handel to remain in London, when Queen Anne died in 1714 and Handel's protector, the Elector of Hannover, became King George I of England. The King bestowed many favors upon the composer and augmented his annuity to 400 pounds sterling. Handel became a British subject in 1727, and Anglicized his name to George Frideric Handel, dropping the original German umlaut. He continued to produce operas, invariably to Italian librettos, for the London stage, including *Silla* (1713) and *Amadigi di Gaula* (1715). In 1716 Handel wrote *Der für die Sünden der Welt gemarterte und sterbende Jesus*, to the text of the poet Heinrich Brockes. In 1717 he produced one of his most famous works, written expressly for King George I, his *Water Music*. On July 17, an aquatic fête on the Thames River was held by royal order; the King's boat was followed by a barge on which an orchestra of 50 musicians played Handel's score, or at least a major portion of it. The final version of the *Water Music* combines two instrumental suites composed at different times: one was written for the barge party; the other is of an earlier provenance.

In 1717 Handel became resident composer to the Duke of Chandos, for whom he wrote the so-called *Chandos Anthems* (1717–1718), 11 in number; the secular oratorio *Acis and Galatea* (1718); and the oratorio *Esther* (1718). He also served as music master to the daughters of the Prince of Wales; for Princess Anne he composed his first collection of *Suites de pièces pour le clavecin* (1720), also known as *The Lessons*, which includes the famous air with variations nicknamed *The Harmonious Blacksmith*; the appellation is gratuitous, and the story that Handel was inspired to compose it after he visited a black-smith shop, where he was impressed by the steady beat of the arti-san's hammer, was a persistent figment of anonymous imagination. In 1719 he was made Master of Musick of a new business venture under the name of the Royal Academy of Music, established for the purpose of presenting opera at the King's Theatre. The first opera he composed for it was *Radamisto* (1720). Between 1721 and 1728 he produced many operas at the King's Theatre; of these, *Giulio Cesare* (1724) and *Rodelinda* (1725) became firmly established in the operat-ic repertoire and had numerous revivals.

In 1727 he composed four grand anthems for the coronation of King George II and Queen Caroline. In the spring of 1728 the Royal Academy of Music ceased operations, and Handel became associated with the management of the King's Theatre. The following year, he went to Italy to recruit singers for a new Royal Academy of Music. Returning to London, he brought out several more operas, of which only *Orlando* (1733) proved to be a lasting success. In 1732, Handel gave a special performance of a revised version of his oratorio *Esther* at the King's Theatre; it was followed in the same year by the revised version of *Acis and Galatea* and the oratorio *Deborah* (1733). In 1733, he produced his oratorio *Athalia* at Oxford, where he also appeared as an organist; he was offered the degree of Mus.D. (*honoris causa*), but declined the honor.

Discouraged by the poor reception of his operas at the King's Theatre, Handel decided to open a new season under a different management. But he quarreled with the principal singer, the famous castrato Senesino, who was popular with audiences, and thus lost the support of a substantial number of his subscribers, who then formed a rival opera company called Opera of the Nobility. It engaged the famous Italian composer Nicola Porpora as director, and opened its first season at Lincoln's Inn Fields on Dec. 29, 1733. Handel's opera

Arianna in Creta had its premiere at the King's Theatre on Jan. 26, 1734, but in July of that year both Handel's company and the rival enterprise were forced to suspend operations. Handel set up his own opera company at Covent Garden, inaugurating his new season with a revised version of *Il Pastor fido* (1734); this was followed by six more operas, all staged between 1735 and 1737; only *Alcina* (1735) sustained a success. In 1741, he produced *Deidamia*, which marked the end of his operatic enterprise.

In historical perspective, Handel's failure as an operatic entrepreneur was a happy turn of events, for he then directed his energy toward the composition of oratorios, in which he achieved greatness. For inspiration, he turned to biblical themes, using English texts. On Jan. 16, 1739, he presented the oratorio *Saul*; on April 4, 1739, there followed *Israel in Egypt*. In the same year, he also wrote an *Ode for St. Cecilia's Day*, after Dryden, and his great set of 12 Concerti grossi, op. 6. Milton's *L' Allegro* and *Il Penseroso* inspired him to write *L' Allegro, il Penseroso, ed il Moderato* (1740).

In 1741 he was invited to visit Ireland, and there he produced his greatest masterpiece, *Messiah*; working with tremendous concentration of willpower and imagination, he completed Part I in six days, Part II in nine days, and Part III in six days. The work on orchestration took him only a few more days; he signed the score on Sept. 14, 1741. The first performance of *Messiah* was given in Dublin on April 13, 1742, and its London premiere was presented on March 23, 1743. If contemporary reports can be trusted, King George II rose to his feet at the closing chords of the "Hallelujah" chorus, and the entire audience followed suit. This established a tradition, at least in England; since then every performance of *Messiah* has moved the listeners to rise during this celebratory chorus. Handel's oratorio *Samson*, produced in London on Feb. 18, 1743, was also successful, but his next oratorio, *Semele* (1744), failed to arouse public admiration. Besides oratorios, mundane events also occupied his attention. To celebrate the Peace of Aachen, he composed the remarkable *Music for the Royal Fireworks*, which was heard for the first time in Green Park in London in 1749.

A parallel between the two great German contemporaries, **J. S. Bach** and Handel, is often drawn. Born a few months apart, Bach in Eisenach, Handel in Halle, at a distance of about 130 kilometers, they never met. Bach visited Halle at least twice, but Handel was then away, in London. The difference between their life's destinies was profound. Bach was a master of the Baroque organ who produced religious works for church use, a schoolmaster who regarded his instrumental music as a textbook for study; he never composed for the stage, and traveled but little. By contrast, Handel was a man of the world who dedicated himself mainly to public spectacles, and who became a British subject. Bach's life was that of a German burgher, and his genius was inconspicuous; Handel shone in the light of public admiration. Bach was married twice; survivors among his 20 children became important musicians in their own right. Handel remained celibate, but he was not a recluse. Physically, he tended toward healthy corpulence; he enjoyed the company of friends, but had a choleric temperament, and could not brook adverse argument. Like Bach, he was deeply religious, and there was no ostentation in his service to his God. Handel's music possessed grandeur of design, majestic eloquence, and lusciousness of harmony. Music-lovers did not have to study Handel's style to discover its beauty, while the sublime art of Bach could be fully understood only after knowledgeable penetration into the contrapuntal and fugal complexities of its structure.

HANDY, W(ILLIAM) C(HRISTOPHER), noted black American composer, known as the "father of the blues"; b. Florence, Alabama, Nov. 16, 1873; d. New York, March 28, 1958. His father and grandfather were ministers. In 1892 he graduated from the Teachers' Agricultural and Mechanical College in Huntsville, Alabama, and became a schoolteacher and also worked in iron mills. He learned to play the cornet and was a soloist at the Chicago World's Fair (1893), and became bandmaster of Mahara's Minstrels. His famous song "Memphis Blues" (published 1912; the second piece to be published as a "blues," and the first blues work to achieve popularity) was originally written as a campaign song for the mayor of Memphis, E.H. Crump (1909). This song, along with his more celebrated "St. Louis Blues" (1914), opened an era in popular music, turning the theretofore prevalent spirit of ragtime gaiety to ballad-like nostalgia, with the lowered third, fifth, and seventh degrees ("blue notes") as distinctive melodic traits. He followed these with more blues: "Yellow Dog"; "Beale Street"; "Joe Turner"; the march, *Hail to the Spirit of Freedom*

(1915); *Ole Miss* for Piano (1916); and the songs, "Aunt Hagar's Children" (1920), "Loveless Love" (1921), and "Aframerican Hymn."

HARRISON, LOU, inventive American composer and performer; b. Portland, Oregon, May 14, 1917. He studied with **Henry Cowell** in San Francisco (1934–1935) and with **Arnold Schoenberg** at the University of California at Los Angeles (1941). His interests are varied: he invented two new principles of clavichord construction; developed a process for direct composing on a phonograph disc; in 1938 proposed a theory of interval control, and in 1942 supplemented it by a device for rhythm control; also wrote plays and versified poematically. He was one of the earliest adherents of an initially small group of American musicians who promoted the music of **Charles Ives, Charles Ruggles, Edgard Varèse**, and Cowell; he prepared for publication Ives's Third Symphony, which he conducted in its first performance in 1946. He visited the Orient in 1961, fortifying his immanent belief in the multiform nature of music by studying Japanese and Korean modalities and rhythmic structures. Seeking new sources of sound production, he organized a percussion ensemble of multitudinous drums and such homely sound makers as coffee cans and flowerpots. He also wrote texts in Esperanto for some of his vocal works. He later composed for the Indonesian gamelan; many of these instruments were constructed by his longtime associate and friend William Colvig.

HAYDN, (FRANZ) JOSEPH, illustrious Austrian composer, brother of **Michael Haydn**; b. Rohrau, Lower Austria, probably March 31, 1732 (baptized, April 1, 1732); d. Vienna, May 31, 1809. He was the second of 12 children born to Mathias Haydn, a wheelwright, who served as village sexton, and Anna Maria Koller, daughter of the market inspector and a former cook in the household of Count Harrach, lord of the village. When Haydn was a small child, his paternal cousin, a choral director, took him to Hainburg, where he gave him instruction in reading, writing, arithmetic, and instrumental playing. When Haydn was eight years old, the Kapellmeister at St. Stephen's Cathedral in Vienna engaged him as a soprano singer in the chorus.

After his voice broke, he lived for a while with a local music teacher, and then was engaged as accompanist to students of Nicolò Porpora, for whom he performed various menial tasks in exchange for composition lessons. Soon, he began to compose keyboard music. In his early twenties, he received commissions for his first string quartets, while he continued to teach harpsichord and singing. In 1759, Haydn was engaged by Count Ferdinand Maximilian von Morzin as Kapellmeister at his estate in Lukave. A year later he was married.

A decided turn in Haydn's life was his meeting with Prince Paul Anton Esterházy. Esterházy had heard one of Haydn's symphonies during a visit to Lukaveč, and engaged him to enter his service as second Kapellmeister at his estate in Eisenstadt; Haydn signed his contract with Esterházy on May 1, 1761. Prince Paul Anton died in 1762, and his brother, Prince Nikolaus Esterházy, known as the "Magnificent," succeeded him. He took Haydn to his new palace at Esterháza, where Haydn was to provide two weekly operatic performances and two formal concerts. Haydn's service at Esterháza was long-lasting, secure, and fruitful. There he composed music of all descriptions, including most of his known string quartets, about 80 of his 104 symphonies, a number of keyboard works, and nearly all his operas; in 1766 he was elevated to the rank of first Kapellmeister.

Prince Nikolaus Esterházy was a cultural patron of the arts, but he was also a stern taskmaster in his relationship to his employees. His contract with Haydn stipulated that each commissioned work had to be performed without delay, and that such a work should not be copied for use by others. Haydn was to present himself in the "antichambre" of the palace each morning and afternoon to receive the Prince's orders, and he was obliged to wear formal clothes, with white hose and a powdered wig with a pigtail or a hairbag; he was to have his meals with the other musicians and house servants. In particular, Haydn was obligated to write pieces that could be performed on the baryton, an instrument that the Prince could play; consequently, Haydn wrote numerous pieces for it. He also wrote three sets of six string quartets each (opp. 9, 17, and 20), which were brought out in 1771–1772. His noteworthy symphonies included No. 49, in F minor, *La passione*; No. 44, in E minor, known as the *Trauersinfonie*; No. 45, in F-sharp minor; and the famous *Abschiedsinfonie* (the *Farewell* Symphony), performed by Haydn at Esterháza in 1772. The last movement of the *Farewell* Symphony ends in a long slow section during which one musician after another ceases to play and leaves the stage, until only the conductor and a single violinist remain to complete the work. The traditional explanation is that Haydn used the charade to suggest to the Prince that his musicians deserved a vacation after their arduous labors, but another and much more plausible version, given by G.G. Ferrari, who personally knew Haydn, is that the Prince had decided to disband the orchestra and that Haydn wished to impress on him the sadness of such a decision; the known result was that the orchestra was retained.

During his visits to Vienna he formed a close friendship with **Mozart**, who was nearly a quarter of a century younger, and for whose genius Haydn had great admiration. If the words of Mozart's father can be taken literally, Haydn told him that Mozart was "the greatest composer known to me either in person or by name." Mozart reciprocated Haydn's regard for him by dedicating to him a set of six string quartets. Prince Nikolaus Esterházy died in 1790, and his son Paul Anton (named after his uncle) inherited the estate. After he disbanded the orchestra, Haydn was granted an annuity of 1,000 florins; nominally he remained in the service of the new Prince as Kapellmeister, but he took up permanent residence in Vienna.

In 1790 Johann Peter Salomon, the enterprising London impresario, visited Haydn and persuaded him to travel to London for a series of concerts. Haydn accepted the offer, arriving in London on Jan. 1, 1791. On March 11 of that year he appeared in his first London concert in the Hanover Square Rooms, presiding at the keyboard. Haydn was greatly feted in London by the nobility; the King himself expressed his admiration for Haydn's art. In July 1791 he went to Oxford to receive the honorary degree of Mus.D. For this occasion, he submitted his Symphony No. 92, in G major, which became known as the *Oxford* Symphony; he composed a three-part canon, *Thy Voice, O Harmony, Is Divine*, as his exercise piece. It was also in England that he wrote his Symphony No. 94, in G major, the *Surprise* Symphony. The surprise of the title was provided by the loud drum strokes at the end of the main theme in the slow movement; the story went that Haydn introduced the drum strokes with the sly intention of awakening the London dowagers, who were apt to doze off at a concert.

On his journey back to Vienna in the summer of 1792, Haydn stopped in Bonn, where young **Beethoven** showed him some of his works, and Haydn agreed to accept him later as his student in Vienna. In 1794 Haydn went to London once more. His first concert, on Feb. 10, met with great success. His *London* symphonies, also known as the *Salomon* symphonies, because Haydn wrote them at Salomon's request, were 12 in number, and they included No. 99, in E-flat major; No. 100, in G major, known as the *Military* Symphony; No. 101, in D major, nicknamed *The Clock* because of its pendulum-like rhythmic accompanying figure; No. 102, in B-flat major; No. 103, in E-flat major, known as the *Drum Roll* Symphony; and No. 104, in D major.

Returning to Vienna, Haydn resumed his contact with the Esterházy family. In 1794 Prince Paul Anton died and was succeeded by his son Nikolaus; the new Prince revived the orchestra at Eisenstadt, with Haydn again as Kapellmeister. Conforming to the new requirements of Prince Nikolaus, Haydn turned to works for the church, including six masses. His Mass in C major was entitled *Missa in tempore belli* (1796), for it was composed during Napoleon's drive toward Vienna. The Second Mass, in B-flat major, the *Heiligmesse*, also dates from 1796. In 1798 he composed the Third Mass, in D minor, which is often called the *Nelsonmesse*, with reference to Lord Nelson's defeat of Napoleon's army at the Battle of the Nile. The Fourth Mass, in B-flat major (1799), is called the *Theresienmesse*, in honor of the Austrian Empress Maria Theresa. The Fifth Mass, in B-flat major, written in 1801, is known as the *Schöpfungsmesse*, for it contains a theme from the oratorio *Die Schöpfung* (*The Creation*). The Sixth Mass, in B-flat major (1802), is referred to as the *Harmoniemesse*, for its extensive use of wind instruments; the word "harmonie" is here used in the French meaning, as the wind instrument section.

Between 1796 and 1798 Haydn composed his great oratorio *Die Schöpfung*, which was first performed at a private concert for the nobility at the Schwarzenburg Palace in Vienna on April 29, 1798. In 1796 he wrote the Concerto in E-flat major for Trumpet, which became a standard piece for trumpet players. In 1797 Haydn was instructed by the Court to compose a hymn-tune of a solemn nature that could be used as the national Austrian anthem. He succeeded triumphantly in this task; he made use of this tune as a theme of a set of variations in his String Quartet in C major, op. 76, no. 3, which itself became known as the *Emperor* Quartet. The original text for the hymn, written by Lorenz Leopold Haschka, began "Gott erhalte Franz den Kaiser." This hymn had a curious history: a new set of words was written by August Heinrich Hoffmann during a period of revolutionary disturbances in Germany preceding the general European revolution of 1848. Its first line, "Deutschland, Deutschland über alles," later assumed the significance of German imperialism; in its original it meant merely, "Germany above all (in our hearts)." Between 1799 and 1801 Haydn completed the oratorio *Die Jahreszeiten*; its text was translated into German from James Thomson's poem *The Seasons*. It was first performed at the Schwarzenburg Palace in Vienna on April 24, 1801. In 1802, beset by illness, Haydn resigned as Kapellmeister to Prince Nikolaus.

Despite his gradually increasing debility, Haydn preserved the saving grace of his natural humor; in response to the many salutations of his friends, he sent around a quotation from his old song *Der Alte*, confessing his bodily weakness. Another amusing musical jest was Haydn's reply to a society lady who identified herself at a Vienna party as a person to whom Haydn had dedicated a lively tune ascending on the major scale; she sang it for him, and he replied wistfully that the tune was now more appropriate in an inversion. Haydn made his last public appearance at a concert given in his honor in the Great Hall of the University of Vienna on March 27, 1808, with Antonio Salieri conducting *Die Schöpfung*. When Vienna capitulated to Napoleon, he ordered a guard of honor to be placed at Haydn's residence. Haydn died on May 31, 1809, and was buried at the Hundsturm Cemetery.

Haydn was often called "Papa Haydn" by his intimates in appreciation of his invariable good humor and amiable disposition. Ironically, he never became a papa in the actual sense of the word. His marriage was unsuccessful; his wife was a veritable termagant; indeed, Haydn was separated from her for most of his life. Still, he corresponded with her and sent her money, even though, according to a contemporary report, he never opened her letters.

In schoolbooks Haydn is usually described as "father of the symphony," the creator of the Classical form of the symphony and string quartet. Historically, this absolute formulation cannot be sustained. The symphonic form was established by Johann Stamitz and his associates at the Mannheim School; the string quartet was of an even earlier provenance. But Haydn's music was not limited to formal novelty; its greatness was revealed in the variety of moods, the excellence of variations, and the contrast among the constituent movements of a symphony. String quartets, as conceived by Haydn, were diminutions of the symphony; both were set in sonata form, consisting in three contrasting movements, Allegro, Andante, Allegro, with a Minuet interpolated between the last two movements. It is the quality of invention that places Haydn above his contemporaries and makes his music a model of Classical composition. Haydn played a historic role in the evolution of functional harmony by adopting four-part writing as a fundamental principle of composition, particularly in his string quartets. This practice has also exercised a profound influence on the teaching of music theory.

Haydn's music naturally lent itself to imaginative nicknames of individual compositions. There are among his symphonies such appellations as *Der Philosoph* and *Der Schulmeister*; some were titled after animals: *L'Ours* and *La Poule*; others derived their names from the character of the main theme, as in *Die Uhr* (The Clock), the *Paukenschlag* (Surprise), and the *Paukenwirbel* (Drum Roll). Among Haydn's string quartets are *La Chasse*, so named because of the hunting horn fanfares; the *Vogelquartett*, in which one hears an imitation of birdcalls; the *Froschquartett*, which seems to invoke a similarity with frog calls in the finale; and the *Lerchenquartett*, containing a suggestion of a lark call. The famous *Toy* Symphony, scored for an ensemble which includes the rattle, the triangle, and instruments imitating the quail, cuckoo, and nightingale, was long attributed to Haydn but is actually a movement of a work by Leopold Mozart.

HAYDN, (JOHANN) MICHAEL, distinguished Austrian composer, brother of **(Franz) Joseph Haydn**; b. Rohrau, Lower Austria (baptized), Sept. 14, 1737; d. Salzburg, Aug. 10, 1806. He was a prolific composer of both sacred and secular music, and particularly esteemed for his mastery of church music. His outstanding Requiem in C minor, *Pro defuncto Archiepiscopo Sigismundo*, was composed in memory of his patron in 1771; it was also performed at Joseph Haydn's funeral. He also wrote a fine Mass, the *Sotto il titulo di S. Teresia*, for the Empress Maria Theresa, who sang the soprano solos under his direction in Vienna in 1801. His secular output included dramatic works, symphonies, serenades, divertimentos, and chamber music. His Symphony in G major (1783) was long attributed to **Mozart** (who composed an introduction to its first movement) as K.444/425a.

HELMHOLTZ, HERMANN (LUDWIG FERDINAND) VON, celebrated German scientist and acoustician; b. Potsdam, Aug. 31, 1821; d. Berlin, Sept. 8, 1894. He studied medicine at the Friedrich Wilhelm Medical Institute in Berlin (M.D., 1843), and also learned to play the piano. After holding various posts, he became professor of physics at the University of Berlin in 1871, and from 1888 served as the first director of the Physico-Technical Institute in Berlin. He was ennobled in 1882. His most important work for those interested in music was his *Lehre von den Tonempfindungen als physiologische Grundlage für die Theorie der Musik* (Braunschweig, 1863; English translation by A. Ellis as *On the Sensations of Tone as a Physiological Basis for the Theory of Music*, 1875; new edition, 1948), in which he established a sure physical foundation for the phenomena manifested by musical tones, either single or combined. He supplemented and amplified earlier theories, furnishing impregnable formulae for all classes of consonant and dissonant tone effects. His labors resulted primarily in instituting the laws governing the differences in quality of tone (tone color) in different instruments and voices, covering the whole field of harmonic, differential, and summational tones, and those governing the nature and limits of musical perception by the human ear.

HENDRIX, JIMI (JAMES MARSHALL), black American rock guitarist, singer, and songwriter; b. Seattle, Nov. 27, 1942; d. as a result of asphyxiation while unconscious after taking an overdose of barbiturates in London, Sept. 18, 1970. Being left-handed, he taught himself to play the guitar upside down, and played in a high school band before dropping out of school during his senior year to join the U.S. Army paratroopers. Following his discharge (1961), he worked with groups in Nashville, Vancouver, and Los Angeles. In 1964 he went to New York, where he joined the Isley Brothers and found a ready response for his wild attire and erotic body locomotions; after working with Curtis Knight's group (1964–65), he formed his own outfit, Jimmy James and the Blue Flames. He then went to England, where he organized the Jimi Hendrix Experience (1966) with bass guitarist Noel Redding and drummer Mitch Mitchell. The live Hendrix experience was replete with the most provocative stage manner, which he frequently culminated by setting his guitar on fire. After recording his first album, *Are You Experienced?* (1967), he made his first appearance in the U.S. with his group at the Monterey (California) Pop Festival that same year. He then recorded the albums *Axis: Bold as Love* (1968) and *Electric Ladyland* (1968), followed by a knockout appearance at the Woodstock Festival (1969). Many more albums were released posthumously.

HENRY, PIERRE, French composer and acoustical inventor; b. Paris, Dec. 9, 1927. He studied with **Olivier Messiaen** at the Paris Conservatoire, and also took courses with Nadia Boulanger. In 1950, Henry was a founder of the Groupe de Recherche de Musique Concrète with Pierre Schaeffer, but in 1958 separated from the group to experiment on his own projects in the field of electro-acoustical music and electronic synthesis of musical sounds. In virtually all of his independent works he applied electronic effects, often with the insertion of prerecorded patches of concrete music and sometimes "objets trouvés" borrowed partially or in their entirety from preexistent compositions.

HENSEL, FANNY (CÄCILIA) (née **Mendelssohn-Bartholdy**), German pianist and composer, sister of **(Jacob Ludwig) Felix Mendelssohn (-Bartholdy)**; b. Hamburg, Nov. 14, 1805; d. Berlin, May 14, 1847. She began her musical training with her mother, then studied piano with Ludwig Berger and composition with Carl Friedrich Zelter, and subsequently studied with Marie Bigot in Paris (1816). She later attended Humboldt's lectures on physical geography and Holtei's lectures on experimental physics in Berlin (1825), but music remained her great love. She married the painter W. Hensel on Oct. 3, 1829. From 1843 she oversaw the Sunday morning concerts at Berlin's Elternhaus. Her untimely death was a great shock to her brother, who died a few months afterward. She was a talented composer; six of her songs were published under her brother's name in his opp. 8 and 9 (*Heimweh, Italien, Suleika und Hatem, Sehnsucht, Verlust*, and *Die Nonne*); other works published under her own name, including some posthumously, include four books of songs, a collection of part-songs entitled *Gartenlieder*, and *Lieder ohne Worte* for Piano.

HILDEGARD VON BINGEN, German composer, poetess, and mystic; b. Bemersheim, near Alzey, 1098; d. Rupertsberg, near Bingen, Sept. 17, 1179. Her noble parents, Hildebert and Mechtild, promised to consecrate her to the Church since she was their 10th child; accordingly, she began her novitiate as a child. She joined with the reclusive mystic Jutta of Spanheim, who with her followers occupied a cell of the Benedictine monastery of Disibodenberg. At 15 Hildegard took the veil, and succeeded Jutta as Mother Superior in 1136. Between 1147 and 1150 she founded a monastery on the Rupertsberg (near Bingen) with 18 sisters; around 1165 she founded another house at Eibingen (near Rüdesheim). She is called "abbess" in letters drawn up by Frederick Barbarossa in 1163. She was known as the "Sybil of the Rhine," and conducted extensive correspondence with popes, emperors, kings, and archbishops. She was thus greatly involved in politics and diplomacy. Several fruitless attempts were made to canonize her, but her name is included in the Roman Martyrology, and her feast is celebrated on Sept. 17.

Hildegard is musically important through her monophonic chants, several of which were settings of her lyric and dramatic poetry. She collected her poems in the early 1150s under the title *Symphonia armonie celestium revelationum*. This volume survives in two sources, both in early German neumes; it comprises 70-odd liturgical poems (the exact number varies, depending on classification), all with melismatic music. The poetry is rich with imagery, and it shares the apocalyptic language of her visionary writings. The music is not typical of plainchant, but involves a technique unique to Hildegard; it is made of a number of melodic patterns recurring in different modal positions, which operate as open structures allowing for internal variation in different contexts. She also wrote a morality play in dramatic verse, *Ordo virtutum*, which includes 82 melodies that are similarly structured but distinctly more syllabic in style. She pointed out that her music is written in a range congenial to women's voices, contrasting with the formal Gregorian modes. Hildegard was also known for her literary works, which include prophecy, medical and scientific treatises, and hagiographies, as well as letters.

HINDEMITH, PAUL, eminent German-born American composer, one of the leading masters of 20th-century music; b. Hanau, near Frankfurt, Nov. 16, 1895; d. Frankfurt, Dec. 28, 1963. He began studying violin at the age of nine; at 14 he entered the Hoch Conservatory in Frankfurt, where he studied violin with Adolf Rebner, and composition with Arnold Mendelssohn. His father was killed in World War I, and Hindemith was compelled to rely on his own resources to make a living. He became concertmaster of the orchestra of the Frankfurt Opera (1915–1923), and later played the viola in the string quartet of his teacher Rebner; from 1922 to 1929 he was violist in the Amar String Quartet, and also appeared as a soloist on the viola and viola d'amore. He later was engaged as a conductor, mainly in his own works. As a composer, he joined the modern movement and was an active participant in the contemporary music concerts at Donaueschingen, and later in Baden-Baden. In 1927 he was appointed instructor in composition at the Berlin Hochschule für Musik. With the advent of the Hitler regime in 1933, Hindemith began to experience increasing difficulties, both artistically and politically. Although his own ethnic purity was never questioned, he was married to Gertrud Rottenberg, daughter of the Jewish conductor Ludwig Rottenberg, and he stubbornly refused to cease ensemble playing with undeniable Jews. Hitler's propaganda minister, Goebbels, accused Hindemith of cultural Bolshevism, and his music fell into an official desuetude. Unwilling to compromise with the barbarous regime, Hindemith accepted engagements abroad.

Beginning in 1934, he made three visits to Ankara at the invitation of the Turkish government, and helped to organize the music curriculum at the Ankara Conservatory. He made his first American appearance at the Coolidge Festival at the Library of Congress in Washington, D.C., in a performance of his Unaccompanied Viola Sonata in 1937. After a brief sojourn in Switzerland, he emigrated to the U.S. He was instructor at the Berkshire Music Center at Tanglewood in the summer of 1940; from 1940 to 1953 he was a professor at Yale University, and was elected a member of the National Institute of Arts and Letters. During the academic year 1950–1951, he was Charles Eliot Norton Lecturer at Harvard University. He became an American citizen in 1946. He conducted concerts in the Netherlands, Italy, and England during the summer of 1947. In 1949, Hindemith revisited Germany for the first time since the war, and conducted the Berlin Philharmonic in a program of his own works. In 1953 he went to Switzerland, giving courses at the University of Zurich, while also conducting orchestras in Germany and Austria. In 1954 he received the prestigious Sibelius Award of $35,000, offered annually to distinguished composers and scientists by a Finnish shipowner. From 1959 to 1961 he conducted guest appearances in the U.S.; in 1963 he visited America for the last time, and then went to Italy, Vienna, and finally Frankfurt, where he died.

Hindemith's early music reflects rebellious opposition to all tradition, including works such as the opera *Mörder, Hoffnung der Frauen* (op. 12, 1921) and *Suite 1922* for Piano (op. 26). At the same time, he cultivated the techniques of constructivism, evident in his theatrical sketch *Hin und Zurück* (op. 45a, 1927), in which *Krebsgang* (retrograde movement) is applied to the action on the stage, so that events are reversed; in a work of a much later period, *Ludus Tonalis* (1943), the postlude is the upside-down version of the prelude. Along constructive lines is Hindemith's cultivation of so-called *Gebrauchsmusik*, that is, music for use. He was also an ardent champion of *Hausmusik*, to be played or sung by amateurs at home; the score of his *Frau Musica* (as revised in 1944) has an obbligato part for the audience to sing. A neo-Classical trend is shown in a series of works, entitled *Kammermusik*, for various instrumental combinations, polyphonically conceived, and Baroque in style. Although he made free use of atonal melodies, he was never tempted to adopt an integral 12-tone method, which he opposed on esthetic grounds. Having made a thorough study of early music, he artfully assimilated its polyphony in his works; his masterpiece of this genre was the opera *Mathis der Maler*.

An exceptionally prolific composer, Hindemith wrote music of all types for all instrumental combinations, including a series of sonatas for each orchestral instrument with piano. His style may be described as a synthesis of modern, Romantic, Classical, Baroque, and other styles, a combination saved from the stigma of eclecticism only by Hindemith's superlative mastery of technical means. As a theorist and pedagogue, he developed a self-consistent method of presentation derived from the acoustical nature of harmonies.

HOLIDAY, BILLIE (ELEANORA) "LADY DAY," remarkable black American jazz singer; b. Philadelphia, April 7, 1915; d. New York, July 17, 1959. She began singing in Harlem nightclubs when she was 14, and was discovered there by the impresario John Hammond, who arranged for her to perform and record with Benny Goodman and his band in 1933. She later worked with bands led by Teddy Wilson (1935), Fletcher Henderson (1936), Count Basie (1937–38), Artie Shaw, and others before setting out on her own. She gave a solo concert at New York's Town Hall and appeared in the movie *New Orleans* in 1946. Her otherwise brilliant career was marred by personal tragedies, which included addiction to narcotics and alcohol; she served time for Federal narcotics charges in 1946, but made a comeback at New York's Carnegie Hall in 1948. She subsequently toured throughout the U.S. and also sang in Europe (1954, 1958). Arrested again on a narcotics charge in 1959, she died in New York's Metropolitan Hospital. Despite the oft-quoted phrase "Lady Day sings the blues," she rarely sang classic blues; with her unique vocal endowments, she made everything she performed—mostly popular tunes of the day—sound "bluesy."

HOLST, GUSTAV(US THEODORE VON), significant English composer; b. Cheltenham, Sept. 21, 1874; d. London, May 25, 1934. He was of Swedish descent. Plagued by suspicions of his German sympathies at the outbreak of World War I in 1914, he removed the Germanic-looking (actually Swedish) nobiliary particle "von" from his surname. Holst's most celebrated work, the large-scale orchestral suite *The Planets*, was inspired by the astrological significance of the planets. It consists of seven movements, each bearing a mythological subtitle, with an epilogue of female voices singing wordless syllables. It was first performed privately in London (Sept. 29, 1918); five movements were played in public (Feb. 15, 1920); and the first complete performance followed (Nov. 15, 1920). The melodic and harmonic style of the work epitomizes Holst's musical convictions, in which lyrical, dramatic, and triumphant motifs are alternately presented in coruscatingly effective orchestra dress. His music in general reflects the influence of English folk songs and the madrigal. He was a master of choral writing; one of his notable works utilizing choral forces was *The Hymn of Jesus* (1917).

HONEGGER, ARTHUR (OSCAR), remarkable French composer; b. Le Havre (of Swiss parents), March 10, 1892; d. Paris, Nov. 27, 1955. He studied violin in Paris with Lucien Capet, and then took courses at the Zurich Conservatory (1909–1911). In the early years of his career, Honegger embraced the fashionable type of urban music, with an emphasis on machine-like rhythms and curt, pert melodies. In 1921 he wrote a sport ballet, *Skating Rink*, and a mock-militaristic ballet, *Sousmarine*. In 1923 he composed the most famous of such machine pieces, *Mouvement symphonique No. 1*, subtitled *Pacific 231*. The score was intended to be a realistic tonal portrayal of a powerful American locomotive, bearing the serial number 231. The music progressed in accelerating rhythmic pulses toward a powerful climax, then gradually slackened its pace until the final abrupt stop; there was a simulacrum of a lyrical song in the middle section of the piece. *Pacific 231* enjoyed great popularity and became in the minds of modern-minded listeners a perfect symbol of the machine age. Honegger's Second *Mouvement symphonique*, composed in 1928, was a musical rendering of the popular British sport rugby. His *Mouvement symphonique No. 3*, however, bore no identifying subtitle. This abandonment of allusion to urban life coincided chronologically with a general trend in his music away from literal representation and toward absolute music in Classical forms, often of historical or religious character. Among his most important works in that genre were *Le Roi David*, to a biblical subject, and *Jeanne d'Arc au bûcher*, glorifying the French patriot saint on the semi-millennium of her martyrdom.

HOROWITZ, VLADIMIR, Russian-born American pianist of legendary fame; b. Berdichev, Oct. 1, 1903; d. New York, Nov. 5, 1989. Reared in a musically inclined Jewish family, he began playing piano in his early childhood under the direction of his mother, a professional pianist and later an instructor at the Kiev Conservatory. He made his first public appearance in a recital in Kiev on in 1920, marking the opening of a fantastically successful career. The revolutionary events in Russia did not prevent him from giving concerts in and around Kiev until he decided to leave Russia; his first official concert abroad took place in Berlin on Jan. 2, 1926. Arriving in Paris in 1928, he took brief instruction with Alfred Cortot, and on Jan. 12 of that same year, he made his American debut in **Tchaikovsky**'s first Piano Concerto with the New York Philharmonic under the direction of Sir Thomas Beecham; he subsequently appeared as soloist with several other American orchestras, earning the reputation of a piano virtuoso of the highest caliber, so that his very name became synonymous with pianistic excellence. He played for President Herbert Hoover at the White House in 1931, and in 1933 married Wanda Toscanini, daughter of Arturo Toscanini; he became an American citizen in 1942.

Horowitz seemed to possess every gift of public success; he was universally admired, and his concerts sold out whenever and wherever he chose to appear. His natural affinity was with the Russian repertoire. He formed a sincere friendship with **Sergei Rachmaninoff**, despite the disparity in their ages; Rachmaninoff himself regarded Horowitz as the greatest pianist of the century, and Horowitz's performance of Rachmaninoff's Third Piano Concerto, which he played numerous times, was his proudest accomplishment. His performances of works by **Chopin, Liszt, Schumann**, and Tchaikovsky were equally incomparable. Yet amid all these successes, he seemed unable to master his own nervous system. He became subject to irrational fears of failure, and once or twice tried to cancel his engagements at the last minute; it took all the devotion and persuasive powers of his wife for him to overcome his psychological difficulties. Horowitz lived for a while in Europe in the hope of a salutary change of environment. Eventually, in 1973, he underwent shock therapy, which appeared to help.

During World War II, he appeared with Toscanini in numerous patriotic concerts; it was for such a celebration in New York's Central Park that he made a vertiginous transcription for piano of Sousa's *Stars and Stripes Forever*, a veritable tour de force of pianistic pyrotechnics, which he performed for years as an encore, to the delight of his audiences. In 1949, he gave the world premiere of **Samuel**

Barber's Piano Sonata in Havana. In 1953, on the 25th anniversary of his American debut, he gave a recital performance in Carnegie Hall in New York. After this recital, he withdrew from the stage, not to return for nearly 12 years. However, he enjoyed making recordings when he was free to change his successive versions in the sanctuary of a studio. He also accepted a few private pupils. He then announced a definite date for a concert in Carnegie Hall: May 9, 1965. Tickets went on sale two weeks in advance, and a line formed whose excitement and agitation would equal and surpass that of a queue of fans for a baseball game. Horowitz himself was so touched by this testimony of devotion that he sent hundreds of cups of coffee to the crowd to make the waiting more endurable on a rainy day.

Despite his agonies over solo performances, Horowitz had no difficulty whatsoever appearing as an accompanist to Dietrich Fischer-Dieskau; he also played trios with Mstislav Rostropovich and Isaac Stern. In 1982, at the behest of the Prince of Wales, he gave a recital in the Royal Festival Hall in London, marking his first appearance in Europe in 31 years. Through his recordings he formed a large following in Japan; to respond to his popularity there, he gave a series of concerts in Tokyo and other Japanese cities (June 1983). The climax of his career, which became a political event as well, was his decision to accept an invitation to revisit Russia for a series of concerts in 1986. His Steinway grand piano was tuned and cleaned and placed on a special plane to Moscow. Horowitz was accompanied on this trip by his wife, a piano tuner, and his cook. Special foods consisting of fresh sole and other delicacies were airmailed to Moscow every day. Horowitz made a short introductory speech in Russian before he played. The Russian music-lovers who filled the hall listened almost tearfully to his playing on his return to Russia after 61 years of absence. His program included works by Rachmaninoff, Tchaikovsky, and **Alexander Scriabin**, and also pieces by **Domenico Scarlatti** and Chopin.

The Russian trip seemed to give Horowitz the necessary spiritual uplift. Returning to New York, he resumed his concert and recording career. He was awarded the U.S. Medal of Freedom by President Reagan in 1986, and the National Medal of Arts in 1989. He made his last recording on Nov. 1 of that year; four days later, in the afternoon, he suddenly collapsed and died of a heart attack. His passing created a universal feeling of loss the world over. His body lay in state in New York and was then flown by his wife to Italy, where it was interred in the Toscanini family plot in Milan.

HORSZOWSKI, MIECZYSLAW, remarkable Polish pianist; b. Lemberg, June 23, 1892; d. Philadelphia, May 22, 1993. He was a certified child prodigy who made his first public appearance at the age of nine playing **Beethoven**'s First Piano Concerto with the Warsaw Philharmonic. He studied piano in Lemberg, and was then sent to Vienna, where Theodor Leschetizky accepted him as a private pupil. On Feb. 16, 1906, he played a solo recital at La Scala in Milan; he subsequently played privately for the Pope and for the King of England, then undertook an extensive concert tour in Europe, and also played chamber music with cellist Pablo Casals. In 1941 he joined the faculty of the Curtis Institute of Music in Philadelphia. Among his most prominent students were Seymour Lipkin, Peter Serkin, and Cecile Licad. In 1981, at the age of 89, he married his longtime companion, the Italian pianist Bice Costa; it was the first marriage for both. Indefatigable, Horszowski continued his career as a concert pianist well into his 90s. His performance in Los Angeles on Jan. 31, 1990, in a program of Bach, Beethoven, Schumann, and Chopin, aroused wonderment for its impeccable interpretation and all but faultless technique.

HOVHANESS (CHAKMAKJIAN), ALAN (VANESS SCOTT), prolific and proficient American composer of Armenian- Scottish descent; b. Somerville, Massachusetts, March 8, 1911. From his earliest attempts at composition, he took great interest in the musical roots of his paternal ancestry, studying the folk songs assembled by the Armenian musician **Komitas**. He gradually came to believe that music must reflect the natural monody embodied in national songs and ancient church hymns. In his music he adopted modal melodies and triadic harmonies. This *parti pris* had the dual effect of alienating him from the milieu of modern composers while exercising great attraction for the music consumer at large. By dint of ceaseless repetition of melodic patterns and relentless dynamic tension, he succeeded in creating a *sui generis* type of impressionistic monody, flowing on the shimmering surfaces of euphony, free from the upsetting intrusion of heterogeneous dissonance. An air of mysticism pervades his music, aided by the programmatic titles that he often assigns to his compositions. A composer of relentless fecundity, he produced over 60 symphonies; several operas, quasi-operas, and pseudo-operas; and an enormous amount of choral music. The totality of his output is in excess of 370 opus numbers. In a laudable spirit of self-criticism, he destroyed seven of his early symphonies and began numbering them anew so that his first numbered symphony (subtitled "Exile") was chronologically his eighth. He performed a similar auto-da-fé on other dispensable pieces. Among his more original compositions is a symphonic score *And God Created Great Whales*, in which the voices of humpback whales recorded on tape is used as a solo with the orchestra.

IBERT, JACQUES (FRANÇOIS ANTOINE), distinguished French composer; b. Paris, Aug. 15, 1890; d. there, Feb. 5, 1962. He studied at the Paris Conservatoire with André Gédalge and **Gustave Fauré** (1911–1914). During World War I, he served in the French navy, returning to the Conservatoire after the Armistice. Ibert received the Prix de Rome in 1919 for his cantata *Le Poète et la fée*; while in Rome, he wrote his most successful work, the symphonic suite *Escales* (Ports of Call), inspired by a Mediterranean cruise he took while serving in the navy. In 1937 he was appointed director of the Académie de France of Rome, and held this post until 1960; he was also administrator of the Réunion des Théâtres Lyriques Nationaux in Paris (1955–56). He was elected a member of the Institut de France in 1956. In his music, Ibert combines the most felicitous moods and techniques of Impressionism and neo-Classicism. His harmonies are opulent; his instrumentation is coloristic. There is an element of humor in his lighter works, such as his popular orchestral *Divertissement* and an even more popular piece, *Le Petit Âne blanc*, from the piano suite *Histoires*. His craftsmanship is excellent; an experimenter in tested values, he never fails to produce the intended effect.

IVES, CHARLES (EDWARD), one of the most remarkable American composers, whose individual genius created music so original, so universal, and yet so deeply national in its sources of inspiration that it profoundly changed the direction of American music; b. Danbury, Connecticut, Oct. 20, 1874; d. New York, May 19, 1954. His father, George, was a bandleader of the First Connecticut Heavy Artillery during the Civil War, and the early development of Charles Ives was, according to his own testimony, deeply influenced by his father. At the age of 12, he played the drums in the band and also received from his father rudimentary musical training in piano and cornet playing. At the age of 13 he played organ at the Danbury Church; soon he began to improvise freely at the piano, without any dependence on school rules. As a result of his experimentation in melody and harmony, encouraged by his father, he began to combine several keys, partly as a spoof, but eventually as a legitimate alternative to traditional music. At 17 he composed his *Variations on America* for organ in a polytonal setting; still earlier he wrote a band piece, *Holiday Quick Step*, which was performed by the Danbury Band in 1888.

In 1894 he entered Yale University, where he took regular academic courses and studied organ with Dudley Buck and composition with Horatio Parker; from Parker he received a fine classical training. While still in college he composed two full-fledged symphonies, written in an entirely traditional manner demonstrating great skill in formal structure, fluent melodic development, and smooth harmonic modulations. After his graduation in 1898, Ives joined an insurance company, and also played organ at the Central Presbyterian Church in New York (1899–1902). In 1907 he formed an insurance partnership with Julian Myrick of New York. He proved himself to be an exceptionally able businessman; the firm of Ives & Myrick prospered, and Ives continued to compose music as an avocation. In 1908 he married Harmony Twichell. In 1918 he suffered a massive heart attack, complicated by a diabetic condition, and was compelled to curtail his work both in business and in music to a minimum because his illness made it difficult for him to handle a pen. He retired from business in 1930, and by that time had virtually stopped composing.

In 1919 Ives published at his own expense his great masterpiece, *Concord Sonata*, for piano, inspired by the writings of Emerson, Hawthorne, the Alcotts, and Thoreau. Although written early in the century, its idiom is so extraordinary, and its technical difficulties so formidable, that the work did not receive a performance in its entirety until John Kirkpatrick played it in New York in 1939. In 1922 Ives brought out, also at his expense, a volume of *114 Songs*, written between 1888 and 1921 and marked by a great diversity of style, ranging from lyrical Romanticism to powerful and dissonant modern invocations. Both the *Concord Sonata* and the *114 Songs* were distributed gratis by Ives to anyone wishing to receive copies. His orchestra masterpiece, *Three Places in New England*, also had to wait nearly two decades before its first performance; of the monumental Fourth Symphony, only the second movement was performed in 1927, and its complete performance was given posthumously in 1965. In 1947 Ives received the Pulitzer Prize for his Third Symphony, written in 1911.

The slow realization of the greatness of Ives and the belated triumphant recognition of his music were phenomena without precedent in music history. Because of his chronic ailment, and also on account of his personal disposition, Ives lived as a recluse, away from the mainstream of American musical life; he never went to concerts and did not own a record player or a radio. While he was well versed in the musical classics, and studied the scores of **Beethoven, Schumann**, and **Brahms**, he took little interest in sanctioned works of modern composers; yet he anticipated many technical innovations, such as polytonality, atonality, and even 12-tone formations, as well as polymetric and polyrhythmic configurations, which were prophetic for his time. In the second movement of the *Concord Sonata* he specified the application of a strip of wood on the white and the black keys of the piano to produce an echo-like sonority. In his unfinished *Universe Symphony* he planned an antiphonal representation of the heavens in chordal counterpoint and the earth in contrasting orchestra groups. He also composed pieces of quarter-tone piano music.

A unique quality of his music was the combination of simple motifs, often derived from American church hymns and popular ballads, with an extremely complex dissonant counterpoint which formed the supporting network for the melodic lines. A curious idiosyncrasy is the frequent quotation of the "fate motive" of Beethoven's Fifth Symphony in many of his works. Materials of his instrumental and vocal works often overlap, and the titles were often changed during the process of composition. In his orchestrations he often indicated interchangeable and optional parts, as in the last movement of the *Concord Sonata*, which has a part for flute obbligato; thus he reworked the original score for large orchestra of his *Three Places in New England* for a smaller ensemble to fit the requirements of Nicolas Slonimsky's Chamber Orchestra of Boston, which gave its first performance, and it was in this version that the work was first published and widely performed until the restoration of the large score was made in 1974.

Ives possessed an uncommon gift for literary expression; his annotations to his works are both trenchant and humorous. He published in 1920 *Essays before a Sonata* as a literary companion volume to the *Concord Sonata*; his *Memos* in the form of a diary, published after his death, reveal an extraordinary power of aphoristic utterance. He was acutely conscious of his civic duties as an American, and once circulated a proposal to have federal laws enacted by popular referendum. His centennial in 1974 was celebrated by a series of conferences at his alma mater, Yale University; in New York, Miami, and many other American cities; and in Europe, including Russia. While during his lifetime he and a small group of devoted friends and admirers had great difficulties in having his works performed, recorded, or published, a veritable Ives cult emerged after his death; eminent conductors gave repeated performances of his orchestral works, and modern pianists were willing to cope with the forbidding difficulties of his works. In terms of the number of orchestra performances, in 1976 Ives stood highest among modern composers on American programs, and the influence of his music on the new generation of composers reached a high mark, so that the adjective "Ivesian" became common in music criticism to describe certain acoustical and coloristic effects characteristic of his music.

JAGGER, MICK (MICHAEL PHILIP), English rock singer and songwriter, the demonic protagonist of the fantastically popular rock group The Rolling Stones; b. Dartford, Kent, July 26, 1944. He studied at the London School of Economics (1962–1964); at the same time, pursued his interest in music, forming The Rolling Stones in 1962. His first success came with "Satisfaction" (1965), a song of candid sexual expression composed by guitarist Keith Richard (his usual writing partner) with lyrics by Jagger. With this frontal assault upon the social sensibilities of the Establishment, the group earned a reputation as the outlaws of rock; Jagger assumed the role of high priest at their subsequent concerts, which often degenerated into mad orgies among the audience, incited by the plenary obscenity of the words and metaphorical gestures of Jagger and his celebrants. He is responsible for such hallucinogenic psychedelic hits as "Midnight Rambler," "Jumpin' Jack Flash," and "Sympathy for the Devil."

JANÁČEK, LEOŠ, greatly significant Czech composer; b. Hukvaldy, Moravia, July 3, 1854; d. Moravska Ostrava, Aug. 12, 1928. Janáček's style of composition underwent numerous transformations, from Romantic techniques of established formulas to bold dissonant combinations. He was greatly influenced by the Russian musical nationalism exemplified by the "realistic" speech inflections in his vocal writing. He visited St. Petersburg and Moscow in 1896 and 1902, and published his impressions of the tour in the press. From

1894 to 1903 he worked assiduously on his most important opera, *Její pastorkyňa* (Her Foster Daughter), to a highly dramatic libretto set in Moravia in the mid-19th century, involving a jealous contest between two brothers for the hand of *Jenůfa* (the innocent heroine), and infanticide at the hands of a foster mother, with an amazing outcome absolving *Jenůfa* and her suitors. The opera encountered great difficulty in securing production in Prague because of its grisly subject, but was eventually produced on various European stages, mostly in the German text, and under the title *Jenůfa*. Another opera by Janáček that attracted attention was *Výlet pana Broučka do XV stoleti* (Mr. Broucek's Excursion to the 15th Century), depicting the imaginary travel of a Czech patriot to the time of the religious struggle mounted by the followers of the nationalist leader Hus against the established church.

Like most artists, writers, and composers of Slavic origin in the old Austro-Hungarian Empire, Janáček had a natural interest in the Pan-Slavic movement, with an emphasis on the common origins of Russian, Czech, Slovak, and other kindred cultures; his *Glagolitic Mass*, to a Latin text translated into the Czech language, is an example. Janáček lived to witness the fall of the old Austrian regime and the national rise of the Slavic populations. He also showed great interest in the emerging Soviet school of composition, even though he refrained from any attempt to join that movement. Inevitably, he followed the striking innovations of the modern school of composition as set forth in the works of **Stravinsky** and **Schoenberg**, but he was never tempted to experiment along those revolutionary lines. He remained faithful to his own well-defined style, and it was as the foremost composer of modern Czech music that he secured his unique place in history.

JONES, "SPIKE" (LINDLEY ARMSTRONG), American bandleader; b. Long Beach, California, Dec. 14, 1911; d. Los Angeles, May 1, 1965. He played drums as a boy; then led a school band. On July 30, 1942, he made a recording of a satirical song, "Der Führer's Face," featuring a Bronx-cheer razzer; then toured the U.S. with his band, The City Slickers, which included a washboard, a Smith and Wesson pistol, anti-bug Flit guns in E-flat, doorbells, anvils, hammers to break glass, and a live goat trained to bleat rhythmically.

Climactically, he introduced the Latrinophone (a toilet seat strung with catgut). With this ensemble, he launched a Musical Depreciation Revue. He retired in 1963, when the wave of extravaganza that had carried him to the crest of commercial success subsided. In his heyday he was known as the "King of Corn."

JOPLIN, JANIS (LYN), American rock and blues singer; b. Port Arthur, Texas, Jan. 19, 1943; d. of an overdose of heroin, Los Angeles, Oct. 4, 1970. After a brief stint in college in San Francisco, she joined the rock group Big Brother and the Holding Company as lead vocalist in 1966, winning acclaim for her rendition of "(Love Is Like a) Ball and Chain" when she appeared with the group at the Monterey International Pop Festival in 1967. Her passionate wailing in a raspy voice immediately established her as an uninhibited representative of the younger generation. After recording the album *Cheap Thrills* (1967), she left Big Brother and struck out on her own, forming her own backup group, the Full Tilt Boogie Band, in 1968 and then appeared in such esoteric emporia as the Psychedelic Supermarket in Boston, Kinetic Playground in Chicago, Whisky A-Go-Go in Los Angeles, and Fillmore East in New York. She produced the albums *I Got Dem Ol' Kozmic Blues Again Mama* and *Pearl* before her early demise. She was arrested in Tampa, Flordia, in 1969 for having hurled porcine epithets at a policeman, which further endeared her to her public. On the more positive side, the Southern Comfort Distillery Co. presented her with a fur coat in recognition of the publicity she gave the firm by her habitual consumption of a quart of Southern Comfort at each of her appearances.

JOPLIN, SCOTT, remarkable black American pianist and composer; b. probably near Marshall, Texas, Nov. 24, 1868; d. New York, April 1, 1917. He learned to play the piano at home, and later studied music seriously with a local German musician. He left home at 17 and went to St. Louis, earning his living by playing piano in local emporia. In 1893 he moved to Chicago, and in 1896 went to Sedalia, Missouri, where he took music courses at George Smith College, a segregated school for blacks.

His first music publications were in 1895, of genteel, maudlin songs and marches, typical of the period. His success as a ragtime composer came with the *Maple Leaf Rag* (1899; the most famous of all piano rags), which he named after a local dance hall, the Maple Leaf Club. The sheet-music edition sold so well that Joplin was able to settle in St. Louis and devote himself exclusively to composition; he even tried to write a ragtime ballet (*The Ragtime Dance*, 1902) and a ragtime opera, *A Guest of Honor* (copyright 1903, but the music is lost). In 1907 he went to New York, where he continued his career as a composer and teacher. Still intent on ambitious plans, he wrote an opera, *Treemonisha*, to his own libretto (the title deals with a black baby girl found under a tree by a woman named Monisha); he completed the score in 1911 and produced it in concert form in 1915 without success. Interest in the opera was revived almost 60 years later; T.J. Anderson orchestrated it from the piano score, and it received its first complete performance in Atlanta in 1972.

Despite Joplin's ambitious attempts to make ragtime "respectable" by applying its principles to European forms, it was with the small, indigenous dance form of the piano rag that he achieved his greatest artistic success. As one noted historian phrased it, these pieces are "the precise American equivalent, in terms of a native dance music, of minuets by Mozart, mazurkas by Chopin, or waltzes by Brahms." Altogether, he wrote about 50 piano rags, in addition to the two operas, and a few songs, waltzes, and marches. The titles of some of these rags reflect his desire to transcend the trivial and create music on a more serious plane: *Sycamore*, "A Concert Rag" (1904); *Chrysanthemum*, "An Afro-American Intermezzo" (1904); *Sugar Cane*, "A Ragtime Classic 2 Step" (1908); *Fig Leaf Rag*, "A High Class Rag" (1908); and *Reflection Rag*, "Syncopated Musings" (1917). In his last years he lamented at having failed to achieve the recognition he felt his music merited. Suffering from syphilis, he became insane and died shortly afterward in a state hospital. More than 50 years later, an extraordinary sequence of events—new recordings of his music and its use in an award-winning film, *The Sting* (1974)—brought Joplin unprecedented popularity and acclaim: among pop recordings, *The Entertainer* (1902) was one of the best-selling discs for 1974; among classical recordings, Joplin albums represented 74 percent of the best-sellers of the year. In 1976 he was awarded exceptional posthumous recognition by the Pulitzer Prize Committee.

KARAJAN, HERBERT VON, preeminent Austrian conductor in the grand Germanic tradition; b. Salzburg, April 5, 1908; d. Anif, near Salzburg, July 16, 1989. He was a scion of a cultured family of Greek-Macedonian extraction whose original name was Karajannis. His father was a medical officer who played the clarinet and his brother was a professional organist. Karajan began his musical training as a pianist, taking lessons at the Salzburg Mozarteum. He further attended the conducting classes of the Mozarteum's director. Eventually he went to Vienna, where he entered the Vienna Academy of Music as a conducting student. In 1928, he made his conducting debut with a student orchestra at the Vienna Academy of Music; shortly afterward, he made his professional conducting debut with the Salzburg Orchestra. He then received an engagement as conductor of the Ulm Stadttheater (1929–1934). From Ulm he went to Aachen, where he was made conductor of the Stadttheater; he subsequently served as the Generalmusikdirektor there (1935–1942).

In 1938, he conducted his first performance with the Berlin Philharmonic, the orchestra that became the chosen medium of his art. Also in 1938, he conducted *Fidelio* at his debut with the Berlin Staatsoper. His capacity of absorbing and interpreting the music at hand and transmitting its essence to the audience became his most signal characteristic; he also conducted all of his scores from memory, including the entire *Ring des Nibelungen*. His burgeoning fame as a master of both opera and symphony led to engagements elsewhere in Europe. In 1938 he conducted opera at La Scala in Milan and also made guest appearances in Belgium, the Netherlands, and Scandinavia. In 1939 he became conductor of the symphony concerts of the Berlin Staatsoper Orchestra.

There was a dark side to Karajan's character, revealing his lack of human sensitivity and even a failure to act in his own interests. He became fascinated by the ruthless organizing solidity of the National Socialist party; on April 8, 1933, he registered in the Salzburg office of the Austrian Nazi party, and barely a month later he joined the German Nazi party in Ulm. He lived to regret these actions after the collapse of the Nazi empire. His personal affairs also began to interfere with his career. He married the operetta singer Elmy Holgerloef in 1938, but divorced her in 1942 to marry Anita Gütermann. Trouble came when the suspicious Nazi genealogists discovered that she was one-quarter Jewish and suggested that he divorce her. But World War II was soon to end, and so was Nazi hegemony. He finally divorced Gütermann in 1958 to marry the French fashion model Eliette Mouret.

Karajan was characteristically self-assertive and unflinching in his personal relationships and in his numerous conflicts with managers and players. Although he began a close relationship with the Vienna Symphony Orchestra in 1948, he left it in 1958. His association as conductor of the Philharmonia Orchestra of London from 1948 to 1954 did more than anything to reestablish his career after World War II, but in later years he disdained his relationship with that ensemble. When Wilhelm Furtwängler, the longtime conductor of the Berlin Philharmonic, died in 1954, Karajan was chosen to lead the orchestra on its first tour of the U.S. However, he insisted that he would lead the tour only on the condition that he be duly elected Furtwängler's successor. Protesters were in evidence for his appearance at New York's Carnegie Hall with the orchestra, but his Nazi past did not prevent the musicians of the orchestra from electing him their conductor.

Karajan soon came to dominate the musical life of Europe as no other conductor had ever done. In addition to his prestigious Berlin post, he served as artistic director of the Vienna Staatsoper from 1956 until he resigned in a bitter dispute with its general manager in 1964. He concurrently was artistic director of the Salzburg Festival (1957–1960), and thereafter remained closely associated with it. From 1969 to 1971 he held the title of artistic adviser of the Orchestra de

Paris. In the meantime, he consolidated his positions in Berlin and Salzburg. In 1963, he conducted the Berlin Philharmonic in a performance of Beethoven's Ninth Symphony at the gala concert inaugurating the orchestra's magnificent new concert hall, the Philharmonie. In 1967 he organized his own Salzburg Easter Festival, which became one of the world's leading musical events; renegotiated his contract and was named conductor-for-life of the Berlin Philharmonic; and made a belated Metropolitan Opera debut in New York, conducting *Die Walküre*. He went on frequent tours of Europe and Japan with the Berlin Philharmonic, and also took the orchestra to the Soviet Union (1969) and China (1979).

In 1985 Karajan celebrated his 30th anniversary as conductor of the Berlin Philharmonic, and in 1988 his 60th anniversary as a conductor. In 1987 he conducted the New Year's Day Concert of the Vienna Philharmonic, which was televised to millions on both sides of the Atlantic. In Feb. 1989 he made his last appearance in the U.S., conducting the Vienna Philharmonic at New York's Carnegie Hall. In April 1989 he announced his retirement from his Berlin post, citing failing health. Shortly before his death, he dictated an autobiographical book to Franz Endler; it was published in an English translation in 1989.

KODÁLY, ZOLTÁN, renowned Hungarian composer, ethnomusicologist, and music educator; b. Kecskemét, Dec. 16, 1882; d. Budapest, March 6, 1967. He became associated with **Béla Bartók**, collecting, organizing, and editing a vast wealth of national folk songs; he made use of these melodies in his own compositions. In 1906 he went to Berlin, and in 1907 proceeded to Paris, where he took some lessons with Charles-Marie Widor, but it was the music of **Claude Debussy** which most profoundly influenced him in his subsequent development as a composer. He was appointed a professor at the Royal Academy of Music in Budapest in 1907. In collaboration with Bartók, he prepared the detailed paper "A Project for a New Universal Collection of Folk Songs" in 1913. They continued their collecting expeditions until World War I intervened. In 1923 he was commissioned to write a commemorative work in celebration of the half-century anniversary of the union of Buda, Pest, and Obuda into Budapest. The resulting work, the oratorio *Psalmus hungaricus* (1923), brought him wide recognition. Another major success was his opera

Háry János (1926); an orchestral suite from this work became highly popular in Hungary and throughout the world. His orchestral works *Marosszéki táncok* (Dances of Marosszék; 1930; based on a piano work) and *Galántai táncok* (Dances of Galánta; for the 80th anniversary of the Budapest Philharmonic Society, 1933) were also very successful. His reputation as one of the most significant national composers was firmly established with the repeated performances of these works. His great interest in music education is reflected in his numerous choral works, which he wrote for both adults and children during the last 30 years of his life. As a composer, Kodály's musical style was not as radical as that of Bartók; he never departed from basic tonality, nor did his experiments in rhythm reach the primitivistic power of Bartók's percussive idiom. He preferred a Romantic treatment of his melodic and harmonic materials, with an infusion of Impressionistic elements.

KOECHLIN, CHARLES (LOUIS EUGÈNE), noted French composer, pedagogue, and writer on music; b. Paris, Nov. 27, 1867; d. Le Canadel, Var, Dec. 31, 1950. He studied for a military career, but was compelled to change his plans when stricken with tuberculosis. While recuperating in Algeria, he took up serious music studies, and then entered the Paris Conservatoire (1890), where he studied with André Gédalge, **Jules Massenet**, and **Gabriel Fauré**, graduating in 1897. He lived mostly in Paris, where he was active as a composer, teacher, and lecturer. With **Maurice Ravel** and Florent Schmitt, he organized the Société Musicale Indépendante (1909) to advance the cause of contemporary music; with **Erik Satie**, Albert Roussel, **Darius Milhaud**, and others, he was a member of the group Les Nouveaux Jeunes (1918–1920), a precursor to Les Six. Although he composed prolifically in all genres, he became best known as a writer on music and as a lecturer. Taking Fauré as his model, he strove as a composer to preserve the best elements in the French Classical tradition. A skillful craftsman, he produced works of clarity and taste, marked by advanced harmonic and polyphonic attributes.

KOMITAS (real name, **Sogomonian**), Armenian ethnomusicologist and composer; b. Kutina, Turkey, Oct. 8, 1869; d. Paris, Oct. 22,

1935. He studied at the Gevorkian Theological Seminary in Vaghars-hapat, and was made a vardapet (archimandrite) in 1894, taking the name Komitas, after a seventh-century Armenian hymn writer. In 1895 he went to Tiflis, where he studied music theory, and then lived in Berlin (1896–1899), where he took courses at Richard Schmidt's private conservatory and at the university. He studiously collected materials on Armenian folk music, publishing articles on the subject and also composing works utilizing Armenian motifs. In 1910 he moved to Constantinople; the Armenian massacre of 1915 so affected him that he became incurably psychotic, and lived from 1919 in a Paris hospital. His body was reburied in the Pantheon of Armenian Artists in Erevan in 1936.

KRAFT, WILLIAM, American percussionist, composer, and conductor; b. Chicago, Sept. 6, 1923. His parental name was Kashareftsky, which his parents Americanized to Kraft. The family moved to California and Kraft began to study piano. He took music courses at San Diego State College and at the University of California at Los Angeles, where he also had professional percussion instruction with Murray Spivack. In 1943 he was called to arms, and served in the U.S. forces as pianist, arranger, and drummer in military bands; while in Europe with the army, he took time to attend music courses at Cambridge University. Returning to the U.S. after his discharge from military duty, he earned a living as percussionist in jazz bands. In the summer of 1948 he enrolled in the Berkshire Music Center in Tanglewood, where he studied composition with Irving Fine and conducting with **Leonard Bernstein**. He continued to perfect his technique as a percussionist, and took lessons with Morris Goldenberg and Saul Goodman; he attained a high degree of virtuosity as a percussion player, both in the classical tradition and in jazz. In 1955 he became a percussionist with the Los Angeles Philharmonic, retaining this position until 1981.

In the meantime he developed his natural gift for conducting; from 1969 to 1972 he served as assistant conductor of the Los Angeles Philharmonic. In a parallel development, he composed assiduously and successfully. From 1981 to 1985 he was composer-in-residence of the Los Angeles Philharmonic, and also founded the Los Angeles Philharmonic New Music Group, presenting programs of modern works for chamber orchestra combinations. As a composer, he explores without prejudice a variety of quaquaversal techniques, including serial procedures; naturally, his music coruscates with a rainbow spectrum of asymmetrical rhythms. There is a tendency in the very titles of his works toward textured constructivism, e.g., *Momentum, Configurations, Collage, Encounters, Translucences, Triangles,* and *Mobiles*; but there are also concrete representations of contemporary events, as in *Contextures: Riots-Decade '60.*

LASSO, ORLANDO DI, great Franco-Flemish composer, also known in Latin as **Orlandus Lassus**, and in French as **Roland de Lassus**; b. Mons, 1532; d. Munich, June 14, 1594. He entered the service of Ferrante Gonzaga when he was about 12 years old, and subsequently traveled with him; then was placed in the service of Constantino Castrioto of Naples at the age of 18. He later proceeded to Rome and entered the service of the Archbishop of Florence, and then was maestro di cappella at St. John Lateran (1553–1554). In 1555, he went to Antwerp, where he enjoyed a fine reputation both socially and artistically. His first works were published that year in Venice, containing 22 madrigals set to poems of Petrarch, along with a collection of madrigals and motets set to texts in Italian, French, and Latin he published in Antwerp. In 1556 he became a singer at the Munich court chapel of Duke Albrecht of Bavaria. He married Regina Wechinger, an aristocratic woman, in 1558. In 1563 he was made maestro di cappella of the Munich court chapel, a position he held with great eminence until his death. He made occasional trips, including to Flanders to recruit singers (1560), to Frankfurt for the coronation of Emperor Maximilian II (1562), to Italy (1567), to the French court (1571; 1573–1574), again to Italy (1574–1579), and to Regensburg (1593). In 1570, he received from the Emperor Maximilian a hereditary rank of nobility.

Lasso represents the culmination of the great era of Franco-Flemish polyphony. His superlative mastery in sacred as well as secular music renders him one of the most versatile composers of his time. He was equally capable of writing in the most elevated style and in the popular idiom. His art was supranational; he wrote Italian madrigals, German lieder, French chansons, and Latin motets. Musicians of his time described him variously as the "Belgian Orpheus" and the "Prince of Music." The sheer scope of his production is amazing: he left more than 2,000 works in various genres.

LEHÁR, FRANZ (actually, **Ferenc**), celebrated Austrian operetta composer of Hungarian descent; b. Komorn, Hungary, April 30, 1870; d. Bad Ischl, Oct. 24, 1948. He began his music training with his father, a military bandmaster. In 1887 Lehár submitted two piano sonatas to **Dvořák**, who encouraged him in his musical career. In 1888 he became a violinist in a theater orchestra in Elberfeld; in 1889, he entered his father's band in Vienna, and assisted him as conductor. From 1890 to 1902 Lehár led military bands in Pola, Trieste, Budapest, and Vienna. Although his early stage works were unsuccessful, he gained some success with his marches and waltzes. With *Der Rastelbinder* (Vienna, Dec. 20, 1902), he established himself as a composer for the theater. His most celebrated operetta, *Die lustige Witwe* (The Merry Widow), was first performed in 1905; it subsequently received innumerable performances throughout the world. Lehár's music exemplifies the spirit of gaiety and frivolity that was the mark of Vienna early in the 20th century. His superlative gift for facile melody and infectious rhythms is combined with genuine wit and irony; a blend of nostalgia and sophisticated humor, undiminished by the upheavals of wars and revolutions, made a lasting appeal to audiences.

LENNON, JOHN (**Winston**; later legally changed to **Ono**), English rock singer, guitarist, poet, and songwriter, member of the celebrated group The Beatles; b. Liverpool, Oct. 9, 1940, during a German air raid on the city; d. New York, Dec. 8, 1980, gunned down in front of his apartment building. He was educated by an aunt after his parents separated (his mother was tragically killed soon afterwards by a hit-and-run driver). Lennon played the mouth organ as a child, and later learned the guitar. Emotionally rocked over by **Elvis Presley**'s animal magnetism, he became infatuated with American popular music, forming his first pop group, the Quarry Men, in 1957. He was soon joined by three other rock-crazed Liverpudlians, Paul McCartney, George Harrison, and Stuart Sutcliffe, in a group he first dubbed the Silver Beatles, later to become simply The Beatles. (Inspired by the success of Buddy Holly and the Crickets, Lennon hit upon the name The Beatles, which possessed the acoustical ring of the coleopterous insect beetle and the rock-associated beat.) The Beatles opened at the pseudo-exotic Casbah Club in Liverpool in 1959, and soon moved to the more prestigious Cavern Club (1961), where they co-opted Pete Best as drummer. In the same year, they played in Hamburg, scoring a gratifyingly vulgar success with the beer-sodden customers by their loud, electrically amplified sound. Back in England, The Beatles crept on to fame. In late 1961, they were taken up by the perspicacious promoter Brian Epstein, who launched an extensive publicity campaign to put them over the footlights. Sutcliffe died of a brain hemorrhage in 1962. Best was ousted from the group and was replaced by Richard Starkey, whose "nom-de-beatle" became Ringo Starr.

The quartet opened at the London Palladium in 1963 and drove the youthful audience to a frenzy, a scene that was to be repeated elsewhere in Europe, America, Japan, and Australia. After a period of shocked recoil, the British establishment acknowledged the beneficial contribution of The Beatles to British art and the Exchequer. In 1965 each Beatle was made a Member of the Order of the British Empire. Although American in origin, the type of popular music plied by Lennon and The Beatles as a group had an indefinably British lilt. The meter was square; the main beat was accentuated; syncopation was at a minimum; the harmony was modal, with a lowered submediant in major keys as a constantly present feature; a propensity for plagal cadences and a proclivity for consecutive triadic progressions created at times a curiously hymnal mood. The lyrics, most of them written by Lennon and McCartney, were distinguished by suggestive allusions, sensuous but not flagrantly erotic, anarchistic but not destructive, cynical but also humane. The Beatles also produced the highly original films *A Hard Day's Night, Help!, Yellow Submarine*, and *Let It Be*. Among the Beatles's most popular songs that were associated with Lennon are "Please Please Me," "I Feel Fine" (supposedly featuring the first recorded example of feedback in rock), "Help!,"

"Ticket to Ride," "Nowhere Man," "In My Life," "Julia" (written in memory of his mother), and "Because."

The Beatles were legally dissolved in 1970. By then Lennon's career had taken a new turn as a result of his relationship with the Japanese-American avant-garde film producer and artist Yoko Ono; through her, Lennon's social consciousness was raised, and he subsequently became an outspoken activist for peace. They appeared nude on the cover of their album *2 Virgins* and celebrated their honeymoon with a "bed-in" for peace. Soon after, he brought out the album *Imagine* (1971); the title cut became his best-known song of the period. Lennon withdrew from public life in 1975, to become, in his own words, a "househusband." He returned in 1980 to the recording studio, collaborating with Ono on his last album, *Double Fantasy*, which achieved great popularity. The shock waves produced by Lennon's senseless murder reverberated throughout the world; crowds in deep mourning marched in New York, Liverpool, and Tokyo; Ono issued a number of declarations urging Lennon's fans not to give way to despair. Not even the death of Elvis Presley generated such outbursts of grief. A photograph taken on the afternoon before his murder, of John in the nude, embracing a fully dressed Ono, was featured on the cover of a special issue of *Rolling Stone* magazine (Jan. 22, 1981). His life was the subject of a touching documentary film, *Imagine*, in 1988.

LEONCAVALLO, RUGGIERO, noted Italian composer; b. Naples, April 23, 1857; d. Montecatini, Aug. 9, 1919. He attended the Naples Conservatory (1866–76), where he studied piano and composition, and at 16 made a pianistic tour. Leoncavallo earned his living as a young man by playing piano in cafés; he continued this life for many years, traveling through Egypt, Greece, Turkey, Germany, Belgium, and the Netherlands before settling in Paris. There he found congenial company, and composed chansonettes and other popular songs, as well as an opera, *Songe d'une nuit d'été* (after Shakespeare's *Midsummer Night's Dream*), which was privately sung in a salon.

He began to study **Richard Wagner**'s scores, and became an ardent Wagnerian; he resolved to emulate the master by producing a trilogy, *Crepusculum*, depicting in epical traits the Italian Renaissance. He spent six years on the basic historical research; having completed the first part, and with the scenario of the entire trilogy sketched, he returned in 1887 to Italy, where the publisher Ricordi became interested in the project, but kept delaying the publication and production of the work. Annoyed, Leoncavallo turned to Sonzogno, the publisher of **Pietro Mascagni**, whose opera *Cavalleria rusticana* had just obtained a tremendous vogue. Leoncavallo submitted a short opera in a similarly realistic vein; he wrote his own libretto based on a factual story of passion and murder in a Calabrian village, and named it *I Pagliacci*. The opera was given with sensational success in Milan under the direction of Arturo Toscanini (1892), and rapidly took possession of operatic stages throughout the world; it is often played on the same evening with Mascagni's opera, both works being of brief duration. Historically, these two operas signalized the important development of Italian operatic *verismo*, which influenced composers of other countries as well.

LIGETI, GYÖRGY (SÁNDOR), eminent Hungarian-born Austrian composer and pedagogue; b. Dicsöszentmárton, Transylvania, May 28, 1923. After the Hungarian revolution was crushed by the Soviet Union in 1956, he fled his homeland for the West; in 1967 he became a naturalized Austrian citizen. He worked at the electronic music studio of the West German Radio in Cologne (1957–58); from 1959 to 1972 he lectured at the Darmstadt summer courses in new music. In 1973 he became a professor of composition at the Hamburg Hochschule für Musik. In his bold and imaginative experimentation with musical materials and parameters, Ligeti endeavors to bring together all aural and visual elements in a synthetic entity, making use of all conceivable effects and alternating tremendous sonorous upheavals with static chordal masses and shifting dynamic colors. He describes his orchestral style as micropolyphony.

LISZT, FRANZ (Ferenc; baptized **Franciscus)**, greatly celebrated Hungarian pianist and composer, creator of the modern form of the symphonic poem, and innovating genius of modern piano technique; b. Raiding, near Odenburg, Oct. 22, 1811; d. Bayreuth, July

31, 1886. His father was an amateur musician who devoted his energies to the education of his son; at the age of nine, young Liszt was able to play a difficult piano concerto by Ferdinand Ries. A group of Hungarian music-lovers provided sufficient funds to finance Liszt's musical education. In 1822 the family traveled to Vienna. **Beethoven** was still living, and Liszt's father bent every effort to persuade Beethoven to come to young Liszt's Vienna concert on April 13, 1823. Legend has it that Beethoven did come and was so impressed that he ascended the podium and kissed the boy on the brow. Liszt perpetuated the legend, and often showed the spot on his forehead where Beethoven was supposed to have implanted the famous kiss. However that might be, Liszt's appearance in Vienna created a sensation; he was hailed by the press as "child Hercules." The link with Beethoven was maintained through Liszt's own teachers: **Carl Czerny**, who was Beethoven's student and friend and with whom Liszt took piano lessons, and the great Antonio Salieri, who was Beethoven's early teacher and who at the end of his life became Liszt's teacher in composition.

Under the guidance of his ambitious father (a parallel with **Mozart**'s childhood suggests itself), Liszt applied for an entrance examination at the Paris Conservatoire, but its powerful director, Luigi Cherubini, declined to accept him, ostensibly because he was a foreigner. Liszt then settled for private lessons in counterpoint from Antonín Reicha, a Parisianized Czech musician who instilled in Liszt the importance of folklore. Liszt's father died in 1837; Liszt remained in Paris, where he soon joined the brilliant company of men and women of the arts. **Niccolò Paganini**'s spectacular performances on the violin in particular inspired Liszt to create a piano technique of transcendental difficulty and brilliance, utilizing all possible sonorities of the instrument. To emphasize the narrative Romantic quality of his musical ideas, he accepted the suggestion of his London manager to use the word "recital" to describe his concerts, and in time the term was widely accepted by other pianists.

In his own compositions, Liszt was a convinced propagandist of program music. He liked to attach descriptive titles to his works, such as *Fantasy, Reminiscence*, and *Illustrations*. The musical form of *Rhapsody* was also made popular by Liszt, but he was not its originator; it was used for the first time in piano pieces by Bohemian composer Wenzel Johann Tomaschek. A true Romantic, Liszt conceived himself as an actor playing the part of his own life, in which he was a child of the Muses. Traveling in Switzerland, he signed his hotel register as follows: "Place of birth—Parnasse. Arriving from—Dante. Proceeding to—Truth. Profession—Musician-philosopher."

Handsome, artistic, a brilliant conversationalist, Liszt was sought after in society. His first lasting attachment was with an aristocratic married woman, the Comtesse Marie d'Agoult; they had three daughters, one of whom, Cosima, married Liszt's friend Hans von Bülow before abandoning him for **Richard Wagner**. D'Agoult was fluent in several European languages and had considerable literary talents, which she exercised under the *nom de plume* of Daniel Stern. Liszt was 22 when he entered his concubinage with her; she was 28. The growing intimacy between Liszt and d'Agoult soon became the gossip of Paris. **Berlioz** warned Liszt not to let himself become too deeply involved with her. D'Agoult rapidly established herself as a salon hostess in Paris; she was a constant intermediary between Liszt and his close contemporary **Chopin**. Indeed, the book on Chopin published under Liszt's name after Chopin's early death was largely written by d'Agoult, whose literary French was much superior to Liszt's.

His second and final attachment was with another married woman, Carolyne von Sayn-Wittgenstein, who was separated from her husband. Her devotion to Liszt exceeded all limits, even in a Romantic age. "I am at your feet, beloved," she wrote him. "I prostrate myself under your footprints." Liszt fully intended to marry Sayn-Wittgenstein, but he encountered resistance from the Catholic Church, to which they both belonged and which forbade marriage to a divorced woman. Thus, Liszt, the great lover of women, never married.

Liszt's romantic infatuations did not interfere with his brilliant virtuoso career. One of his greatest successes was his triumphant tour in Russia in 1842. Russian musicians and music critics exhausted their flowery vocabulary to praise Liszt as the miracle of the age. His Majesty Czar Nicholas I himself attended a concert given by Liszt in St. Petersburg, and expressed his appreciation by sending him a pair of trained Russian bears. Liszt acknowledged the imperial honor, but did not venture to take the animals with him on his European tour. Liszt was a consummate showman. In Russia, as elsewhere, he had two grand pianos installed on the stage at right angles, so that the keyboards were visible from the right and the left respectively and he could alternate his playing on both. He appeared on the stage wearing a long cloak and white gloves, discarding both with a spectacular gesture. Normally he needed eyeglasses, but he was too vain to wear them in public.

It is not clear why, after all his triumphs in Russia and elsewhere in Europe, Liszt decided to abandon his career as a piano virtuoso and devote his entire efforts to composition. He became associated with Wagner, his son-in-law, as a prophet of "music of the future." Indeed, Liszt anticipated Wagner's chromatic harmony in his works. Inevitably, Liszt and Wagner became objects of derision on the part of conservative music critics.

As a composer, Liszt made every effort to expand the technical possibilities of piano technique; in his two piano concertos, and particularly in his *Études d'exécution transcendante*, he made use of the grand piano, which expanded the keyboard in both the bass and the extreme treble. He also extended the field of piano literature with his brilliant transcriptions of operas. These transcriptions were particularly useful at the time when the piano was the basic musical instrument at home. Liszt never wrote a full-fledged opera, but he composed several sacred oratorios that were operatic in substance. In his secular works he was deeply conscious of his Hungarian heritage, but he gathered his material mainly from Gypsy dances that he heard in public places in Budapest.

In his Weimar years, Liszt aged rapidly. Gone were the classical features that had so fascinated his contemporaries, especially women, during his virtuoso career. Photographs taken in Weimar show him with snow-white hair descending upon his shoulders. He walked with difficulty, dragging his feet. He suffered attacks of phlebitis in his legs and had constant intestinal difficulties. He neglected his physical state, and finally developed double pneumonia and died during his sojourn in Bayreuth at the age of 74.

Liszt was a great musical technician. He organized his compositions with deliberate intent to create music that is essentially new. Thus he abandons the traditional succession of two principal themes in sonata form. In his symphonic poem *Les Préludes*, the governing melody dominates the entire work. In his popular Third *Liebestraum* for Piano, the passionate melody modulates by thirds rather than by Classically anointed fifths and fourths. The great *Faust* symphony is more of a literary essay on Goethe's great poem than a didactic composition. His two piano concertos are free from the dialectical contrasts of the established Classical school. The chromatic opening of the First Concerto led Hans von Bülow to improvise an insulting line to accompany the theme, "Sie sind alle ganz verrückt!" ("They're all completely crazy!"), and the introduction of the triangle solo aroused derisive whoops from the press. Liszt was indifferent to such outbursts. He was the master of his musical fate in the ocean of sounds.

LUENING, OTTO (CLARENCE), multifaceted American composer, teacher, flutist, and conductor; b. Milwaukee, June 15, 1900. He gave his first concert as a flutist in Munich on March 27, 1916. When America entered World War I in 1917, Luening went to Switzerland, where he studied at the Zurich Conservatory; he also had an opportunity to take private lessons with **Ferruccio Busoni**. It was during this period he began to compose; his First Violin Sonata and a Sextet were performed there. Luening returned to the U.S. in 1920; he earned a living as a flutist and conductor in theater orchestras.

An important development in Luening's career as a composer took place in 1952, when he began to experiment with the resources of magnetic tape. He composed a strikingly novel piece, *Fantasy in Space*, in which he played the flute with its accompaniment electronically transmuted on tape; Stokowski featured it on his program in New York on Oct. 28, 1952, along with Luening's two other electronic pieces, *Low Speed* and *Invention*. He found a partner in Vladimir Ussachevsky, who was also interested in musical electronics. Together, they produced the first work that combined real sounds superinduced on an electronic background, *Rhapsodic Variations* for Tape Recorder and Orchestra, performed by the Louisville Orchestra in 1954; its performance anticipated by a few months the production of **Edgard Varèse**'s similarly constructed work, *Déserts*. Another electronic work by Luening and Ussachevsky, *A Poem in Cycles and Bells* for Tape Recorder and Orchestra, was played by the Los Angeles Philharmonic, also in 1954. **Leonard Bernstein** conducted the first performance of still another collaborative composition by Luening and Ussachevsky, *Concerted Piece* for Tape Recorder and Orchestra, with the New York Philharmonic in 1960.

Thenceforth, Luening devoted a major part of his creative effort to an integration of electronic sound into the fabric of a traditional orchestra, without abondoning the fundamental scales and intervals; most, but not all, of these works were in collaboration with Ussachevsky. Unaided, he produced *Synthesis* for Electronic Tape and Orchestra (1960) and *Sonority Canon* (1962). He also wrote straightforward pieces without electronics, the most important of which is *A Wisconsin Symphony*, a sort of musical memoir of the Wisconsin-born composer; it was performed in Milwaukee, Luening's birthplace, on Jan. 3, 1976.

LULLY, JEAN-BAPTISTE (originally, **Giovanni Battista Lulli**), celebrated Italian-born French composer; b. Florence, Nov. 28, 1632; d. Paris, March 22, 1687. The son of a poor Florentine miller, he learned to play the guitar at an early age. His talent for singing brought him to the attention of the Chevalier de Guise, and he was taken to Paris in 1646 as a page to Mlle. d'Orléans, a young cousin of Louis XIV. He quickly adapted to the manner of the French court; although he mastered the language, he never lost his Italian accent. At some time before 1656 he became conductor of Les Petits Violons du Roi, a smaller offshoot of the *grande bande*. This ensemble was heard for the first time in 1656 in *La Galanterie du temps*. Thanks to Lully's strict discipline with regard to organization and interpretation, Les Petits Violons soon came to rival the parent ensemble; the two groups were combined in 1664.

Lully became a naturalized French citizen in 1661, the same year in which he was appointed surintendant de la musique et compositeur de la musique de la chambre; he also became maître de la musique de la famille royale in 1662. His association with Molière commenced in 1664; he provided Molière with the music for a series of *comedies-ballets*, culminating with *Le Bourgeois Gentilhomme* in 1670. Lully acquired the sole right to form an Académie Royale de Musique in 1672, and thus gained the power to forbid performances of stage works by any other composer. From then until his death he produced a series of *tragédies lyriques*, most of which were composed to texts by the librettist Philippe Quinault. The subject matter for several of these works was suggested by the King, who was extravagantly praised and idealized in their prologues. Lully took great pains in perfecting these texts, but was often content to leave the writing of the inner voices of the music to his pupils.

Lully's monopoly of French musical life created much enmity. In 1674 Henri Guichard attempted to establish an Académie Royale des Spectacles, and their ensuing rivalry resulted in Lully accusing Guichard of trying to murder him by mixing arsenic with his snuff. Lully won the court case that followed, but the decision was reversed on appeal. The King continued to support Lully, however, in spite of the fact that the composer's homosexuality had become a public scandal (homosexuality at the time was a capital offense). Lully's acquisition of titles culminated in 1681, when noble rank was conferred upon him with the title Secrétaire du Roi. In his last years he turned increasingly to sacred music. It was while he was conducting his *Te Deum* on Jan. 8, 1687, that he suffered a symbolic accident, striking his foot with a pointed cane used to pound out the beat. Gangrene set in, and he died of blood poisoning two months later. Lully's historical importance rests primarily upon his music for the theater. He developed what became known as the French overture, with its three contrasting slow-fast-slow movements. He further replaced the Italian *recitativo secco* style with accompanied French recitative. Thus, through the Italian-born Lully, French opera came of age.

MACDOWELL, EDWARD (ALEXANDER), greatly significant American composer; b. New York, Dec. 18, 1860; d. there, Jan. 23, 1908. His father was a Scotch-Irish tradesman; his mother, an artistically inclined woman who encouraged his musical studies. He studied from 1876 to 1878 at the Paris Conservatoire, while also studying piano with Antoine- François Marmontel and solfège with Marmontel's son, Antonín. He withdrew from the Conservatoire in 1878, and went to Wiesbaden for further study. In 1879 he enrolled at the Hoch Conservatory in Frankfurt, taking classes with Joachim Raff (the conservatory director) in composition, among others. Raff's class had a visit from **Liszt**; two years later MacDowell visited Liszt in Weimar, and played his own first Piano Concerto for him. Liszt recommended MacDowell to his publishers, who subsequently brought out the first works of MacDowell's to appear in print, the *Modern Suites* for piano, opp. 10 and 14.

Despite his youth, MacDowell was given a teaching position at the Darmstadt Conservatory. He also accepted private pupils, among them Marian Nevins of Connecticut; they were secretly married in 1884. In 1888 he returned to the U.S., where he was welcomed in artistic circles as a famous composer and pianist; musical America at the time was virtually a German colony, and MacDowell's German training was a certificate of his worth. In 1888, MacDowell made his American debut as a composer and pianist at a Boston concert of the Kneisel String Quartet, featuring his *Modern Suite*, op. 10. In 1889, he was the soloist in the premiere performance of his Second Piano Concerto with the New York Philharmonic.

In 1896 Columbia University invited MacDowell to become its first professor of music. In the academic year 1902–1903, he took a sabbatical, playing concerts throughout the U.S. and in Europe. During his sabbatical, Columbia University replaced its president with Nicholas Murray Butler, whose ideas about the role of music in the university were diametrically opposed to MacDowell's. MacDowell resigned in 1904 and subsequently became a *cause célèbre*, resulting in much acrimony on both sides. It was not until some time later that the Robert Center Chair that MacDowell had held was renamed the Edward MacDowell Chair of Music to honor its first recipient.

Through the combination of the trauma resulting from this episode, an accident with a hansom, and the development of what appears to have been tertiary syphilis, MacDowell rapidly deteriorated mentally. He showed signs of depression, extreme irritability, and a gradual loss of vital functions. He eventually lapsed into total insanity, and spent the last two years of his life in a childlike state, unaware of his surroundings. MacDowell was only 47 years old when he died.

Among American composers, MacDowell occupies a historically important place as the first American whose works were accepted as comparable in quality and technique with those of the average German composers of his time. His music adhered to the prevalent representative Romantic art. Virtually all of his works bear titles borrowed from mythical history, literature, or painting; even his piano sonatas, set in Classical forms, carry descriptive titles, indicative of the mood of melodic resources, or as an ethnic reference. German musical culture was decisive in shaping his musical development; even the American rhythms and melodies in his music seem to be European reflections of an exotic art. A parallel with **Grieg** is plausible, for Grieg was also a regional composer trained in Germany. But Grieg possessed a much more vigorous personality, and he succeeded in communicating the true spirit of Norwegian song modalities in his works. Lack of musical strength and originality accounts for MacDowell's gradual decline in the estimation of succeeding generations; his Romanticism was apt to lapse into salon sentimentality. The frequency of performance of his works in concert (he never wrote for the stage) declined in the decades following his death, and his influence on succeeding generations of American composers receded to a faint recognition of an evanescent artistic period.

MAHLER, GUSTAV, great Austrian composer and conductor; b. Kalischt, Bohemia, July 7, 1860; d. Vienna, May 18, 1911. He attended school in Iglau, and in 1875 entered the Vienna Conservatory; he also took academic courses in history and philosophy at the University of Vienna (1877–1880). In the summer of 1880 he received his first engagement as a conductor, at the operetta theater in the town of Hall in Upper Austria. Subsequently, he held posts as theater conductor in several Austrian cities and towns until 1885, when he attained the post of second Kapellmeister at the Prague Opera, where he gave several performances of Wagner's operas. From 1886 to 1888 he was assistant conductor at the Leipzig Opera; in 1888 he received the important appointment of music director of the Royal Opera in Budapest. In 1891 he was engaged as conductor at the Hamburg Opera; during his tenure there, he developed a consummate technique for conducting.

In 1897 he received a tentative offer as music director of the Vienna Court Opera, but there was an obstacle to overcome. Mahler was Jewish, and although there was no overt anti-Semitism in the Austrian government, an imperial appointment could not be given to a Jew. Mahler was never orthodox in his religion, and had no difficulty in converting to Catholicism, which was the prevailing faith in Austria. He held this position at the Vienna Court Opera for 10 years; under his guidance, it reached the highest standards of artistic excellence. In 1898 Mahler was engaged to succeed Hans Richter as conductor of the Vienna Philharmonic. Here, as in his direction of opera, he proved a great interpreter, but he also allowed himself considerable freedom in rearranging the orchestration of classical scores when he felt it would redound to greater effect. He also aroused antagonism among the players by his autocratic behavior toward them. He resigned from the Vienna Philharmonic in 1901; in 1907 he also resigned from the Vienna Court Opera. In the meantime, he became immersed in strenuous work as a composer. He confined himself exclusively to composition of symphonic music, sometimes with vocal parts; because of his busy schedule as conductor, he could compose only in the summer months, in a villa on the Wörthersee in Carinthia. In 1902 he married Alma Schindler; they had two daughters. The younger daughter, Anna Mahler, was briefly married to Ernst Krenek; the elder daughter died in infancy. Alma Mahler studied music with Alexander Zemlinsky, the brother-in-law of **Arnold Schoenberg**.

Having exhausted his opportunities in Vienna, Mahler accepted the post of principal conductor of the Metropolitan Opera in New York in 1907. He made his American debut there on Jan. 1, 1908, conducting *Tristan und Isolde*. In 1909 he was appointed conductor of the New York Philharmonic. His performances both at the Metropolitan and with the New York Philharmonic were enormously successful with the audiences and the New York music critics, but inevitably he had conflicts with the board of trustees in both organizations. He resigned from the Metropolitan Opera; on Feb. 21, 1911, he conducted his last concert with the New York Philharmonic and then returned to Vienna; he died there of pneumonia on May 18, 1911, at the age of 50.

Mahler's symphonies were sharply condemned in the press as being too long, too loud, and too discordant. It was not until the second half of the 20th century that Mahler became fully recognized as a composer, the last great Romantic symphonist. Mahler's symphonies were drawn on the grandest scale, and the technical means employed for the realization of his ideas were correspondingly elaborate. The sources of his inspiration were twofold: the lofty concepts of universal art, akin to those of **Anton Bruckner**, and ultimately stemming from Wagner; and the simple folk melos of the Austrian countryside, in pastoral moods recalling the intimate episodes in **Beethoven**'s symphonies. True to his Romantic nature, Mahler attached descriptive titles to his symphonies: the first was named the *Titan*; the second, *Resurrection*; the third, *Ein Sommermorgentraum*; and the fifth, *The Giant*. The great eighth became known as "symphony of a thousand" because it required about 1,000 instrumentalists, vocalists, and soloists for performance; however, this sobriquet was the inspiration of Mahler's agent, not of Mahler himself. Later in life Mahler tried to disassociate his works from their programmatic titles; he even claimed that he never used them in the first place, contradicting the evidence of the manuscripts, in which the titles appear in Mahler's own handwriting.

Mahler was not an innovator in his harmonic writing; rather, he brought the Romantic era to a culmination by virtue of the expansiveness of his emotional expression and the grandiose design of his musical structures. Morbid by nature, he brooded upon the inevitability of death. One of his most poignant compositions was the cycle for voice and orchestra *Kindertotenlieder*; he wrote it shortly before the death of his little daughter, and somehow he blamed himself for this seeming anticipation of his personal tragedy. In 1910 he consulted Sigmund Freud, but the treatment was brief and apparently did not help Mahler to resolve his psychological problems. Unquestionably, he suffered from an irrational feeling of guilt. In the third movement of his unfinished 10th Symphony, significantly titled *Purgatorio*, he wrote on the margin, "Madness seizes me, annihilates me," and appealed to the Devil to take possession of his soul. But he never was clinically insane. He died of a heart attack brought on by a bacterial infection. Mahler's importance to the evolution of modern music is very great; the early works of Schoenberg and **Berg** show the influence of Mahler's concepts.

MASCAGNI, PIETRO, famous Italian opera composer; b. Livorno, Dec. 7, 1863; d. Rome, Aug. 2, 1945. He composed industriously; in 1888 he sent the manuscript of his one-act opera *Cavalleria rusticana* to the music publisher Sonzogno for a competition, and won first prize. The opera was performed at the Teatro Costanzi in Rome in 1890, with sensational success. The dramatic story of village passion, and Mascagni's emotional score, laden with luscious music, combined to produce an extraordinary appeal to opera lovers. The short opera made the tour of the world stages with amazing rapidity, productions being staged all over Europe and America with never-failing success; the opera was usually presented in two parts, separated by an "intermezzo sinfonico" (which became a popular orchestral number performed separately). *Cavalleria rusticana* marked the advent of the operatic style known as *verismo*, in which stark realism was the chief aim and the dramatic development was condensed to enhance the impressions. When, two years later, another "veristic" opera, Leoncavallo's *I Pagliacci*, was taken by Sonzogno, the two operas became twin attractions on a single bill. Ironically, Mascagni could never duplicate or even remotely approach the success of his first production, although he continued to compose industriously, and opera houses all over the world were only too eager to stage his successive operas.

MASSENET, JULES (-EMILE-FRÉDÉRIC), illustrious French composer; b. Montaud, near St-Etienne, Loire, May 12, 1842; d. Paris, Aug. 13, 1912. At the age of nine he was admitted to the Paris Conservatoire. After taking first prize for piano (1859), he carried off the Grand Prix de Rome with the cantata *David Rizzio* (1863). In 1878 he was appointed professor of composition at the Conservatoire, and at the same time was elected a member of the Académie des Beaux-Arts; he continued to teach at the Conservatoire until 1896. As a pedagogue, he exercised a profound influence on French opera. After **Gounod**, Massenet was the most popular French opera composer. He possessed a natural sense of graceful melody in a distinctive French style. His best operas, *Manon, Werther*, and *Thaïs*, enjoy tremendous popularity in France; the celebrated Meditation for Violin and Orchestra from *Thaïs* was a regular repertoire number among violinists.

MCFERRIN, BOBBY (ROBERT), gifted African American popular vocalist, son of opera singer Robert McFerrin; b. New York, March 11, 1950. He studied music theory from the age of six and played piano in high school, forming a quartet that copied the styles of Henry Mancini and Sergio Mendes. In 1970 he heard Miles Davis's fusion album *Bitches Brew* and completely changed his musical direction. He studied music at Sacramento State University and at Cerritos College; then played piano professionally until 1977, when he began to develop his voice. He toured in 1980 with jazz vocalist Jon Hendricks, and debuted a solo act in 1982. His best-known recording is *Simple Pleasures* (1988), which includes the hit song "Don't Worry, Be Happy;" he has also sung with Herbie Hancock, Yo-Yo Ma, Manhattan Transfer, and others. In 1989 he established the 11-voice ensemble Voicestra, with which he created the sound track for *Common Threads*, a 1989 documentary on the AIDS quilt; the group's first concert tour, in 1990, received critical acclaim. McFerrin began studying conducting in 1989, making his debut with a performance of **Beethoven**'s Symphony No. 7 with the San Francisco Symphony in 1990. Technically, McFerrin is a virtuoso, using a remarkable range of voices with sophisticated control and accompanying them with body percussion, breath, and other self-generated sounds. Esthetically, he fuses a number of musical styles, including jazz, rock, and New Age, in a brilliant palette. His solo and ensemble shows are based on various improvisatory structures through which he produces highly polished, expertly burnished works.

MENDELSSOHN, FANNY. See **HENSEL, FANNY CÄCILIA**.

MENDELSSOHN (-BARTHOLDY), (JACOB LUDWIG) FELIX, famous German composer, pianist, and conductor; b. Hamburg, Feb. 3, 1809; d. Leipzig, Nov. 4, 1847. He was a grandson of the philosopher Moses Mendelssohn and the son of the banker Abraham Mendelssohn. The family was Jewish, but, upon its settlement in Berlin, the father decided to become a Protestant and added Bartholdy to his surname. Mendelssohn received his first piano lessons from his mother, and subsequently studied piano with Ludwig Berger and violin with Carl Wilhelm Henning and Eduard Rietz. He also had regular lessons in foreign languages and in painting (he showed considerable talent in drawing with pastels). His most important teacher in his early youth was Carl Friedrich Zelter, who understood the magnitude of Mendelssohn's talent; in 1821 Zelter took him to Weimar and introduced him to Goethe, who took considerable interest in the boy after hearing him play. Zelter arranged for Mendelssohn to become a member of the Singakademie in Berlin in 1819 as an alto singer; on Sept. 18, his *19th Psalm* was performed by the Akademie. In 1825 Mendelssohn's father took him to Paris to consult Luigi Cherubini (the director of the Conservatoire) on Mendelssohn's prospects in music; however, he returned to Berlin, where he had better opportunities for development.

Mendelssohn was not only a precocious musician, both in performing and in composition; what is perhaps without a parallel in music history is the extraordinary perfection of his works written during adolescence. He played in public for the first time at the age of nine, on Oct. 28, 1818, in Berlin, performing the piano part of a trio by Joseph Wölfl. He wrote a remarkable octet at the age of 16; at 17 he composed the overture for the incidental music to Shakespeare's *A Midsummer Night's Dream*, an extraordinary manifestation of his artistic maturity, showing a mastery of form equal to that of the remaining numbers of the work, which were composed 15 years later. He proved his great musicianship when he conducted **J. S. Bach**'s *St. Matthew Passion* in the Berlin Singakademie in 1829, an event that gave an impulse to the revival of Bach's vocal music.

In the spring of 1829 Mendelssohn made his first journey to England, where he conducted his Symphony in C minor; later he performed in London the solo part in **Beethoven**'s *Emperor* Concerto. He then traveled through Scotland, where he found inspiration for the composition of his overture *Fingal's Cave* (*Hebrides*), which he conducted for the first time during his second visit to London, in 1832; he also played the solo part of his G minor Concerto and his *Capriccio brillante*. He became a favorite of the English public. Queen Victoria was one of his most fervent admirers, and altogether he made 10 trips to England as a pianist, conductor, and composer. From 1830 to 1832 he traveled in Germany, Austria, Italy, and Switzerland, and also went to Paris. In May 1833 he led the Lower-Rhine Music Festival in Düsseldorf; then conducted at Cologne in June 1835.

He was still a very young man when, in 1835, he was offered the conductorship of the celebrated Gewandhaus Orchestra in Leipzig; the University of Leipzig bestowed upon him an honorary degree of Ph.D. Mendelssohn's leadership of the Gewandhaus Orchestra was of the greatest significance for the development of German musical culture; he engaged the violin virtuoso Ferdinand David as concertmaster of the orchestra, which soon became the most prestigious symphonic organization in Germany. On March 28, 1837, he married Cécile Charlotte Sophie Jeanrenaud of Frankfurt, the daughter of a French Protestant clergyman. Five children were born to them, and their marriage was exceptionally happy. At the invitation of King Friedrich Wilhelm IV, Mendelssohn went in 1841 to Berlin to take charge of the music of the court and in the cathedral; he received the title of Royal Generalmusikdirektor, but residence in Berlin was not required.

Returning to Leipzig in 1842, he organized the famous "Conservatorium." Its splendid faculty comprised, besides Mendelssohn (who taught piano, ensemble playing, and later composition), **Robert Schumann**, who taught classes in piano and composition; Moritz Hauptmann, in music theory; David, in violin; Constantin Becker, in organ; and Louis Plaidy and Ernst Wenzel, in piano. The Conservatorium was officially opened on April 3, 1843.

In the summer of 1844 he conducted the Philharmonic concerts in London, during his eighth visit to England; during his ninth visit he conducted the first performance of his oratorio *Elijah* in Birmingham in 1846. It was in England that the "Wedding March" from Mendelssohn's music to *A Midsummer Night's Dream* began to be used to accompany the bridal procession; it became particularly fashionable after it was played at the wedding of the Princess Royal in 1858. He made his tenth and last visit to England in the spring of 1847; this was a sad period of his life, for his favorite sister, Fanny, died on May 14, 1847. Mendelssohn's own health began to deteriorate, and he died at the age of 38. The exact cause of his early death is not determined; he suffered from severe migraines and chills before he died, but no evidence could be produced by the resident physicians for either a stroke or heart failure. The news of his death produced a profound shock in the world of music; not only in Germany and England, where he was personally known and beloved, but in distant America and Russia as well, there was genuine sorrow among musicians.

Mendelssohn's influence on German, English, American, and Russian music was great and undiminishing through the years; his symphonies, concertos, chamber music, piano pieces, and songs became perennial favorites in concerts and at home, the most popular works being the overture *Hebrides*, the ubiquitously played Violin Concerto, the *Songs without Words* for Piano, and the "Wedding March" from incidental music to *A Midsummer Night's Dream*.

MESSIAEN, OLIVIER (EUGÈNE PROSPER CHARLES), outstanding French composer and pedagogue; b. Avignon, Dec. 10, 1908; d. Paris, April 27, 1992. A scion of an intellectual family (his father was a translator of English literature; his mother, Cécile Sauvage, a poet), he absorbed the atmosphere of culture and art as a child. He learned to play piano; at the age of eight composed a song, *La Dame de Shalott*, to a poem by Tennyson. At the age of 11 he entered the Paris Conservatoire, specializing in organ, improvisation, and composition; he carried first prizes in all these departments. After graduation in 1930, he became organist at the Trinity Church in Paris. He taught at the École Normale de Musique and at the Schola Cantorum (1936–1939). He also organized, with André Jolivet, Ives Baudrier, and Daniel-Lesur, the group La Jeune France, with the aim of promoting modern French music. He was in the French army at the outbreak of World War II in 1939, and was taken prisoner. He spent two years in a German prison camp in Görlitz, Silesia; he composed there his *Quatuor pour la fin du temps*, and was repatriated in 1941 and resumed his post as organist at the Trinity Church in Paris. He was professor of harmony and analysis at the Paris Conservatoire (from 1948). He also taught at the Berkshire Music Center in Tanglewood (1948) and in Darmstadt (1950–1953). Young composers seeking instruction in new music became his eager pupils, including **Pierre Boulez, Karlheinz Stockhausen,** and **Iannis Xenakis**. He married the pianist Yvonne Loriod in 1961.

Messiaen is one of the most original of modern composers; in his music he makes use of a wide range of resources, from Gregorian chant to Oriental rhythms. A mystic by nature and Catholic by religion, he strives to find a relationship between progressions of musical sounds and religious concepts. In his theoretical writing he strives to postulate an interdependence of modes, rhythms, and harmonic structures. Ever in quest of new musical resources, he employs in his scores the Ondes Martenot and exotic percussion instruments; a synthesis of these disparate tonal elements finds its culmination in his grandiose orchestral work *Turangalîla-Symphonie*. One of the most fascinating aspects of Messiaen's innovative musical vocabulary is the phonetic emulation of bird song in several of his works; in order to attain ornithological fidelity, he made a detailed study notating the rhythms and pitches of singing birds in many regions of several countries. The municipal council of Parowan, Utah, where Messiaen wrote his work Des canyons aux étoiles, glorifying the natural beauties of the state of Utah, resolved to name a local mountain Mt. Messiaen in 1978. In 1983, his first opera, St. François d'Assise, was premiered, to international acclaim, at the Paris Opéra.

MEYERBEER, GIACOMO (real name, **Jakob Liebmann Beer**), famous German composer; b. Vogelsdorf, near Berlin, Sept. 5, 1791; d. Paris, May 2, 1864. He was a scion of a prosperous Jewish family of merchants. He added the name Meyer to his surname, and later changed his first name for professional purposes. He went to Italy early in 1816, and there turned his attention fully to dramatic composition. His six Italian operas brought him fame, placing him on a par with the celebrated **Rossini** in public esteem. The immense success of *Il Crociato in Egitto* (1824) in particular led to a successful staging at London's King's Theatre, followed by a triumphant Paris production, both in 1825, which made Meyerbeer famous throughout Europe. To secure his Paris position, he revamped his earlier *Margherita d'Angiù* (1820) for the French stage as *Margherita d'Anjou* (1826).

He began a long and distinguished association with the dramatist and librettist Eugene Scribe in 1827 as work commenced on the opera *Robert le diable*. It was produced at the Paris Opéra in 1831, with extraordinary success. He began work on what was to become the opera *Les Huguenots* in 1832; set to a libretto mainly by Scribe, it was accorded a spectacular premiere at the Opéra in 1836. Late in 1836 he and Scribe began work on a new opera, *Le Prophète*. He also commenced work on the opera *L'Africaine* in August 1837, again utilizing a libretto by Scribe; it was initially written for the famous soprano Marie-Cornélie Falcon. However, after the loss of her voice, Meyerbeer set the score aside; it was destined to occupy him on and off for the rest of his life. In 1839 **Richard Wagner** sought out Meyerbeer in Boulogne. Impressed with Wagner, Meyerbeer extended him financial assistance and gave him professional recommendations. However, Wagner soon became disenchanted with his prospects and berated Meyerbeer in private, so much so that Meyerbeer was compelled to disassociate himself from Wagner. The ungrateful Wagner retaliated by giving vent to his anti-Semitic rhetoric.

Meyerbeer established himself as the leading composer of French grand opera in 1831 with *Robert le diable*, a position he retained with distinction throughout his career. Indeed, he became one of the most celebrated musicians of his era. Although the grandiose conceptions and stagings of his operas proved immediately appealing to audiences, his dramatic works were more than mere theatrical spectacles. His vocal writing was truly effective, for he often composed and tailored his operas with specific singers in mind. Likewise, his gift for original orchestration and his penchant for instrumental experimentation placed his works on a high level. Nevertheless, his stature as a composer was eclipsed after his death by Richard Wagner. As a consequence, his operas disappeared from the active repertoire, although revivals and several recordings saved them from total oblivion in the modern era.

MILHAUD, DARIUS, eminent French composer; b. Aix-en-Provence, Sept. 4, 1892; d. Geneva, June 22, 1974. He was the descendant of an old Jewish family, settled in Provence for many centuries. His father was a merchant of almonds; there was a piano in the house, and Milhaud improvised melodies as a child, and then began to take violin lessons. He entered the Paris Conservatoire in 1909, almost at the age limit for enrollment. He received first "accessit" in violin and counterpoint, and second in fugue, and won the Prix Lepaulle for composition. While still a student, he wrote music in a bold modernistic manner, and became associated with **Erik Satie**, poet Jean Cocteau, and the philosopher Paul Claudel. When Claudel was appointed French minister to Brazil, he engaged Milhaud as his secretary; they sailed for Rio de Janeiro early in 1917, and returned to Paris (via the West Indies and New York) shortly after the armistice in 1918. Milhaud's name became known to a larger public as a result of a newspaper article by critic Henri Collet, grouping him with five other French composers of modern tendencies (**Georges Auric**, Louis Durey, **Arthur Honegger, Francis Poulenc**, and Germaine Tailleferre) under the sobriquet Les Six, even though the association was stylistically fortuitous.

In 1922 he visited the U.S.; lectured at Harvard University, Princeton University, and Columbia University, and appeared as pianist and composer in his own works. In 1925, he traveled in Italy, Germany, Austria, and Russia; returning to France, he devoted himself mainly to composition and teaching. At the outbreak of World War II, he was in Aix-en-Provence. In July 1940 he went to the U.S., and taught at Mills College in Oakland, California. In 1947 he returned to France, and was appointed professor at the Paris Conservatoire, but continued to visit the U.S. as conductor and teacher almost annually, despite arthritis, which compelled him to conduct while seated. He retained his post at Mills College until 1971, and then settled in Geneva.

Exceptionally prolific from his student days, he wrote a great number of works in every genre, introducing a modernistic type of music drama, "opéra à la minute," and also the "miniature symphony." He experimented with new stage techniques, incorporating cinematic interludes, and also successfully revived the Greek type of tragedy with vocal accompaniment. He composed works for electronic instruments, and demonstrated his contrapuntal skill in such compositions as his two string quartets (No. 14 and No. 15), which can be played together as a string octet. He was the first to exploit polytonality in a consistent and deliberate manner. He applied the exotic rhythms of Latin America and the West Indies in many of his lighter works; of these, his *Saudades do Brasil* are particularly popular, and Brazilian movements are also found in his *Scaramouche* and *Le Boeuf sur le toit*. In some of his works he drew upon the resources of jazz. His ballet *La Création du monde* (1923), portraying the Creation in terms of African-American cosmology, constitutes the earliest example of the use of the blues and jazz in a symphonic score, anticipating **Gershwin** in this respect. Despite this variety of means and versatility of forms, Milhaud succeeded in establishing a style that was distinctly and identifiably his own. His melodies are nostalgically lyrical or vivaciously rhythmical, according to mood; his instrumental writing is of great complexity and difficulty, and yet entirely within the capacities of modern virtuoso technique. He arranged many of his works in several versions.

MONK, MEREDITH (JANE), American composer, singer, and filmmaker; b. Lima, Peru (of American parents), Nov. 20, 1942. She studied Dalcroze eurythmics, the educational method that relates music to movement, from an early age. She was educated at Sarah Lawrence College (B.A., 1964), then was a pupil in voice of Vicki Starr, John Devers, and Jeanette Lovetri, in composition of Ruth Lloyd, Richard Averee, and Glenn Mack, and in piano of Gershon Konikow. She pursued an active career as a singer, filmmaker, director, choreographer, recording artist, and composer. Her powerful soprano vocalizations employ a wide range of ethnic and avant-garde influences. As one of the first and most natural of performance artists, she developed a flexible, imaginative theatrical style influenced by dream narrative and physical movement.

MONTEVERDI, CLAUDIO (GIOVANNI ANTONIO), great Italian composer; b. Cremona (baptized), May 15, 1567; d. Venice, Nov. 29, 1643. He was the son of an apothecary who practiced medicine as a barber-surgeon. He studied singing and theory with the maestro di cappella at the Cathedral of Cremona; he also learned to play the organ. He acquired the mastery of composition at a very early age. He was only 15 when a collection of his three-part motets was published in Venice; there followed several sacred madrigals (1583) and canzonettas (1584). He married Claudia de Cattaneis, one of the Mantuan court singers, on May 20, 1599; they had two sons, and a daughter who died in infancy. In 1601 he was appointed maestro di cappella in Mantua following the death of Benedetto Pallavicino. The publication of two books of madrigals in 1603 and 1605 further confirmed his mastery of the genre.

Having already composed some music for the stage, he now turned to the new form of the opera. *L' Orfeo*, his first opera, was presented in Mantua in 1607. In this pastoral, he effectively moved beyond the Florentine model of recitative-dominated drama by creating a more flexible means of expression; the score is an amalgam of monody, madrigal, and instrumental music of diverse kinds. He suffered a grievous loss in the death of his wife in 1607. Although greatly depressed, he accepted a commission to compose an opera to celebrate the marriage of the heir-apparent to the court of Mantua to Margaret of Savoy; the result was *L' Arianna* (1608). Although the complete manuscript has been lost, the extant versions of the "Lamento d'Arianna" from the score testify to Monteverdi's genius in expressing human emotion in moving melodies.

In 1614 he prepared his sixth book of madrigals, as well as writing two more works for wedding celebrations, the prologue to the pastoral play *L' Idropica* (not extant), and the French-style ballet *Il ballo delle ingrate*. His patron, Duke Vincenzo of Mantua, died in 1612. However, Monteverdi had the good fortune of being called to Venice in 1613 to occupy the vacant post of maestro di cappella at San Marco, at a salary of 300 ducats, which was raised to 400 ducats in 1616. His post at San Marco proved to be the most auspicious of his career, and he retained it for the rest of his life. He composed mostly church music, but did not neglect the secular madrigal forms. He accepted important commissions from Duke Ferdinando of Mantua, including the ballet *Tirsi e Clori* (1616).

In 1619 he published his seventh book of madrigals, significant in its bold harmonic innovations. In 1624 his dramatic cantata, *Il combattimento di Tancredi e Clorinda*, was performed at the home of a Venetian nobleman. The score is noteworthy for the effective role played by the string orchestra. Following the plague of 1630–1631, he wrote a mass of thanksgiving for performance at San Marco (the *Gloria* is extant); in 1632 he took Holy Orders. His *Scherzi musicali* for one and two voices was published in 1632. Then followed his *Madrigali guerrieri et amorosi*, an extensive retrospective collection covering some 30 years, which was published in 1638. In 1637 the first public opera houses were opened in Venice, and Monteverdi found a new outlet there for his productions. His operas *Il ritorno d'Ulisse in patria* (1640), *Le nozze d'Enea con Lavinia* (1641; not extant), and *L'incoronazione di Poppea* (1642) were all given in Venice. The extant operas may be considered the first truly modern operas in terms of dramatic viability. Monteverdi died at the age of 76 and was accorded burial in the Church of the Frari in Venice. A commemorative plaque was erected in his honor, and a copy remains in the church to this day.

Monteverdi's place in the history of music is of great magnitude. He established the foundations of modern opera conceived as a drama in music. For greater dynamic expression, he enlarged the orchestra, in which he selected and skillfully combined the instruments accompanying the voices. He was one of the earliest, if not the first, to employ such coloristic effects as string tremolo and pizzicato; his recitative assumes dramatic power, at times approaching the dimensions of an arioso. In harmonic usage he introduced audacious innovations, such as the use of the dominant seventh chord and other dissonant chords without preparation. He is widely regarded as having popularized the terms "prima prattica" and "secunda prattica" to demarcate the polyphonic style of the 16th century from the largely monodic style of the 17th century, corresponding also to the distinction between "stile antico" and "stile moderno." For this he was severely criticized by the Bologna theorist Giovanni Maria

Artusi, who published in 1600 a vitriolic pamphlet against Monteverdi, attacking the "musica moderna" that allowed chromatic usages in order to achieve a more adequate expression.

MORLEY, THOMAS, famous English composer; b. Norwich, 1557 or 1558; d. London, Oct. 1602. He studied with **William Byrd**. From 1583 to 1587 he was organist and master of the choristers at Norwich Cathedral. In 1588 he received his B.Mus. from Oxford, and about this time he became organist at St. Paul's Cathedral. By 1591 he had turned spy for the government of Queen Elizabeth I. In 1592 he was sworn in as a Gentleman of the Chapel Royal and was made Epistler and then Gospeller. He was also active as a printer, holding a monopoly on all music published under a patent granted to him by the government in 1598. In addition to publishing his own works, he acted as editor, arranger, translator, and publisher of music by other composers. Notable among his editions was *The Triumphes of Oriana* (1601), a collection of madrigals by 23 composers. He gained distinction as a music theorist; his *A Plaine and Easie Introduction to Practicall Musicke* (1597) became famous as an exposition of British musical schooling of his time.

MORTON, "JELLY ROLL" (**Ferdinand Joseph Lemott, LaMothe**, or **La Menthe**), famous African American (actually, a "Creole-of-color," having mixed African and French-American ancestry) ragtime, blues, and jazz pianist and composer; b. New Orleans, Oct. 20, 1890; d. Los Angeles, July 10, 1941. Born into a French-speaking family that proudly recalled its former days of wealth and position, Morton grew up surrounded by musical instruments, and frequently attended performances at the New Orleans French Opera House. He took up piano when he was 10 and began working in the bordellos of Storyville when he was 12; by the time he was 14, he was traveling throughout Louisiana, Mississippi, Alabama, and Florida while making New Orleans his main haunt. He was a colorful and flamboyant figure, given to extravagant boasting and flashy living; in addition to being a musician, he was a professional gambler (cards and billiards), nightclub owner, and producer, making and losing several fortunes. As a result of his travels, he assimiliated various black, white, and Hispanic musical idioms to produce a form of music akin to jazz. After performing in Los Angeles (1917–1922), he went to Chicago, where he made his first solo recordings in 1923 of his own *New Orleans Blues* (1902), *Jelly Roll Blues* (1905), and *King Porter Stomp* (1906) and, with a sextet of his own, *Big Foot Ham* (1923); with his own New Orleans-style band, the Red Hot Peppers, he recorded *Grandpa's Spells* (1911), *The Pearls* (1919), and *Black Bottom Stomp* (1925) in 1926–1927. He went to New York in 1928, but found himself outside the mainstream of jazz developments; later, he ran a jazz club in Washington, D.C., where he made infrequent appearances as a pianist. By the mid-thirties he was living and performing in New York City. In 1938 Alan Lomax, the folklorist, recorded him for the Library of Congress, capturing him on disc playing piano, singing, relating anecdotes, and preserving his view of the history of jazz; these sessions were the basis for Lomax's book, *Mr. Jelly Lord*. This aroused the interest of the commercial Commodore label, which cut Morton's last solo and band dates.

MOZART, WOLFGANG AMADEUS (baptismal names, **Johannes Chrysostomus Wolfgangus Theophilus**), supreme Austrian genius of music whose works in every genre are unsurpassed in lyric beauty, rhythmic variety, and effortless melodic invention, son of (Johann Georg) Leopold; b. Salzburg, Jan. 27, 1756; d. Vienna, Dec. 5, 1791. He and his sister, tenderly nicknamed "Nannerl," were the only two among the seven children of Anna Maria and Leopold Mozart to survive infancy. Mozart's sister was four-and-a-half years older; she took harpsichord lessons from her father, and Mozart as a very young child eagerly absorbed the sounds of music. He soon began playing the harpsichord himself, and later studied the violin.

Leopold was an excellent musician, but he also appreciated the theatrical validity of the performances that Wolfgang and Nannerl began giving in Salzburg. On Jan. 17, 1762, he took them to Munich, where they performed before the Elector of Bavaria. In Sept. 1762 they played for Emperor Francis I at his palace in Vienna. The family returned to Salzburg in Jan. 1763, and in June 1763 the children were taken to Frankfurt, where Wolfgang showed his skill in improvising at the keyboard. In November they arrived in Paris, where they played before Louis XV; it was in Paris that Wolfgang's first compositions were printed (four sonatas for Harpsichord, with Violin ad libitum).

In April 1764 they proceeded to London; there Wolfgang played for King George III. In London he was befriended by **J. S. Bach**'s son **Johann Christian Bach**, who gave exhibitions improvising four-hands at the piano with the child Mozart. By that time Mozart had tried his ability in composing serious works; he wrote two symphonies for a London performance, and the manuscript of another very early symphony, purportedly written by him in London, was discovered in 1980. In July 1765 they journeyed to the Netherlands, then set out for Salzburg, visiting Dijon, Lyons, Geneva, Bern, Zurich, Donaueschingen, and Munich on the way. Arriving in Salzburg in Nov. 1766, Wolfgang applied himself to serious study of counterpoint under the tutelage of his father.

In September 1767 the family proceeded to Vienna, where Wolfgang began work on an opera, *La finta semplice*; his second theater work was a singspiel, *Bastien und Bastienne*, which was produced in Vienna at the home of Dr. Franz Mesmer, the protagonist of the famous method of therapy by "animal magnetism," which became known as Mesmerism. In 1768, Mozart led a performance of his *Missa solemnis* in C minor before the royal family and court at the consecration of the Waisenhauskirche. Upon Mozart's return to Salzburg in Jan. 1769, Archbishop Sigismund von Schrattenbach named him his Konzertmeister; however, the position was without remuneration. Still determined to broaden Mozart's artistic contacts, his father took him on an Italian tour. He was commissioned to compose an opera; the result was *Mitridate, rè di Ponto*, which was performed in Milan in 1770; Mozart himself conducted three performances of this opera from the harpsichord. After a short stay in Salzburg, they returned to Milan in 1771, where he composed the serenata *Ascanio in Alba* for the wedding festivities of Archduke Ferdinand (Oct. 17, 1771). He returned to Salzburg late in 1771; his patron, Archbishop Schrattenbach, died about that time, and his successor, Archbishop Hieronymus Colloredo, seemed to be indifferent to Mozart as a musician. Once more Mozart went to Italy, where his newest opera, *Lucio Silla*, was performed in Milan in 1772. He returned to Salzburg in March 1773, but in July of that year he went to Vienna, where he became acquainted with the music of **Haydn**, who greatly influenced his instrumental style. Returning to Salzburg once more, he supervised the production of his opera *Il Rè pastore* (1775).

In March 1778 Mozart visited Paris again for a performance of his "Paris" Symphony at a Concert Spirituel. His mother died in Paris on July 3. Returning to Salzburg in Jan. 1779, he resumed his duties as Konzertmeister and also obtained the position of court organist at a salary of 450 gulden. In 1780 the Elector of Bavaria commissioned from him an opera seria, *Idomeneo*, which was successfully produced in Munich on Jan. 29, 1781. In May 1781 Mozart lost his position with the Archbishop in Salzburg and decided to move to Vienna, which became his permanent home. There he produced the operatic masterpiece *Die Entführung aus dem Serail*, staged at the Burgtheater in 1782, with excellent success. On Aug. 4, he married Constanze Weber, the sister of Aloysia Weber, with whom he had previously been infatuated. Two of his finest symphonies—No. 35 in D major, "Haffner," written for the Haffner family of Salzburg, and No. 36 in C major, the "Linz"—date from 1782 and 1783, respectively.

From this point forward Mozart's productivity reached extraordinary dimensions, but despite the abundance of commissions and concert appearances, he was unable to earn enough to sustain his growing family. Still, melodramatic stories of Mozart's abject poverty are gross exaggerations. He apparently felt no scruples in asking prosperous friends for financial assistance. Periodically he wrote to Michael Puchberg, a banker and a brother Freemason (Mozart joined the Masonic Order in 1784), with requests for loans (which he never repaid); invariably Puchberg obliged, but usually granting smaller amounts than Mozart requested.

In 1785 Mozart completed a set of six string quartets which he dedicated to Haydn; unquestionably the structure of these quartets owed much to Haydn's contrapuntal art. In 1786, Mozart's great opera buffa, *Le nozze di Figaro*, was produced in Vienna, obtaining a triumph with the audience; it was performed in Prague early in 1787 with Mozart in attendance. It was during that visit that Mozart wrote his 38th Symphony, in D major, known as the "Prague" Symphony; it was in Prague, also, that his operatic masterpiece *Don Giovanni* was produced, on Oct. 29, 1787. In Nov. 1787 Mozart was appointed Kammermusicus in Vienna as a successor to **Gluck**, albeit at a smaller salary.

The year 1788 was a glorious one for Mozart and for music history; it was the year when he composed his last three symphonies: No. 39 in E-flat major; No. 40 in G minor; and No. 41 in C major, known under the name "Jupiter" (the Jovian designation was apparently attached to the work for the first time in British concert programs). In the spring of 1789 Mozart went to Berlin; on the way he appeared as soloist in one of his piano concertos before the Elector of Saxony in Dresden, and also played the organ at the Thomaskirche in Leipzig. His visits in Potsdam and Berlin were marked by his private concerts at the court of Friedrich Wilhelm II; the King commissioned from him a set of six string quartets and a set of six piano sonatas, but Mozart died before completing these commissions. Returning to Vienna, he began work on his opera buffa *Così fan tutte* (an untranslatable sentence because tutte is the feminine plural, so that the full title would be "Thus do all women"). The opera was first performed in Vienna in 1790. In 1791, during his last year of life, he completed the score of *Die Zauberflöte*, with a German libretto by Emanuel Schikaneder; it was performed for the first time on Sept. 30, in Vienna.

The immediate cause of Mozart's death at the age of 35 has been the subject of much speculation. Almost immediately after the sad event, myths and fantasies appeared in the press; the most persistent of them all was that Mozart had been poisoned by Antonio Salieri out of professional jealousy. The story was further elaborated upon by a report that Salieri confessed his unspeakable crime on his deathbed in 1825. Pushkin used the tale in his drama *Mozart and Salieri*, which **Rimsky-Korsakov** set to music in his opera of the same title. A fanciful dramatization of the Mozart-Salieri rivalry was made into a successful play, *Amadeus*, by Peter Shaffer, which was produced in London in 1979 and in New York in 1980; it subsequently gained wider currency through its award-winning film version of 1984. The notion of Mozart's murder also appealed to the Nazis; in the ingenious version propagated by some German writers of the Hitlerian persuasion, Mozart was a victim of a double conspiracy of Masons and Jews who were determined to suppress the flowering of racial Germanic greatness. The Masons, in this interpretation, were outraged by his revealing of their secret rites in *Die Zauberflöte*, and allied themselves with plutocratic Jews to prevent further spread of his dangerous revelations. Another myth related to Mozart's death that found its way into the majority of Mozart biographies and even into respectable reference works was that a blizzard raged during his funeral and that none of his friends could follow his body to the cemetery; this story is easily refuted by the records of the Vienna weather bureau for the day. It is also untrue that Mozart was buried in a pauper's grave; his body was removed from its original individual location because the family neglected to pay the mandatory dues.

The universal recognition of Mozart's genius during the two centuries since his death has never wavered among professional musicians, amateurs, and the general public. In his music, smiling simplicity was combined with somber drama; lofty inspiration was contrasted with playful diversion; profound meditation alternated with capricious moodiness; religious concentration was permeated with human tenderness. Devoted as Mozart was to his art and respectful as he was of the rules of composition, he was also capable of mocking the professional establishment. A delightful example of this persiflage is his little piece *Ein musikalischer Spass*, subtitled "Dorf Musikanten," a "musical joke" at the expense of "village musicians," in which Mozart all but anticipated developments of modern music, two centuries in the future; he deliberately used the forbidden consecutive fifths, allowed the violin to escape upward in a whole-tone scale, and finished the entire work in a welter of polytonal triads.

The variety of technical development in Mozart's works is all the more remarkable considering the limitations of instrumental means in his time; the topmost note on his keyboard was F above the third ledger line, so that in the recapitulation in the first movement of his famous C major Piano Sonata, the subject had to be dropped an octave lower to accommodate the modulation. The vocal technique displayed in his operas is amazing in its perfection; to be sure, the human voice has not changed since Mozart's time, but he knew how to exploit vocal resources to the utmost. This adaptability of his genius to all available means of sound production is the secret of the eternal validity of his music.

MUSSORGSKY, MODEST (PETROVICH), great Russian composer; b. Karevo, Pskov district, March 21, 1839; d. St. Petersburg, March 28, 1881. He received his first instruction on the piano from his mother. At the age of 10, he was taken to St. Petersburg, where he had piano lessons with Anton Herke, remaining his pupil until 1854. In 1852 he entered the cadet school of the Imperial Guard, and composed a piano piece entitled *Porte enseigne Polka*, which was published. After graduation (1856), he joined the regiment of the Guard. In 1857, he met Alexander Dargomyzhsky, who introduced him to César Cui and **Mily Balakirev**; he also became friendly with the critic and chief champion of Russian national music, Vladimir Stasov. These associations prompted his decision to become a professional composer. He eagerly sought professional advice from his friends Stasov (for general esthetics) and **Rimsky-Korsakov** (for problems of harmony). To the end of his life, he regarded himself as being only half-educated in music, and constantly acknowledged his inferiority as a craftsman. But he yielded to no one in his firm faith in the future of national Russian music. When a group of composers from Bohemia visited St. Petersburg in 1867, Stasov published an article in which he for the first time referred to the "mighty handful of Russian musicians" pursuing the ideal of national art. The expression was picked up derisively by some journalists, but it was accepted as a challenge by Mussorgsky and his comrades-in-arms, Balakirev, **Alexander Borodin**, Cui, and Rimsky-Korsakov, the "Mighty Five" of Russian music. In 1869 he once more entered government service, this time in the forestry department. He became addicted to drink, and had epileptic fits; he died a week after his forty-second birthday.

The significance of Mussorgsky's genius did not become apparent until some years after his death. Most of his works were prepared for publication by Rimsky-Korsakov, who corrected some of his harmonic crudities, and reorchestrated the symphonic works. Original versions of his music were preserved in manuscript, and eventually published. But despite the availability of the authentic scores, his works continue to be performed in Rimsky-Korsakov's editions, made familiar to the whole musical world. In his dramatic works, and in his songs, Mussorgsky draws a boldly realistic vocal line, in which inflections of speech are translated into a natural melody. His first attempt in this genre was an unfinished opera, *The Marriage*, to Gogol's comedy; here he also demonstrated his penetrating sense of musical humor. His ability to depict tragic moods is revealed in his cycle *Songs and Dances of Death*; his understanding of intimate poetry is shown in the children's songs. His greatest work is the opera *Boris*

Godunov (to Pushkin's tragedy), which has no equal in its stirring portrayal of personal destiny against a background of social upheaval. In it, Mussorgsky created a true national music drama, without a trace of the Italian conventions that had theretofore dominated the operatic works by Russian composers. Although Mussorgsky was a Russian national composer, his music influenced many composers outside Russia, and he came to be regarded as the most potent talent of the Russian national school.

NANCARROW, CONLON, remarkable American-born Mexican composer, innovator in the technique of recording notes on a player-piano roll; b. Texarkana, Arkansas, Oct. 27, 1912. He played the trumpet in jazz orchestras, and then took courses at the Cincinnati College-Conservatory of Music (1929–1932). He subsequently traveled to Boston, where he became a private student of **Nicolas Slonimsky**, Walter Piston, and **Roger Sessions**. In 1937 he joined the Abraham Lincoln Brigade and went to Spain to fight in the ranks of the Republican Loyalists against the brutal assault of General Franco's armies. Classified as a premature anti-Fascist after the Republican defeat in Spain, he was refused a U.S. passport and moved to Mexico City, where he remained for 40 years, eventually obtaining Mexican citizenship (1956). In 1981, with political pressures defused in the U.S., Nancarrow was able to revisit his native land and to participate in the New American Music Festival in San Francisco. In 1982 he was a composer-in-residence at the Cabrillo Music Festival in Aptos, California; he also traveled to Europe, where he participated at festivals in Austria, Germany, and France. An extraordinary event occurred in his life in 1982, when he was awarded the "genius grant" of $300,000 by the MacArthur Foundation of Chicago, enabling him to continue his work without any concerns about finances.

The unique quality of Nancarrow's compositions is that they can be notated only by perforating player-piano rolls to mark the notes and rhythms, and can be performed only by activating such piano rolls. This method of composition gives him total freedom in conjuring up the most complex contrapuntal, harmonic, and rhythmic combinations that no human pianist or number of human pianists could possibly perform. The method itself is extremely laborious; a bar containing a few dozen notes might require an hour to stamp out on the piano roll. Some of his studies were published in normal notation in Cowell's *New Music Quarterly*. In 1984, Nancarrow gave a concert of his works in Los Angeles, in a program including his *Prelude and Blues for Acoustic Piano* and several of his studies. An audiovisual documentary on Nancarrow was presented on slides by Eva Soltes. A number of Nancarrow's *Studies for Player Piano* that could be adequately notated were published in *Soundings 4* (1977), accompanied with critical commentaries by Gordon Mumma, Charles Amirkhanian, **John Cage**, Roger Reynolds, and James Tenney. In 1988, his third String Quartet was given its premiere performance in Cologne by the London-based Arditti Quartet, perhaps the only ensemble in the world capable of realizing Nancarrow's exceedingly complex score.

OFFENBACH, JACQUES (actually, **Jacob**), famous French composer of German descent; b. Cologne, June 20, 1819; d. Paris, Oct. 5, 1880. He was the son of a Jewish cantor, whose original surname was Eberst; Offenbach was the town where his father lived. He studied violin before taking up the cello when he was nine. After training in Cologne, he settled in Paris (1833). Following cello studies at the Conservatoire (1833–1834), he played in the orchestra of the Opéra-Comique. He then pursued a career as a soloist and chamber music artist (from 1838), subsequently working as a conductor at the Théâtre-Français (1850–1855). Offenbach is a master of the operetta; his music is characterized by an abundance of flowing, rollicking melodies, seasoned with ironic humor, suitable to the extravagant burlesque of the situations. His irreverent treatment of mythological characters gave Paris society a salutary shock; his art mirrored the atmosphere of precarious gaiety during the second Empire.

ORFF, CARL, outstanding German composer; b. Munich, July 10, 1895; d. there, March 29, 1982. He initiated a highly important method of musical education, which was adopted not only in Germany but in England, America, and Russia. It stemmed from the Günther School for gymnastics, dance, and music that Orff founded in 1924 with dancer Dorothee Günther in Munich, with the aim of promoting instrumental playing and understanding of rhythm among children. He commissioned the piano manufacturer Karl

Maendler to construct special percussion instruments that would be extremely easy to play; these "Orff instruments" became widely adopted in American schools. Orff's ideas of rhythmic training owe much to the eurhythmics of Jacques-Dalcroze, but he simplified them to reach the elementary level. As a manual, he compiled a set of musical exercises, *Schulwerk* (1930–1935, rev. 1950–1954). He also taught composition at the Munich Staatliche Hochschule für Musik (1950–1955).

As a composer, Orff sought to revive the early monodic forms and to adapt them to modern tastes by means of dissonant counterpoint, with lively rhythm in asymmetrical patterns, producing a form of "total theater." His most famous score is the scenic oratorio *Carmina Burana* (1937); the words (in Latin and German) are from 13th-century student poems found in the Benediktbeuren monastery in Bavaria ("Burana" is the Latin adjective of the locality).

PACHELBEL, JOHANN, celebrated German organist, pedagogue, and composer; b. Nuremberg (baptized), Sept. 1, 1653; d. there (buried), March 9, 1706. In 1673 he went to Vienna as deputy organist at St. Stephen's Cathedral, assuming the position of court organist in Eisenach four years later. In 1678 he became organist at the Protestant Predigerkirche in Erfurt, where he established his reputation as a master organist, composer, and teacher. He was a friend of the Bach family, and was the teacher of Johann Christoph Bach, who in turn taught **Johann Sebastian Bach**. In 1690 he accepted an appointment as Württemberg court musician and organist in Stuttgart. However, with the French invasion in the fall of 1692, he fled to Nuremberg; in November of that year he became town organist in Gotha. In 1695 he succeeded Georg Kaspar Wecker as organist at St. Sebald in Nuremberg, a position he held until his death.

Pachelbel was one of the most significant predecessors of J. S. Bach. His liturgical organ music was of the highest order, particularly his splendid organ chorales. His non-liturgical keyboard music was likewise noteworthy, especially his fugues and variations (of the latter, his *Hexachordum Apollinis* of 1699 is extraordinary). He was equally gifted as a composer of vocal music. His motets, sacred concertos, and concertato settings of the Magnificat are fine examples of German church music. He was a pioneer in notational symbolism of intervals, scales, and pitch levels arranged to correspond to the meaning of the words. Thus, his setting of the motet *Durch Adams Fall* is accomplished by a falling figure in the bass; exaltation is expressed by a rising series of arpeggios in a major key; steadfast faith is conveyed by a repeated note; satanic evil is translated into an ominous figuration of a broken diminished-seventh-chord. Generally speaking, joyful moods are portrayed by major keys, mournful states of soul by minor keys, a practice which became a standard mode of expression through the centuries.

PADEREWSKI, IGNACY (JAN), celebrated Polish pianist and composer; b. Kurylowka, Podolia (Russian Poland), Nov. 18, 1860; d. New York, June 29, 1941. On March 3, 1888, he gave his first Paris recital, and on Nov. 10, played a concert in Vienna, both with excellent success. He also began receiving recognition as a composer. Anna Essipoff (who was married to Theodor Leschetizky) played his piano concerto in Vienna under the direction of Hans Richter. Paderewski made his London debut in 1890. A year later, he played for the first time in New York, and was acclaimed with an adulation rare for pianists; by some counts he gave 107 concerts in 117 days in New York and other American cities and attended 86 dinner parties. His wit, already fully developed, made him a social lion in wealthy American salons. Paderewski eclipsed even **Enrico Caruso** as an idol of the masses.

Although cosmopolitan in his culture, Paderewski remained a great Polish patriot. During the First World War he donated the entire proceeds from his concerts to a fund for the Polish people caught in the war between Russia and Germany. After the establishment of the independent Polish state, Paderewski served as its representative in Washington. In 1919 he was named prime minister of the Polish Republic, the first musician to occupy such a post in any country at any period; Paderewski resigned his post on Dec. 10. He reentered politics in 1920 in the wake of the Russian invasion of Poland that year, when he became a delegate to the League of Nations; he resigned on May 7, 1921, and resumed his musical career. On Nov. 22, 1922, he gave his first concert after a hiatus of many years at Carnegie Hall in New York. In 1939 he made his last American tour. Once more during his lifetime Poland was invaded, this time by both Germany and Russia, and once more Paderewski was driven to political action. He joined the Polish government-in-exile in France and was named president of its parliament on

Jan. 23, 1940. He returned to the U.S. on Nov. 6, a few months before his death.

As an artist, Paderewski was a faithful follower of the Romantic school, which allowed free, well-nigh improvisatory declensions from the written notes, tempi, and dynamics. Judged by 20th-century standards of precise rendering of the text, Paderewski's interpretations appear surprisingly free, but this very personal freedom of performance moved contemporary audiences to ecstasies of admiration. Also, Paderewski's virtuoso technique, which astonished his listeners, has been easily matched by any number of pianists of succeeding generations. Yet his position in the world of the performing arts remains undiminished by the later achievements of younger men and women pianists. As a composer, Paderewski also belongs to the Romantic school. At least one of his piano pieces, the *Menuet in G* (which is a movement of his set of six *Humoresques* for piano), achieved enormous popularity. His other compositions, however, never sustained a power of renewal and were eventually relegated to the archives of unperformed music.

PAGANINI, NICCOLÒ, legendary Italian violinist; b. Genoa, Oct. 27, 1782; d. Nice, May 27, 1840. His father, a poor dockworker, gave him his first lessons on the mandolin and violin; he then studied with a violinist in the theater orchestra. By this time the young Paganini was already composing; he also began to study harmony with Francesco Gnecco, and subsequently studied violin with Giacomo Costa, who arranged for him to play in local churches. His first documented public appearance took place at the Church of S. Filippo Neri in 1794. It was about this time that he was indelibly impressed by the Franco-Polish violin virtuoso Auguste Frédéric Durand (later billed as Duranowski), who was a brilliant showman.

As a soloist, Paganini captivated his auditors by his pyrotechnics. During an engagement in Livorno he so impressed a wealthy French merchant that he was rewarded with a valuable violin. With the arrival of Princess Elisa Baciocchi, the sister of Napoleon, as ruler of Lucca (1805), musical life there was reorganized. The two major orchestras were dissolved and replaced by a chamber orchestra. Paganini was retained as second violinist, and then was made solo court violinist (1807). After the chamber orchestra itself was dissolved in 1808, he played in the court string quartet and also served as violin teacher to Prince Felix Baciocchi. Dissatisfied with his position, he broke with the court in Dec. 1809, and pursued a career as a virtuoso.

He came to national prominence in 1813 with a series of sensationally successful concerts in Milan. He subsequently toured throughout Italy, his renown growing from year to year and his vast technical resources maturing and augmenting such that he easily displaced his would-be rivals. When he left Italy for his first tour abroad in 1828, he immediately gained a triumph with his opening concert in Vienna. He gave 14 concerts during his stay in Vienna, and was accorded the honorary title of chamber virtuoso by the Emperor and presented with the city's medal of St. Salvator. He made his first appearance in Berlin in 1829, also playing in Frankfurt, Darmstadt, Mannheim, and Leipzig. In 1831 he made his Paris and London debuts. He subsequently gave concerts throughout Great Britain (1831–1833).

Paganini's artistic fortunes began to decline in 1834; his long-precarious health was ruined, but he had managed to retain his fame and considerable wealth. He continued to give sporadic concerts in subsequent years, but he spent most of his time at his villa in Parma, making occasional visits to Paris. A critical illness in Oct. 1838 led to the loss of his voice; in Nov. 1839 he went to Nice for his health, and died there the following spring.

Paganini's stupendenous technique, power, and control, as well as his romantic passion and intense energy, made him the marvel of his time. He also was not above employing certain tricks of virtuosity, such as tuning up the A string of his violin by a semitone or playing the *Witches' Dance* on one string after severing the other three on stage, in sight of his audience, with a pair of scissors. He was also a highly effective composer for the violin, and gave regular performances of his works at his concerts with great success. Outstanding among his compositions are the *24 Caprices* for Solo Violin, the *Moto perpetuo* for Violin and Orchestra, and several of the violin concertos.

PALESTRINA, GIOVANNI PIERLUIGI DA, great Italian composer; b. probably in Palestrina, near Rome, 1525 or 1526; d. Rome, Feb. 2, 1594. In his letters he customarily signed his name as

Giovanni Petraloysio. He is first listed as a choirboy at S. Maria Maggiore in 1537. In 1544 he was appointed organist of the Cathedral of S. Agapit in Palestrina, where his duties also included teaching music to the canons and choirboys. In 1547, he married Lucrezia Gori; they had three sons. In 1550 the bishop of Palestrina was elected pope, taking the name of Julius III; a year later, he appointed Palestrina maestro of the Cappella Giulia, and Palestrina dedicated his first book of masses to him in 1554. In Jan. 1555, the pope rewarded him by making him a member of the Cappella Sistina even though he was a married man, but in September, Pope Paul IV dismissed Palestrina and two other singers after invoking the celibacy rule of the chapel, although he granted each of them a small pension.

In 1555, Palestrina became maestro di cappella of the great Church of St. John Lateran, where his son Rodolfo joined him as a chorister. Palestrina's tenure was made difficult by inadequate funds for the musical establishment, and he resigned his post in July 1560. From 1561 to 1566 he was maestro di cappella of S. Maria Maggiore. In 1562–1563 the Council of Trent took up the matter of sacred music. Out of its discussions arose a movement to advance the cause of intelligibility of sacred texts when set to music. Palestrina's role with this Council remains a matter of dispute among historians, but his *Missa Pape Marcelli* is an outstanding example of a number of its reforms. From 1564 he was also in charge of the music at the summer estate of Cardinal Ippolito II d'Este in Tivoli, near Rome. He apparently took up a full-time position in the Cardinal's service from 1567 to 1571. From 1566 to 1571 he likewise taught at the Seminario Romano, where his sons Rodolfo and Angelo were students. In 1568 the court of Emperor Maximilian II offered him the position of imperial choirmaster in Vienna, but Palestrina demanded so high a salary that the offer was tacitly withdrawn.

In April 1571, upon the death of Giovanni Animuccia, he resumed his post as maestro of the Cappella Giulia. In 1577, at the request of Pope Gregory XIII, Palestrina and Annibale Zoilo began the revision of the plainsongs of the Roman Gradual and Antiphoner. Palestrina never completed his work on this project; the revision was eventually completed by others and published as *Editio Medicaea* in 1614. In 1580, having lost his eldest sons and his wife to the plague, he made a decision to enter the priesthood; he soon changed his mind, however, and instead married Virginia Dormoli, the widow of a wealthy furrier, on Feb. 28, 1581. In succeeding years he devoted much time to managing her fortune while continuing his work as a musician. In 1584 he published his settings of the *Song of Solomon*. In 1593 he began plans to return to Palestrina as choirmaster of the cathedral, but he was overtaken by death early the next year. He was buried in the Cappella Nuova of old St. Peter's Church.

With his great contemporaries **William Byrd** and **Orlando di Lasso**, Palestrina stands as one of the foremost composers of his age. He mastered the polyphonic style of the Franco-Flemish school, creating works of unsurpassing beauty and technical adroitness. His sacred music remains his most glorious achievement. Highly prolific, he composed 104 masses, over 375 motets, 68 offertories, over 65 hymns, 35 Magnificats, over 140 madrigals (both sacred and secular), Lamentations, litanies, and Psalms.

PARTCH, HARRY, innovative American composer, performer, and instrument maker; b. Oakland, California, June 24, 1901; d. San Diego, Sept. 3, 1974. Largely autodidact, he began experimenting with instruments capable of producing fractional intervals, which led him to the formulation of a 43-tone scale. Among new instruments constructed by him are elongated violas, a chromelodeon, kitharas with 72 strings, harmonic canons with 44 strings, boos (made of giant Philippine bamboo reeds), cloud-chamber bowls, blow-boys (a pair of bellows with an attached automobile horn). Seeking intimate contact with American life, he wandered across the country, collecting indigenous expressions of folkways, inscriptions on public walls, and so forth, for texts in his productions.

PENDERECKI, KRZYSZTOF, celebrated Polish composer; b. Debica, Nov. 23, 1933. After a few works of an academic nature, he developed a hyper-modern technique of composition in a highly individual style, in which no demarcation line is drawn between consonances and dissonances, tonal or atonal melody, or traditional or innovative instrumentation; an egalitarian attitude prevails toward all available resources of sound. While his idiom is naturally complex, he does not disdain tonality, even in its overt triadic forms. In his creative evolution, he has bypassed orthodox serial procedures; his music follows an athematic course, in constantly varying metrical and rhythmic patterns. He utilizes an entire spectrum of modern sonorities, expanding the domain of tone to unpitched elements, making use of such effects as shouting, hissing, and verbal ejaculations in vocal parts, at times reaching a climax of aleatory glossolalia; tapping, rubbing, or snapping the fingers against the body of an instrument; striking the piano strings by mallets, etc. For this he designed an optical notation, with symbolic ideograms indicating the desired sound: thus a black isosceles triangle denotes the highest possible pitch; an inverted isosceles triangle, the lowest possible pitch; a black rectangle for a sonic complex of white noise within a given interval; etc. He applies these modern devices to religious music, including masses in the orthodox Roman Catholic ritual. Penderecki's most impressive and most frequently performed work is his *Tren pamieci ofiarom Hiroszimy* (Threnody in Memory of Victims of Hiroshima) for 52 String Instruments (1959–1960), rich in dynamic contrasts and ending on a tone cluster of two octavefuls of icositetraphonic harmony.

PERGOLESI, GIOVANNI BATTISTA, remarkable Italian composer; b. Jesi, near Ancona, Jan. 4, 1710; d. Pozzuoli, near Naples, March 16, 1736. The original family name was Draghi; the name Pergolesi was derived from the town of Pergola, where Pergolesi's ancestors lived. He became highly proficient as a violinist, playing at the Conservatorio and throughout Naples. His first work to be performed was the dramma sacro *Li prodigi della divina grazia nella conversione di S. Guglielmo Duca d'Aquitania*, which was given by the Conservatorio at the monastery of S. Agnello Maggiore in 1731. He graduated shortly thereafter, and received a commission for his first opera, *La Salustia* (Naples, 1732). In Dec. 1732 he composed several sacred works for performance at the Church of S. Maria della Stella as a votive offering following a series of severe earthquakes in Naples. He was next commissioned to write an opera seria to celebrate the birthday of the empress on Aug. 28, 1733. However, the premiere of the resulting *Il Prigionier superbo* was delayed until Sept. 5; it contained the two-act intermezzo *La Serva padrona*, which became his most celebrated stage work. By 1735 his health had seriously declined, most likely from tuberculosis. Early in 1736 he went to the Franciscan monastery in Pozzuoli, where he soon died at the age of 26. He was buried in the common grave adjacent to the cathedral. Following his death, his fame spread rapidly through performances of *La Serva padrona* and several other stage works. The Paris revival of the work in 1752 precipitated the so-called *querelle des bouffons* between the partisans of the Italian and French factions. His fame was further increased by performances of the *Salve regina* in C minor and the *Stabat Mater* in F minor.

POULENC, FRANCIS (JEAN MARCEL), brilliant French composer; b. Paris, Jan. 7, 1899; d. there, Jan. 30, 1963. He was born into a wealthy family of pharmaceutical manufacturers; his mother taught him music in his childhood. A decisive turn in his development as a composer occurred when he attracted the attention of **Erik Satie**, the *arbiter elegantiarum* of the arts and social amenities in Paris. Deeply impressed by Satie's fruitful eccentricities in the then-shocking manner of Dadaism, Poulenc joined an ostentatiously self-descriptive musical group called the Nouveaux Jeunes. In a gratuitous parallel with the Russian "Mighty Five," the French critic Henri Collet dubbed the "New Youths" Le Groupe de Six, and the label stuck under the designation Les Six. The six musicians included, besides Poulenc, **Georges Auric**, Louis Durey, **Artur Honegger**, **Darius Milhaud,** and Germaine Tailleferre. Although quite different in their styles of composition and artistic inclinations, they continued collective participation in various musical events. An excellent pianist, Poulenc became in 1935 an accompanist to the French baritone Pierre Bernac, for whom he wrote numerous songs.

Compared with his fortuitous comrades-in-six, Poulenc appears a Classicist. He never experimented with the popular devices of "machine music," asymmetrical rhythms, and polyharmonies as cultivated by Honegger and Milhaud. Futuristic projections had little interest for him; he was content to follow the gentle neo-Classical formation of **Maurice Ravel**'s piano music and songs. Among his other important artistic contacts was the ballet impresario Diaghilev, who commissioned him to write music for his Ballets Russes. Apart from his fine songs and piano pieces, Poulenc revealed himself as an inspired composer of religious music, of which his choral works

Stabat Mater and *Gloria* are notable. He also wrote remarkable music for the organ, including a concerto that became a minor masterpiece. A master of artificial simplicity, he pleases even sophisticated listeners by his bland triadic tonalities, spiced with quickly passing diaphonous discords.

PRAETORIUS, MICHAEL, great German composer, organist, and music theorist; b. Creuzburg an der Werra, Thuringia, Feb. 15, 1571; d. Wolfenbüttel, Feb. 15, 1621. The surname of the family was Schultheiss (sometimes rendered as Schultze), which he latinized as Praetorius. He studied with the cantor of the Torgau Lateinschule. In 1582 he entered the University of Frankfurt an der Oder, continuing his studies in 1584 at the Lateinschule in Zerbst, Anhalt. From 1587 to 1590 he was organist of St. Marien in Frankfurt. In 1595 he entered the service of Duke Heinrich Julius of Braunschweig-Wolfenbüttel as an organist; in 1604 he also assumed the duties of court Kapellmeister. Upon the death of his patron in 1613, the Elector Johann Georg of Saxony obtained his services as deputy Kapellmeister at the Dresden court. He retained his Dresden post until 1616, and then resumed his duties in Wolfenbüttel. Praetorius devoted only a part of his time to Wolfenbüttel, for he had been named Kapellmeister to the administrator of the Magdeburg bishopric and prior of the monastery at Ringelheim in 1614. He also traveled a great deal, visiting various German cities. These factors, coupled with a general decline in his health, led to the decision not to reappoint him to his Wolfenbüttel post in 1620. He died the following year a wealthy man. Deeply religious, he directed that the greater portion of his fortune go to organizing a foundation for the poor. Praetorius was one of the most important and prolific German composers of his era. His *Musae Sioniae*, a significant collection of over 1,200 settings of Lutheran chorales, is a particularly valuable source for hymnology.

PRESLEY, ELVIS (ARON), fantastically popular American rock-'n'-roll singer and balladeer; b. Tupelo, Mississippi, Jan. 8, 1935; d. Memphis, Tennessee, Aug. 16, 1977. His father was a poor, ne'er-do-well farmer; his mother an overly protective housewife. His twin brother died in infancy. The family eked out a subsistence living, moving to Memphis, Tennessee early in the singer's life in search of regular employment. Elvis was employed as a mechanic and truck driver in his early youth, picking up guitar playing in his leisure hours. Determined to break into the big time, he hung out at the small recording studio of Sun Records, cutting a custom birthday recording for his mother in 1953. Producer Sam Phillips of Sun was struck by something in the quality of the young singer, and invited him back to work with two local musicians, guitarist "Scotty" Moore and bass player Bill Black. Elvis's first single, "That's Alright," was a cover of a well-known rhythm-and-blues song, and was released in 1954. Within a year, he was a nationwide phenomenon; almost effortlessly he captivated multitudes of adolescents by the hallucinogenic monotone of his vocal delivery, enhanced by rhythmic pelvic gyrations (hence the invidious appellation "Elvis the Pelvis"). He switched to major label RCA, signed with manager "Colonel" Tom Parker (an ex-carnival barker turned mega-music manager, who also handled country crooner Hank Snow), and began to appear in a series of forgettable teen movies. In 1958, Presley was drafted, and served two years in Germany; along with the death of his mother in the same year, this ended the greatest period of his recordings. Returning to civilian life in 1960, he spent many years in Hollywood turning out B movies, while performing for the supper-club crowd in Las Vegas. A much-heralded "comeback" occurred in 1968, when Presley returned to his Memphis roots. He continued to record, although an increased dependency on drugs (both legal and illegal) led him to withdraw into the splendours of his mansion outside of Memphis, known as Graceland.

Presley's death (of cardiac arrhythmia aggravated by an immoderate use of tranquilizers and other drugs) precipitated the most extraordinary outpouring of public grief over an entertainment figure since the death of Rudolph Valentino. His entombment in the family mausoleum in Memphis was the scene of mob hysteria, during which two people were run over and killed by an automobile; two men were arrested for an alleged plot to spirit away his body and hold it for ransom. Entrepreneurs avid for gain put out a mass of memorial literature, souvenirs, and gewgaws, sweat shirts emblazoned with Presley's image in color, Elvis dolls, and even a life-size effigy, as part of a multimillion-dollar effort to provide solace to sorrowing humanity. Presley's home, turned into a sanctuary at suburban Whitehaven, in Memphis, was opened to the public on June 7, 1982, and was visited by mobs, not only by drug-besotted local rock fans, but by delegations from fan clubs in civilized nations (even the U.K.). Souvenirs included an "Always Elvis" brand of wine; license plates of out-of-town motorists bore the legend ELVIS-P. In the early '90s, a nationwide referendum was held as to whether to issue a stamp portraying the young, up-and-coming Elvis or the older, gone-to-seed crooner; the young star won out, and it became the best-selling stamp ever issued by the U.S. post office.

PROKOFIEV (PROKOFIEFF), SERGEI (SERGEIEVICH), great Russian composer of modern times, creator of new and original formulas of rhythmic, melodic, and harmonic combinations that became the recognized style of his music; b. Sontsovka, near Ekaterinoslav, April 27, 1891; d. Moscow, March 5, 1953. Prokofiev received his first piano lessons from his mother, who was an amateur pianist. He improvised several pieces, and then composed a children's opera, *The Giant* (1900), which was performed in a domestic version. Following his bent for the theater, he put together two other operas, *On Desert Islands* (1902) and *Ondine* (1904–1907); fantastic subjects obviously possessed his childish imagination. He was 11 years old when he met the great Russian master, Sergei Taneyev, who arranged for him to take systematic private lessons with Reinhold Glière, who became his tutor at Sontsovka during the summers of 1903 and 1904 and by correspondence during the intervening winter. Under Glière's knowledgeable guidance in theory and harmony, Prokofiev composed a symphony in piano version and still another opera, *Plague*, based upon a poem by Pushkin.

Finally, in 1904, at the age of 13, he enrolled in the St. Petersburg Conservatory, where he studied composition and piano; later he was accepted by no less a master than **Rimsky-Korsakov**, who instructed him in orchestration. During the summers, he returned to Sontsovka or traveled in the Caucasus and continued to compose, already in quite an advanced style; the Moscow publisher Jurgenson accepted his first work, a piano sonata, for publication. It was premiered in Moscow on March 6, 1910. It was then that Prokofiev made his first visit to Paris, London, and Switzerland

(1913); in 1914 he graduated from the St. Petersburg Conservatory, receiving the Anton Rubinstein Prize (a grand piano) as a pianist-composer with his Piano Concerto No. 1, which he performed publicly at the graduation concert.

Because of audacious innovations in his piano music (he wrote one piece in which the right and left hands played in different keys), he was described in the press as a "futurist," and because of his addiction to dissonant and powerful harmonic combinations, some critics dismissed his works as "football music." This idiom was explicitly demonstrated in his *Sarcasms* and *Visions fugitives*, percussive and sharp, yet not lacking in lyric charm. Grotesquerie and irony animated his early works; he also developed a strong attraction toward subjects of primitive character. His important orchestral work, the *Scythian Suite* (arranged from music written for a ballet, *Ala and Lolly*, 1915), draws upon a legend of ancient Russian sun- worship rituals. While a parallel with Stravinsky's *Le Sacre du printemps* may exist, there is no similarity between the styles of the two works. Another Prokofiev score, primitivistic in its inspiration, was the cantata *Seven, They Are Seven*, based upon incantations from an old Sumerian religious ritual. During the same period, Prokofiev wrote his famous *Classical Symphony* (1916–17), in which he adopted with remarkable acuity the formal style of **Haydn**'s music. While the structure of the work was indeed classical, the sudden modulatory shifts and subtle elements of grotesquerie revealed decisively a new modern art.

In 1920 Prokofiev settled in Paris, where he established an association with Diaghilev's Ballets Russes, which produced his ballets *Chout* (a French transliteration of the Russian word for buffoon), *Le Pas d'acier* (descriptive of the industrial development in Soviet Russia), and *L' Enfant prodigue*. In 1921 Prokofiev again visited the U.S. to attend the production of his opera commissioned by the Chicago Opera Company, *The Love of Three Oranges*. In 1927 he was invited to be the pianist for a series of his own works in Russia. He gave a number of concerts in Russia again in 1929, and eventually decided to remain there. In Russia he wrote some of his most popular works, including the symphonic fairy tale *Peter and the Wolf*, staged by a children's theater in Moscow, the historical cantata *Alexander Nevsky*, the ballet *Romeo and Juliet*, and the opera *War and Peace*.

Unexpectedly, Prokofiev became the target of the so-called proletarian group of Soviet musicians who accused him of decadence, a major sin in Soviet Russia at the time. His name was included in the official denunciation of modern Soviet composers issued by reactionary Soviet politicians. He meekly confessed that he had been occasionally interested in atonal and polytonal devices during his stay in Paris, but insisted that he had never abandoned the ideals of classical Russian music. Indeed, when he composed his Seventh Symphony, he described it specifically as a youth symphony, reflecting the energy and ideals of new Russia. Prokofiev died suddenly of heart failure on March 5, 1953, a few hours before the death of Stalin. Curiously enough, the anniversary of Prokofiev's death is duly commemorated, while that of his once powerful nemesis is officially allowed to be forgotten.

PUCCINI, GIACOMO (ANTONIO DOMENICO MICHELE SECONDO MARIA), celebrated composer; b. Lucca, Dec. 22, 1858; d. Brussels, Nov. 29, 1924. He was the fifth of seven children of composer/pedagogue Michele Puccini, who died when Giacomo was only five. His musical training was thus entrusted to his uncle, a pupil of his father; however, Giacomo showed neither inclination nor talent for music. His mother, determined to continue the family tradition, sent him to the local Istituto Musicale Pacini, where Carlo Angeloni— its director, who had also studied with Michele Puccini—became his teacher. After Angeloni's untiring patience had aroused interest, and then enthusiasm, in his pupil, progress was rapid and he soon became a proficient pianist and organist. He began serving as a church organist in Lucca and environs when he was 14, and began composing when he was 17. After hearing *Aida* in Pisa in 1876, he resolved to win laurels as a dramatic composer. Having written mainly sacred music, it was self-evident that he needed further training after graduating from the Istituto (1880). With financial support from his granduncle, and a stipend from Queen Margherita, he pursued his studies with Antonio Bazzini and Amilcare Ponchielli at the Milan Conservatory (1880–83). For his graduation, he wrote a *Capriccio sinfonico*, which was presented at a conservatory concert, eliciting unstinting praise from the critics.

In the same year, Ponchielli introduced Puccini to the librettist Fontana, who furnished him the text of a one-act opera. They produced one further opera together in 1889, but Puccini became convinced that, in order to write a really effective opera, he needed a better libretto than Fontana had provided. Accordingly, he commissioned Domenico Oliva to write the text of *Manon Lescaut*; during the composition, however, Puccini and the publisher Ricordi practically rewrote the entire book, and in the published score Oliva's name is not mentioned. With *Manon Lescaut*, first produced at the Teatro Regio in Turin in 1893, Puccini won a veritable triumph, which was even surpassed by his next work, *La Bohème*, produced at the same theater in 1896. These two works not only carried their composer's name throughout the world, but also have found and maintained their place in the repertoire of every opera house. With fame came wealth, and in 1900 he built at Torre del Lago, where he had been living since 1891, a magnificent villa.

His next opera, *Tosca*, produced in Rome in 1900, is Puccini's most dramatic work; it has become a fixture of the standard repertoire, and contains some of his best-known arias. At its premiere at La Scala in 1904, *Madama Butterfly* was hissed. Puccini thereupon withdrew the score and made some slight changes (the original two-act work was divided into three acts, and the tenor aria was added in the last scene). This revised version was greeted with frenzied applause in Brescia on May 28 of the same year.

Puccini was now the acknowledged ruler of the Italian operatic stage, his works rivaling those of **Verdi** in the number of performances. The first performance of *Madama Butterfly* at the Metropolitan Opera in New York in 1907 took place in the presence of the composer, whom the management had invited especially for the occasion. It was then suggested that he write an opera on an American subject, the premiere to take place at the Metropolitan. He found his subject when he witnessed a performance of Belasco's *The Girl of the Golden West*; he commissioned C. Zangarini and G. Civinini to write the libretto, and in the presence of the composer the world premiere of *La Fanciulla del West* occurred, amid much enthusiasm, at the Metropolitan in 1910. While it never equaled the success of his *Tosca* or *Madama Butterfly*, it returned to favor in the 1970s as a period piece. Puccini then brought out *La Rondine* (1917) and the three one-act operas *Il Tabarro* (after Didier Gold's *La Houppelande*), *Suor Angelica*, and *Gianni Schicchi* (all first performed at the Metropolitan

Opera, 1918). His last opera, *Turandot* (after Gozzi), was left unfinished; the final scene was completed by Franco Alfano and performed at La Scala in 1926.

PURCELL, HENRY, great English composer; b. London, 1659; d. Dean's Yard, Westminster, Nov. 21, 1695. His parentage remains a matter of dispute, since documentary evidence is lacking. Whatever the case, the young Henry Purcell became a chorister of the Chapel Royal (1669), and also received instruction from composer/organist John Blow. When his voice broke (1673), he was appointed assistant keeper of the instruments, and subsequently was named composer-in-ordinary for the violins (1677). He became Blow's successor as organist of Westminster Abbey (1679), and one of the three organists of the Chapel Royal (1682), and was named organ maker and keeper of the king's instruments a year later. His first printed work was a song in Playford's *Choice Ayres* (volume I, 1675); volume II (1679) contains other songs and an elegy on the death of Matthew Locke. In 1680 he published one of his finest instrumental works, the *Fantasias* for Strings. In that same year he began writing odes and welcome songs; although their texts are almost invariably stupid or bombastic, he succeeded in clothing them in some of his finest music. His incidental music for the stage also dates from that year. He wrote the anthem *My Heart is Inditing* for the coronation of King James II (1685). With *Dido and Aeneas* (1689) he produced the first great English opera.

Purcell lies in the north aisle of Westminster Abbey, and his burial tablet well expresses contemporary estimation of his worth: "Here lyes Henry Purcell, Esq.; who left this life, and is gone to that blessed place where only his harmony can be exceeded." His church music shows him to be an original melodist, and a master of form, harmony, and all contrapuntal devices. His music for the stage is equally rich in invention, dramatic instinct, and power of characterization. His chamber works surpass those of his predecessors and contemporaries.

RACHMANINOFF, SERGEI (VASSILIEVICH), greatly renowned Russian-born American pianist, conductor, and composer; b. Semyonovo, April 1, 1873; d. Beverly Hills, California, March 28, 1943. He was of a musical family. His grandfather, father, and mother were amateur pianists; his mother gave him his initial training at their estate. He met **Tchaikovsky**, who appreciated his talent and gave him friendly advice. He graduated from the Moscow Conservatory as a pianist (1891) and as a composer (1892), winning the gold medal with his opera *Aleko*, after Pushkin. Then followed his Prelude in C-sharp minor (1892); published that same year, it quickly became one of the most celebrated piano pieces in the world. Rachmaninoff launched a career as a piano virtuoso, and also took up a career as a conductor, joining the Moscow Private Russian Orchestra (1897). Plagued by depression, he underwent treatment by hypnosis, and then began work on his Second Piano Concerto. He played the first complete performance of the score in Moscow in 1901; this concerto became the most celebrated work of its genre written in the 20th century, and its singular charm has never abated since. It is no exaggeration to say that it became a model for piano concertos by a majority of modern Russian composers, and also of semi-popular virtuoso pieces for piano and orchestra written in America.

On May 12, 1902, Rachmaninoff married his cousin Natalie Satina; they spent some months in Switzerland, then returned to Moscow. After conducting at Moscow's Bolshoi Theater (1904–6), he

decided to spend most of his time in Dresden, where he composed
his Second Symphony, one of his most popular works. Having composed another major work, his Third Piano Concerto, he took it on
his first tour of the U.S. in 1909. His fame was so great that twice he
was offered the conductorship of the Boston Symphony Orchestra,
but he declined. He lived in Russia from 1910 until after the
Bolshevik Revolution of 1917, at which time he left Russia with his
family, never to return. From 1918 until 1939 he made annual tours
of Europe as a pianist; also of the U.S. (from 1918 until his death),
where he spent much of his time. He also owned a villa in Lucerne
(1931–1939), and it was there that he composed one of his most
enduring scores, the *Rhapsody on a Theme of Paganini* (1934). After
the outbreak of World War II (1939), he spent his remaining years in
the U.S. He became a naturalized U.S. citizen a few weeks before his
death, having made his last appearance as a pianist in Knoxville,
Tennessee, on Feb. 15, 1943.

Among Russian composers, Rachmaninoff occupies a very
important place. The sources of his inspiration lie in the Romantic
tradition of 19th-century Russian music; the link with Tchaikovsky's
lyrical art is very strong. Melancholy moods prevail and minor keys
predominate in his compositions, as in Tchaikovsky's; but there is an
unmistakable stamp of Rachmaninoff's individuality in the broad,
rhapsodic sweep of the melodic line, and particularly in the fully
expanded sonorities and fine resonant harmonies of his piano writing. Its technical resourcefulness is unexcelled by any composer since
Liszt. Despite the fact that Rachmaninoff was an émigré and stood
in avowed opposition to the Soviet regime (until the German attack
on Russia in 1941 impelled him to modify his stand), his popularity
never wavered in Russia; after his death, Russian musicians paid
spontaneous tribute to him. Rachmaninoff's music is much less popular in Germany, France, and Italy; on the other hand, in England
and America it constitutes a potent factor on the concert stage.

RAMEAU, JEAN-PHILIPPE, great French composer, organist, and
music theorist; b. Dijon (baptized), Sept. 25, 1683; d. Paris, Sept. 12,
1764. His father was organist of St. Étienne in Dijon. He learned to
play the harpsichord as a small child. From age 10 to 14 he attended

the Jesuit Collège des Godrans in Dijon, where he took up singing and composing instead of concentrating on his academic studies. At 18 his father sent him to Milan, where he stayed for only a brief time before joining the orchestra of a traveling French opera troupe as a violinist. He succeeded his father as organist at Notre Dame Cathedral in Avignon in 1709; became organist to the Jacobins in Lyons in 1713; and then was organist at Clermont Cathedral from 1715 to 1723. There he wrote his famous *Traité de l'harmonie* (1722). This epoch-making work, though little understood at the time, attracted considerable attention and roused opposition, so that when he settled definitely in Paris a year later he was by no means unknown. In 1732 he became organist at Ste-Croix-de-la-Bretonnerie, and soon was recognized as the foremost organist in France. In 1726 appeared his *Nouveau système de musique théorique*, an introduction to the *Traité*. The leading ideas of his system of harmony are (1) chord-building by thirds; (2) the classification of a chord and all its inversions as one and the same, thus reducing the multiplicity of consonant and dissonant combinations to a fixed and limited number of root chords; and (3) his invention of a fundamental bass (*basse fondamentale*), which is an imaginary series of root tones forming the real basis of the varied chord progressions employed in a composition.

The stir that these novel theories occasioned, and his reputation as the foremost French organist, by no means satisfied Rameau's ambition; his ardent desire was to bring out a dramatic work at the Opéra. He had made a modest beginning with incidental music to Alexis Piron's comedy *L'Endriague* in 1723. After contributing further incidental music to Piron's comedies *L'Enrôlement d'Arlequin* (1726) and *La Robe de dissension, ou Le Faux prodigue* (1726), he became music master to the wife of the "fermier-général" La Pouplinière; the latter obtained from Voltaire a libretto for *Samson*, which Rameau set to music, but it was rejected on account of its biblical subject. A second libretto, by Abbé Pellegrin, was accepted, and *Hippolyte et Aricie* was produced at the Opéra in 1733. Its reception was cool, despite its undeniable superiority over the operas of **Lully** and his following. Rameau considered abandoning composing any further works for the theater, but the persuasions of his friends, who also influenced public opinion in his favor, were effective. In 1735 he brought out the successful opera-ballet *Les Indes galantes*, and in 1737 his masterpiece,

Castor et Pollux, a work that for years held its own beside the operas of **Gluck**. A career of uninterrupted prosperity commenced. He was recognized as the leading theorist of the time, and his instruction was eagerly sought; for the next 30 years his operas dominated the French stage; and he was named compositeur du cabinet du roy in 1745, and was ennobled four months before his death.

From the beginning of his dramatic career Rameau roused opposition, and at the same time found ardent admirers. The first war of words was waged between the "Lullistes" and the "Ramistes." This had scarcely been ended by a triumphant revival of *Pygmalion* in 1751 when the production of **Pergolesi**'s *La Serva padrona* (1752) caused a more prolonged and bitter controversy between the adherents of Rameau and the "Encyclopédistes," a struggle known as "La Guerre des Bouffons," in which Rameau participated by writing numerous essays defending his position. Practically the same charges were made against him as would be made a century later against **Wagner**: unintelligible harmony, lack of melody, preponderance of discords, noisy instrumentation, etc. But when 25 years later the war between Gluckists and Piccinnists was raging, Rameau's works were praised as models of beauty and perfection. It is a matter for regret that Rameau was indifferent to the quality of his librettos. He relied so much upon his musical inspiration that he never could be brought to a realization of the importance of a good text; hence the inequality of his operas. Nevertheless, his operas mark a decided advance over Lully's in musical characterization, expressive melody, richness of harmony, variety of modulation, and expert and original instrumentation.

RAVEL, (JOSEPH) MAURICE, great French composer; b. Ciboure, Basses-Pyrénées, March 7, 1875; d. Paris, Dec. 28, 1937. His father was a Swiss engineer, and his mother of Basque origin. The family moved to Paris when he was an infant. He began to study piano at the age of seven and harmony at 12. He entered the Paris Conservatoire in 1889, won first medal (1891), and then passed to the advanced class of Charles de Bériot. He left the Conservatoire in 1895 and that same year completed work on his song *Un Grand sommeil noir*, the *Menuet antique* for Piano, and the *Habañera* for Two Pianos (later included in the *Rapsodie espagnole* for Orchestra); these pieces, written at the age of 20, already reveal great originality in the treatment of old modes and of Spanish motifs. However, he continued to study; in 1897 he returned to the Conservatoire to study with **Gabriel Fauré** (composition) and André Gédalge (counterpoint and orchestration); his well-known *Pavane pour une infante défunte* for Piano was written during that time (1899). On May 27, 1899, he conducted the premiere of his overture *Shéhérazade* in Paris; some elements of this work were incorporated in his song cycle of the same name (1903). In 1901 he won the second Prix de Rome with the cantata *Myrrha*; but ensuing attempts to win the Grand Prix de Rome were unsuccessful. At his last try (1905) he was eliminated in the preliminaries, and so was not allowed to compete; the age limit then set an end to his further effort to enter.

By 1905, Ravel had written a number of his most famous compositions, and was regarded by most French critics as a talented disciple of **Debussy**. No doubt Ravel's method of poetic association of musical ideas paralleled that of Debussy; his employment of unresolved dissonances and the enhancement of the diatonic style into pandiatonicism were techniques common to Debussy and his followers. But there were important differences: whereas Debussy adopted the scale of whole tones as an integral part of his musical vocabulary, Ravel resorted to it only occasionally; similarly, augmented triads appear much less frequently in Ravel's music than in Debussy's. In his writing for piano, Ravel actually anticipated some of Debussy's usages. In France, and soon in England and other European countries, Ravel's name became well-known, but for many years he was still regarded as an ultramodernist. Actually, he mastered a wide range of styles. Inspired evocation of the past was one aspect of Ravel's creative genius; in this style are his *Pavane pour une infante défunte*, *Le Tombeau de Couperin*, and *La Valse*. Luxuriance of exotic colors marks his ballet *Daphnis et Chloé*, his opera *L'Heure espagnole*, the song cycles *Shéhérazade* and *Chansons madécasses*, and his virtuoso pieces for Piano *Miroirs* and *Gaspard de la nuit*. Other works are deliberately austere, even ascetic, in their pointed classicism: the piano concertos, the Piano Sonatina, and some of his songs with piano accompaniment. His association with Diaghilev's Ballets Russes was most fruitful; for Diaghilev he wrote one of his masterpieces, *Daphnis et Chloé*. Another ballet, *Boléro*, commissioned by Ida Rubinstein and performed at her dance recital at the Paris Opéra in 1928, became Ravel's most spectacular success as an orchestral piece.

In 1929 he was honored by his native town by the inauguration of the Quai Maurice Ravel. Shortly afterward, he began to experience difficulties in muscular coordination, and suffered from attacks of aphasia, symptoms indicative of a cerebral malady. He underwent brain surgery on Dec. 19, 1937, but it was not successful; he died nine days later.

RESPIGHI, OTTORINO, eminent Italian composer; b. Bologna, July 9, 1879; d. Rome, April 18, 1936. He studied violin and composition at Bologna's Liceo Musicale (1891–1900). In 1900 he went to Russia, and played first viola in the orchestra of the Imperial Opera in St. Petersburg; there he took lessons with **Rimsky-Korsakov**, which proved a decisive influence in Respighi's coloristic orchestration. His style of composition is a highly successful blend of songful melodies with full and rich harmonies; he was one of the best masters of modern Italian music in orchestration. His power of evocation of the Italian scene and his ability to sustain interest without prolixity is incontestable. Although he wrote several operas, he achieved his greatest success with two symphonic poems, *Le fontane di Roma* and *I pini di Roma*, each consisting of four tone paintings of the Roman landscape. A great innovation for the time was the insertion of a phonograph recording of a nightingale into the score of *I pini di Roma*.

RIMSKY-KORSAKOV, NIKOLAI (ANDREIEVICH), great Russian composer; b. Tikhvin, near Novgorod, March 18, 1844; d. Liubensk, near St. Petersburg, June 21, 1908. He remained in the country until he was 12 years old; in 1856 he entered the Naval School in St. Petersburg, graduating in 1862. He took piano lessons as a child with provincial teachers, and later with a professional musician, Theodore Canille, who introduced him to **Mily Balakirev**; he also met César Cui and **Alexander Borodin**. In 1862 he was sent on the clipper Almaz on a voyage that lasted two-and-a-half years; returning to Russia in the summer of 1865, he settled in St. Petersburg, where he remained most of his life. During his travels he maintained contact with Balakirev, and continued to report to him the progress of his musical composition. He completed his First Symphony (which was also the earliest significant work in this form by a Russian composer), and it was performed under Balakirev's direction in 1865, at a concert of the Free Music School in St. Petersburg.

In 1871 Rimsky-Korsakov was engaged as a professor of composition and orchestration at the St. Petersburg Conservatory, even though he was aware of the inadequacy of his own technique. He remained on the faculty until his death, with the exception of a few months in 1905, when he was relieved of his duties as professor for his public support of the rebellious students during the revolution of that year. As a music educator, Rimsky-Korsakov was of the greatest importance to the development and maintenance of the traditions of the Russian national school; among his students were Alexander Glazunov, Nikolai Tcherepnin, and Maximilian Steinberg. **Igor Stravinsky** studied privately with him from 1903 on.

In 1873 Rimsky-Korsakov was appointed to the post of inspector of the military orchestras of the Russian navy, until it was abolished in 1884. From 1883 to 1894 he was also assistant director of the Court Chapel and led the chorus and the orchestra there. Although he was not a gifted conductor, he gave many performances of his own orchestral works. He made his debut at a charity concert for the victims of the Volga famine, in St. Petersburg in 1874; the program included the first performance of his Third Symphony. From 1886 until 1900 he conducted the annual Russian symphony concerts; in June 1889 he conducted two concerts of Russian music at the World Exposition in Paris; in 1890 and 1900 he conducted similar concerts of Russian music in Brussels. His last appearance abroad was in the spring of 1907, when he conducted in Paris two historic concerts of Russian music arranged by Diaghilev; in the same year he was elected corresponding member of the French Academy, to succeed **Edvard Grieg**.

These activities, however, did not distract him from his central purpose as a national Russian composer. His name was grouped with those of Cui, Borodin, Balakirev, and **Modest Mussorgsky** as the "Mighty Five," and he maintained an intimate friendship with most of them. At Mussorgsky's death he collected his manuscripts and prepared them for publication, revising Mussorgsky's opera *Boris Godunov*; it was in Rimsky-Korsakov's version that the opera became famous. Later some criticism was voiced against Rimsky-Korsakov's reduction of Mussorgsky's original harmonies and melodic lines to an academically acceptable standard. He helped publish a great number of works by Russian composers of the St. Petersburg group, although only a small part of these sumptuously printed scores represents the best in Russian music. Although he was far from being a revolutionary, he freely expressed his disgust at the bungling administration of Czarist Russia; he was particularly indignant about the attempts of the authorities to alter Pushkin's lines in his own last opera, *The Golden Cockerel*, and refused to compromise. He died, of angina pectoris, with the situation still unresolved; the opera was produced posthumously, with the censor's changes; the original text was not restored until the revolution of 1917.

Rimsky-Korsakov was one of the greatest masters of Russian music. His source of inspiration was **Mikhail Glinka**'s operatic style. He made use of both the purely Russian idiom and coloristic Oriental melodic patterns; such works as his symphonic suite *Scheherazade* and *The Golden Cockerel* represent Russian Orientalism at its best. In the purely Russian style, the opera *Snow Maiden* and the *Russian Easter* overture are outstanding examples. The influence of **Wagner** and **Liszt** in his music was small; only in his opera *The Legend of the Invisible City of Kitezh* are there perceptible echoes from *Parsifal*. In the art of orchestration, Rimsky-Korsakov had few equals; his treatment of instruments, in solo passages and in ensemble, was invariably idiomatic. In his treatise on orchestration he selected only passages from his own works to demonstrate the principles of practical and effective application of registers and tone colors. Although an academician in his general esthetics, he experimented boldly with melodic progressions and ingenious harmonies that pointed toward modern usages. He especially favored the major scale with the lowered submediant and the scale of alternating whole tones and semitones (which in Russian reference works came to be termed as "Rimsky-Korsakov's scale"). In *The Golden Cockerel* and *Kashchei the Immortal* he applied dissonant harmonies in unusual superpositions. But he set for himself a definite limit in innovation, and severely criticized **Richard Strauss**, Debussy, and Vincent d'Indy for their modernistic practices.

ROREM, NED, brilliant American composer, pianist, and writer; b. Richmond, Indidana, Oct. 23, 1923. His father was a medical economist and a founder of Blue Cross; his mother was active in various peace movements. He developed as a composer of substance and originality, proclaiming that music must sing, even if it is written for instruments. Between times he almost unexpectedly discovered an astonishing talent as a writer. An elegant stylist in both French and English, he published a succession of personal journals, recounting with gracious insouciance his encounters in Paris and New York. He proudly declared that he wrote music for an audience and that he did not wish to indulge in writing songs and symphonic poems for an indefinite, abstract group. Rorem is regarded as one of the finest song composers in America; a born linguist, he has a natural feeling for vocal line and for prosody of text.

ROSSINI, GIOACHINO (ANTONIO), great Italian opera composer possessing an equal genius for shattering melodrama in tragedy and for devastating humor in comedy; b. Pesaro, Feb. 29, 1792; d. Paris, Nov. 13, 1868. He came from a musical family: his father served as town trumpeter in Lugo and Pesaro, and played brass instruments in provincial theaters; his mother sang opera as seconda donna. When his parents traveled, he was usually boarded in Bologna. In 1808, his cantata *Il pianto d'Armonia sulla morte d'Orfeo* was performed at the Liceo Musicale in Bologna and received a prize. About the same time he wrote his first opera, *Demetrio e Polibio*. Six more operas followed between 1810 and 1811, including a commission from La Scala of Milan; the resulting work, *La pietra del paragone*, was a fine success. In 1813 he produced three operas for Venice; of them, the last, *L'Italiana in Algeri*, became a perennial favorite. His next three operas were unsuccessful.

By that time Rossini, still a very young man, had been approached by the famous impresario Barbaja, the manager of the Teatro San Carlo and the Teatro Fondo in Naples, with an offer for an exclusive contract, under the terms of which Rossini was to supply two operas annually for Barbaja. The first opera Rossini wrote for him was *Elisabetta, regina d'Inghilterra*, produced in Naples in 1815; the title role was entrusted to the famous Spanish soprano Isabella Colbran, who was Barbaja's favorite mistress. An important innovation in the score was Rossini's use of *recitativo stromentato* in place of the usual *recitativo secco*. His next opera, *Torvaldo e Dorliska*, produced in Rome in 1815, was an unfortunate failure.

Rossini now determined to try his skill in composing an opera buffa, based on the famous play by Beaumarchais, *Le Barbier de Seville*; it was an audacious decision on Rossini's part, since an Italian opera on the same subject by Giovanni Paisiello, *Il Barbiere di Siviglia*, originally produced in 1782, was still playing with undiminished success. To avoid confusion, Rossini's opera on this subject was performed in Rome under a different title, *Almaviva, ossia L'inutile precauzione*. Rossini was only 23 years old when he completed the score, which proved to be his greatest accomplishment and a standard opera buffa in the repertoire of theaters all over the world.

Rossini arrived in London late in 1823 and was received by King George IV. He conducted several of his operas, and was also a guest at the homes of the British nobility, where he played piano as an accompanist to singers, at very large fees. In 1824 he settled in Paris, where he became director of the Théâtre-Italien. For the coronation of King Charles X, he composed *Il viaggio a Reims*, which was performed in Paris under his direction in 1825. He used parts of this *pièce d'occasion* in his opera *Le Comte Ory*. In Paris he met **Meyerbeer**, with whom he established an excellent relationship. After the expiration of his contract with the Théâtre-Italien, he was given the nominal titles of "Premier Compositeur du Roi" and "Inspecteur Général du Chant en France" at an annual salary of 25,000 francs. He was now free to compose for the Paris Opéra; there, he produced revised versions of two of his earlier operas in 1826 and 1827, and then *Le Comte Ory* (1828). In May 1829 Rossini was able to obtain an agreement with the government of King Charles X guaranteeing him a lifetime annuity of 6,000 francs. In return, he promised to write more works for the Paris Opéra. On Aug. 3, 1829, his *Guillaume Tell* was given its premiere at the Opéra; it became immensely popular. And then, at the age of 37, Rossini stopped writing operas. The French revolution of July 1830, which dethroned King Charles X, invalidated his contract with the French government.

What were the reasons for Rossini's decision to stop writing operas? Rumors flew around Paris that he was unhappy about the cavalier treatment he received from the management of the Paris Opéra, and he spoke disdainfully of yielding the operatic field to "the Jews" (Meyerbeer and Fromental Halévy), whose operas captivated the Paris audiences. The report does not bear the stamp of truth, for Rossini was friendly with Meyerbeer until Meyerbeer's death in 1864. Besides, he was not in the habit of complaining; he enjoyed life too well. He was called "Le Cygne de Pesaro" ("The Swan of Pesaro," his birthplace). The story went that a delegation arrived from Pesaro with a project of building a monument to Rossini; the town authorities had enough money to pay for the pedestal, but not for the statue itself. Would Rossini contribute 10,000 francs for the completion of the project? "For 10,000 francs," Rossini was supposed to have replied, "I would stand on the pedestal myself." He had a healthy sense of self-appreciation, but he invariably put it in a comic context. While his mother was still living, he addressed his letters to her as "Mother of the Great Maestro."

The circumstance that Rossini was born on a leap-year day was the cause of many a *bon mot* on his part. On Feb. 29, 1868, he decided to celebrate his 19th birthday, for indeed, there had been then only 19 leap years since his birth. He was superstitious; like many Italians, he stood in fear of Friday the 13th. He died on Nov. 13, 1868, which was a Friday. In 1887 his remains were taken to Florence for entombment in the Church of Santa Croce.

RUBINSTEIN, ARTHUR (actually **Artur**), celebrated Polish-born American pianist; b. Lodz, Jan. 28, 1887; d. Geneva, Dec. 20, 1982. He was a product of a merchant family with many children, of whom he alone exhibited musical propensities. He became emotionally attached to the piano as soon as he saw and heard the instrument; at the age of seven, he played pieces by **Mozart, Schubert**, and **Mendelssohn** at a charity concert in Lodz. After studying piano locally, he was taken to Warsaw, where he had piano lessons with Alexander Różycki, and then went to Berlin in 1897 to study with Heinrich Barth. In 1900 he appeared as soloist in Mozart's A major Concerto, K.488, in Potsdam; he repeated his success that same year when he played the work again in Berlin under Joseph Joachim's direction; and then toured in Germany and Poland. After further studies with **Ignacy Paderewski** in Switzerland (1903), he went to Paris, where he played with the Lamoureux Orchestra and met **Ravel**, Paul Dukas, and Jacques Thibaud. He also played the G minor Piano Concerto by **Saint-Saëns** in the presence of the composer, who commended him.

The ultimate plum of artistic success came when Rubinstein received an American contract. He made his debut at Carnegie Hall in New York on Jan. 8, 1906, as soloist with the Philadelphia Orchestra in his favorite Saint-Saëns concerto. In 1915 he appeared as soloist with the London Symphony Orchestra. During the season 1916–17, he gave numerous recitals in Spain, a country in which he was to become extremely successful; from Spain he went to South America, where he also became a great favorite. He developed a flair for Spanish and Latin American music, and his renditions of the piano works of Isaac Albéniz and **Manuel de Falla** were models of authentic Hispanic modality. **Villa-Lobos** dedicated to Rubinstein his *Rudepoema*, regarded as one of the most difficult piano pieces ever written. Symbolic of his cosmopolitan career was the fact that he maintained apartments in New York, Beverly Hills, Paris, and Geneva. He was married to Aniela Mlynarska in 1932; in 1946 he became an American citizen. In 1958, Rubinstein gave his first postwar concert in Poland; in 1964 he played in Moscow, Leningrad, and Kiev. In Poland and in Russia he was received with tremendous emotional acclaim. But he forswore any appearances in Germany as a result of the Nazi extermination of the members of his family during World War II. On April 30, 1976, at the age of 89, he gave his farewell recital in London.

Rubinstein was one of the finest interpreters of **Chopin**'s music, to which his fiery temperament and poetic lyricism were particularly congenial. His style of playing tended toward bravura in Classical compositions, but he rarely indulged in mannerisms; his performances of Mozart, Beethoven, Schumann, and Brahms were particularly inspiring. In his characteristic spirit of robust humor, he made jokes about the multitude of notes he claimed to have dropped, but asserted that a worse transgression against music would be pedantic inflexibility in tempo and dynamics. He was a bon vivant, an indefatigable host at parties, and a fluent, though not always grammatical, speaker in most European languages, including Russian and his native Polish. In Hollywood, he played on the sound tracks for the motion pictures *I've Always Loved You* (1946), *Song of Love* (1947), and *Night Song* (1947). He also appeared as a pianist, representing himself, in the films *Carnegie Hall* (1947) and *Of Men and Music* (1951). A film documentary entitled *Artur Rubinstein, Love of Life* was produced in 1975; a 90-minute television special, *Rubinstein at 90*, was broadcast to mark his entry into that nonagenarian age in 1977.

During the last years of his life, he was afflicted with retinitis pigmentosa, which led to his total blindness; but even then he never lost his joie de vivre. He once said that the slogan "wine, women, and song" as applied to him was 80% women and only 20% wine and song. And in a widely publicized interview he gave at the age of 95 he declared his ardent love for Annabelle Whitestone, the English-woman who was assigned by his publisher to help him organize and edit his autobiography, which appeared as *My Young Years* (New York, 1973) and *My Many Years* (New York, 1980). He slid gently into death in his Geneva apartment, as in a pianissimo ending of a Chopin noc-turne, ritardando, morendo . . . Rubinstein had expressed a wish to be buried in Israel; his body was cremated in Switzerland; the ashes were flown to Jerusalem to be interred in a separate emplacement at the cemetery, since the Jewish law does not permit cremation.

RUGGLES, CARL (CHARLES SPRAGUE), remarkable American composer; b. Marion, Massachusetts, March 11, 1876; d. Bennington, Vermont, Oct. 24, 1971. He learned to play violin as a child; then went to Boston, where he took violin and theory, and later enrolled as a special student at Harvard University, where he attended the com-position classes of John Knowles Paine. Impressed with the widely assumed supremacy of the German school of composition (of which Paine was a notable representative), Ruggles Germanized his given name from Charles to Carl. Ruggles wrote relatively few works, which he constantly revised and rearranged, and they were mostly in small forms. He did not follow any particular modern method of composi-tion, but instinctively avoided needless repetition of thematic notes, which made his melodic progressions atonal. His use of dissonances, at times quite strident, derived from the linear proceedings of chro-matically inflected counterpoint. A certain similarity with the 12-tone method of composition of **Arnold Schoenberg** resulted from this process, but Ruggles never adopted it explicitly. In his sources of inspiration, he reached for spiritual exaltation with mystic connota-tions, scaling the heights and plumbing the depths of musical expres-sion. Such music could not attract large groups of listeners and repelled some critics. Unable and unwilling to withstand the prevail-ing musical mores, Ruggles removed himself from the musical scene; he went to live on his farm in Arlington, Vermont, and devoted him-self mainly to his avocation, painting; his pictures, mostly in the man-ner of Abstract Expressionism, were occasionally exhibited in New

York galleries. In 1966 he moved to a nursing home in Bennington, where he died at the age of 95. A striking revival of interest in his music took place during the last years of his life, and his name began to appear with increasing frequency on the programs of American orchestras and chamber music groups. His manuscripts were recovered and published; virtually all of his compositions have been recorded.

RUSSOLO, LUIGI, Italian inventor, painter, and Futurist composer; b. Portogruaro, April 30, 1885; d. Cerro di Laveno, Varese, Feb. 4, 1947. In 1909 he joined the Futurist movement of Filippo Marinetti, formulating the principles of "art of noises" in his book, *L'arte dei rumori* (1916). He constructed a battery of noise-making instruments ("intonarumori"), with which he gave concerts in Milan (1914) and Paris (1921), creating such a commotion in the concert hall that on one occasion a group of outraged concertgoers mounted the stage and physically attacked Russolo and his fellow noisemakers. The titles of his works sing the glory of the machine and of urban living: *Convegno dell'automobili e dell'aeroplani, Il Risveglio di una città,* and *Si pranza sulla terrazza dell'Hotel*. In his "futurist manifesto" of 1913 the noises are divided into six categories, including shrieks, groans, clashes, explosions, etc. In 1929 he constructed a noise instrument which he called "Russolophone." Soon the novelty of machine music wore out, the erstwhile marvels of automobiles and airplanes became commonplace, and the future of the Futurists turned into a yawning past. Russolo gradually retreated from cultivation of noise and devoted himself to the most silent of all arts, painting. His pictures, influenced by the modern French school, and remarkable for their vivid colors, had several successful exhibitions in Paris and New York.

SADRA, I WAYAN, significant Indonesian composer, performer, and writer on music; b. Denpasar, Bali, Aug. 1, 1953. He attended the local high school conservatory, Konservatori Karawitan (KOKAR; graduated, 1972), where he specialized in traditional Balinese music, particularly gender wayang (music for the Balinese shadow play). In 1973–1974 he worked with the well-known experimental Indonesian choreographer Sardono W. Kusumo. After touring with his group in Europe and the Middle East, Sadra settled in Jakarta, where he studied painting and taught Balinese gamelan at Institut Kesenian Jakarta (IKJ, Jakarta Fine Arts Institute; 1975–1978). He also taught Balinese music at the Indonesian University (1978–1980), and experimental composition, Balinese gamelan, and music criticism at Sekolah Tinggi Seni Indonesia Surakarta (STSI, National College of the Arts; from 1983), where he earned a degree in composition (1988). He concurrently wrote new-music criticism for various Indonesian newspapers. He appeared widely as a performer with traditional Indonesian ensembles, performing throughout Indonesia and Europe, and in Singapore, Japan, Hong Kong, Australia, and Seoul. In 1988 he was keynote speaker at the national Pekan Komponis (Composers' Festival) in Jakarta; in 1989, appeared in California at the Pacific Rim Festival; and in 1990, was a featured participant at Composer-to-Composer in Telluride, Colorado.

Concurrent with the development of Indonesia's national identity has come an increase of national new-music festivals, increased interaction among artists from different regions, and the greater degree of individual freedom to create autonomous music; all have contributed to the emergence of a distinct Indonesian esthetic and a contemporary art music. Sadra is one of the outstanding young composers to emerge from this period, and his works have contributed much to the development of "musik kontemporer," "komposisi," and "kreasi baru" ("new creations"). He is also concerned with the social context of performance, considering audience development as important as the development of new works. His compositions are often scored for unusual combinations of instruments. In an experimental piece performed at the Telluride Institute, raw eggs were thrown at a heated black panel; as the eggs cooked and sizzled, they provided both a visual and sonic element for the closing of the piece. He also proposed to the mayor of Solo, Central Java, a new work entitled *Sebuah Kota Yang Bermain Musik* (A City That Plays Music), wherein the entire population of the city would make sounds together for a specified five minutes; the proposal was not accepted, but Sadra hopes for its realization in the future.

SAINT-SAËNS, (CHARLES-) CAMILLE, celebrated French composer; b. Paris, Oct. 9, 1835; d. Algiers, Dec. 16, 1921. His widowed mother sent him to his great-aunt, Charlotte Masson, who taught him to play piano. He proved exceptionally gifted, and gave a performance in a Paris salon before he was five. At six he began to compose, and at seven he became a private pupil of Camille Stamaty. So rapid was his progress that he made his pianistic debut in 1846, playing a **Mozart** concerto and a movement from **Beethoven**'s C minor Concerto, with Orchestra. In 1853, his first numbered symphony was performed; **Gounod** wrote him a letter of praise, containing a prophetic phrase regarding the "obligation de devenir un grand maître." Saint-Saëns was one of the founders of the Société Nationale de Musique (1871), established for the encouragement of French composers, but withdrew in 1886 when Vincent d'Indy proposed to include works by foreign composers in its program. He visited the U.S. for the first time in 1906, and was a representative of the French government at the Panama-Pacific Exposition in 1915, conducting his choral work *Hail California*, which was written for the occasion. In 1916, at the age of 81, he made his first tour of South America. He continued to appear in public as conductor of his own works almost to the time of his death. He played a program of his piano pieces at the Saint-Saëns museum in Dieppe on Aug. 6, 1921. For the winter he went to Algiers, where he died.

The position of Saint-Saëns in French music was very important. Solidity of contrapuntal fabric, instrumental elaboration, fullness of sonority in orchestration, and a certain harmonic saturation are the chief characteristics of his music, qualities that were not yet fully exploited by French composers at the time, the French public preferring the lighter type of music. However, Saint-Saëns overcame this initial opposition, and toward the end of his life was regarded as an embodiment of French traditionalism. He was unalterably opposed to modern music, and looked askance at **Debussy**; he regarded later manifestations of musical modernism as outrages, and was outspoken in his opinions. That Saint-Saëns possessed a fine sense of musical characterization, and true Gallic wit, is demonstrated by his ingenious suite *Carnival of the Animals*, which he wrote in 1886 but did not allow to be published during his lifetime.

SATIE, ERIK (ALFRED-LESLIE), celebrated French composer who elevated his eccentricities and verbal virtuosity to the plane of high art; b. Honfleur, May 17, 1866; d. Paris, July 1, 1925. He played in various cabarets in Montmartre; in 1884 he published a piano piece which he numbered, with malice aforethought, op. 62. His whimsical ways and Bohemian manner of life attracted many artists and musicians. He met **Debussy** in 1891, and joined the Rosicrucian Society in Paris in 1892. Satie began to produce short piano pieces with eccentric titles intended to ridicule modernistic fancies and Classical pedantries alike. Debussy thought highly enough of him to orchestrate two numbers from his piano suite *Gymnopédies* (1888). Satie was almost 40 when he decided to pursue serious studies at the Paris Schola Cantorum, taking courses in counterpoint, fugue, and orchestration (1905–8). In 1898 he had moved to Arcueil, a suburb of Paris; there he held court for poets, singers, dancers, and musicians, among whom he had ardent admirers. **Darius Milhaud**, Henri Sauguet, and Roger Desormière organized a group, which they called only half-facetiously "École d'Arcueil," in honor of Satie as master and leader.

But Satie's eccentricities were not merely those of a Parisian poseur; rather, they were adjuncts to his esthetic creed, which he enunciated with boldness and total disregard for professional amenities (he was once brought to court for sending an insulting letter to a music critic). Interestingly enough, he attacked modernistic aberrations just as assiduously as reactionary pedantry, publishing "manifestos" in prose and poetry. Although he was dismissed by most serious musicians as an uneducated person who tried to conceal his ignorance of music with persiflage, he exercised a profound influence on the young French composers of the first quarter of the 20th century. Moreover, his stature as an innovator in the modern idiom grew after his death, so that the avant-garde musicians of the later day accepted him as inspiration for their own experiments; thus "space music" could be traced back to Satie's *musique d'ameublement*, in which players were stationed at different parts of a hall playing different pieces in different tempi. The instruction in his piano piece *Vexations*, to play it 840 times in succession, was carried out literally in New York on Sept. 9, 1963, by a group of five pianists working in relays overnight, thus setting a world's record for duration of any musical composition. When critics accused Satie of having no idea of form, he published *Trois Morceaux en forme de poire*, the eponymous pear being reproduced in color on the cover; other pieces bore self-contradictory titles, such as *Heures séculaires et instantanées* and *Crépuscule matinal de midi*. In his ballets he introduced jazz for the first time in Paris; at the performance of his ballet *Relâche* (1924), the curtain bore the legend "Erik Satie is the greatest musician in the world; whoever disagrees with this notion will please leave the hall."

SCARLATTI, (GIUSEPPE) DOMENICO, famous Italian composer, harpsichordist, and teacher, son of (Pietro) Alessandro (Gaspare) Scarlatti; b. Naples, Oct. 26, 1685; d. Madrid, July 23, 1757. Nothing is known about his musical training. In 1701, he was appointed organist and composer at the Royal Chapel in Naples, where his father was maestro di cappella. The two were granted a leave of absence in June 1702, and they went to Florence; later that year Domenico returned to Naples without his father, and resumed his duties. His first opera, *Ottavia ristituita al trono*, was performed in Naples in 1703. He was sent to Venice by his father in 1705, but nothing is known of his activities there. In 1708 he went to Rome, where he entered the service of Queen Maria Casimira of Poland; he remained in her service until 1714, and composed a number of operas and several other works for her private palace theater. He became assistant to Tommaso Bai, the maestro di cappella at the Vatican, in 1713; upon Bai's death the next year, he was appointed his successor. He also became maestro di cappella to the Portuguese ambassador to the Holy See in 1714. He resigned his positions in 1719; by 1724 he was in Lisbon, where he took up the post of mestre at the patriarchal chapel. His duties included teaching the Infanta Maria Barbara, daughter of King John V, and the King's younger brother. In 1728 Maria Barbara married the Spanish Crown Prince Fernando, and moved to Madrid. Scarlatti accompanied her, remaining in Madrid for the rest of his life. In 1724 he visited Rome, where he met German flutist Johann Joachim Quantz. In 1725 he saw his father for the last time in Naples; three years later in Rome he married his first wife, Maria Caterina Gentili. When Maria Barbara became Queen in 1746, he was appointed her maestro de cámera. His last years were spent quietly in Madrid; from 1752 until 1756, Antonio Soler studied with him. So closely did he become associated with Spain that his name eventually appeared as Domingo Escarlatti.

Scarlatti composed over 500 single-movement sonatas for solo keyboard. Although these works were long believed to have been written for the harpsichord, the fact that Maria Barbara used pianos in her residences suggests that some of these works were written for that instrument as well; at least three were written for the organ. His sonatas reveal his gifts as one of the foremost composers in the "free style" (a homophonic style with graceful ornamentation, in contrast to the former contrapuntal style). He also obtained striking effects by the frequent crossing of hands, tones repeated by rapidly changing fingers, etc.

SCHENKER, HEINRICH, outstanding Austrian music theorist; b. Wisniowczyki, Galicia, June 19, 1868; d. Vienna, Jan. 13, 1935. He studied jurisprudence at the University of Vienna (D.Jur., 1890), and concurrently took courses with **Anton Bruckner** at the Vienna Conservatory. He composed some songs and piano pieces; **Brahms** liked them sufficiently to recommend Schenker to his publisher. For a while Schenker served as accompanist to the baritone Johannes

Messchaert; he then returned to Vienna and devoted himself entirely
to the development of his theoretical research. He endeavored to
derive the basic laws of musical composition from a thoroughgoing
analysis of the standard masterworks. The result was the contention
that each composition represents a horizontal integration, through
various stages, of differential triadic units derived from the overtone
series. By a dialectical manipulation of the thematic elements and
linear progressions of a given work, Schenker succeeded in preparing a formidable system in which the melody is the "Urlinie" (basic
line), the bass is "Grundbrechung" (broken ground), and the ultimate formation is the "Ursatz" (background). The result seems as
self-consistent as the Ptolemaic planetary theory of epicycles. Arbitrary as the Schenker system is, it proved remarkably durable in
academia; some theorists even attempted to apply it to modern
works lacking in the triadic content essential to Schenker's theories.

SCHOENBERG (originally, **Schönberg**), **ARNOLD (Franz Walter)**,
great Austrian-born American composer whose new method of musical organization in 12 different tones related only to one another
profoundly influenced the entire development of modern techniques
of composition; b. Vienna, Sept. 13, 1874; d. Los Angeles, July 13,
1951. He studied at the Realschule in Vienna, learning to play the
cello, and also became proficient on the violin. In 1899 he wrote his
first true masterpiece, *Verklärte Nacht*, set for string sextet, which was
first performed in Vienna by the Rosé Quartet and members of the
Vienna Philharmonic on March 18, 1902. It is a fine work, deeply
imbued with the spirit of Romantic poetry, with its harmonic idiom
stemming from **Wagner**'s modulatory procedures; it remains Schoenberg's most frequently performed composition, known principally
through its arrangement for string orchestra. About 1900 he was
engaged as conductor of several amateur choral groups in Vienna
and its suburbs; this increased his interest in vocal music. He then
began work on a choral composition, *Gurre-Lieder*, of monumental
proportions, to the translated text of a poem by the Danish writer
Jens Peter Jacobsen. It calls for five solo voices, a speaker, three male
choruses, an eight-part mixed chorus, and a very large orchestra. He
completed the first two parts of *Gurre-Lieder* in the spring of 1901,

but the composition of the remaining section was delayed by 10 years; it was not until 1913, that its complete performance was given by the Vienna Philharmonic and its choral forces.

In March 1904 Schoenberg organized with Alexander Zemlinsky the Vereinigung Schaffender Tonkünstler for the purpose of encouraging performances of new music. Under its auspices he conducted the first performance of his symphonic poem *Pelleas und Melisande* (1905); this score features the first use of a trombone glissando. There followed a performance in 1907, of *Kammersymphonie*, op. 9, with the participation of the Rosé Quartet and the wind instrumentalists of the Vienna Philharmonic; the work produced much consternation in the audience and among critics because of its departure from traditional tonal harmony, with chords built on fourths and nominal dissonances used without immediate resolution. About the same time, he turned to painting, which became his principal avocation. In his art, as in his music, he adopted the tenets of Expressionism, that is, freedom of personal expression within a self-defined program. Schoenberg's reputation as an independent musical thinker attracted to him such progressive-minded young musicians as **Alban Berg, Anton von Webern**, and Egon Wellesz, who followed Schoenberg in their own development.

In 1909, Schoenberg completed his piano piece op. 11, no. 1, which became the first musical composition to dispense with all reference to tonality. In 1911 he completed his important theory book *Harmonielehre*, dedicated to the memory of **Mahler**; it comprises a traditional exposition of chords and progressions, but also offers illuminating indications of possible new musical developments, including fractional tones and melodies formed by the change of timbre on the same note. In 1912 he brought out a work that attracted a great deal of attention: *Five Orchesterstücke*. The critical reception was that of incomprehension, with a considerable measure of curiosity. The score was indeed revolutionary in nature, each movement representing an experiment in musical organization. In the same year, Schoenberg produced another innovative work, a cycle of 21 songs with instrumental accompaniment, entitled *Pierrot Lunaire*, and consisting of 21 "melodramas," to German texts translated from verses by the Belgian poet Albert Giraud. Here he made systematic use of *Sprechstimme*, with a gliding speech-song replacing precise pitch. The work was given, after some 40 rehearsals, in Berlin, and the reaction was startling, the purblind critics drawing upon the stronges invective in their vocabulary to condemn the music.

Discouraged by his inability to secure performances for himself and his associates in the new music movement, he organized in Vienna, in 1918, the Verein für Musikalische Privataufführungen (Society for Private Musical Performances), from which critics were demonstratively excluded, and which ruled out any vocal expression of approval or disapproval. The organization disbanded in 1922. About that time, Schoenberg began work on his *Suite* for Piano, op. 25, which was to be the first true 12-tone piece consciously composed in that idiom. In 1925 he was appointed professor of a master class at the Prussian Academy of Arts in Berlin. With the advent of the beastly Nazi regime, the German Ministry of Education dismissed him from his post as a Jew. As a matter of record, Schoenberg had abandoned his Jewish faith in Vienna in 1898, and in a spirit of political accommodation converted to Lutheranism; 35 years later, horrified by the hideous persecution of Jews at the hands of the Nazis, he was moved to return to his ancestral faith and was reconverted to Judaism in Paris in 1933. With the rebirth of his hereditary consciousness, he turned to specific Jewish themes in works such as *Survivor from Warsaw* and *Moses und Aron*. Although Schoenberg was well known in the musical world, he had difficulty obtaining a teaching position; he finally accepted the invitation of Joseph Malkin, founder of the Malkin Conservatory of Boston, to join its faculty. He arrived in the U.S. on Oct. 31, 1933. After teaching in Boston for a season, he moved to Hollywood. In 1935 he became a professor of music at the University of Southern California, and in 1936 accepted a similar position at the University of California in Los Angeles, where he taught until 1944, when he reached the mandatory retirement age of 70.

In 1924 Schoenberg's creative evolution reached the all-important point at which he found it necessary to establish a new governing principle of tonal relationship, which he called the "method of composing with 12 different notes related entirely to one another." This method was adumbrated in his music as early as 1914, and is used partially in his *Five Klavierstücke*, op. 23, and in his *Serenade*, op. 24. It was employed for the first time in its integral form in the piano *Suite*, op. 25 (1924); in it, the thematic material is based on a group of 12 different notes arrayed in a certain prearranged order. Such a tone row was henceforth Schoenberg's mainspring of thematic invention. Development was provided by the devices of inversion, retrograde, and retrograde inversion of the basic series; allowing for transposition, 48 forms were obtainable in all, with counterpoint and harmony, as well as melody, derived from the basic tone row. Immediate repetition of thematic notes was admitted; the realm of rhythm remained free.

As with most historic innovations, the 12-tone technique was not the creation of Schoenberg alone but was, rather, a logical development of many currents of musical thought. Schoenberg's great achievement was the establishment of the basic 12-tone row and its changing forms as foundations of a new musical language; using this idiom, he was able to write music of great expressive power. In general usage, the 12-tone method is often termed "dodecaphony," from Greek *dodeca*, "12," and *phone*, "sound." The tonal composition of the basic row is devoid of tonality; an analysis of Schoenberg's works shows that he avoided using major triads in any of their inversions, and allowed the use of only the second inversion of a minor triad. He deprecated the term "atonality" that was commonly applied to his music. He suggested, only half in jest, the term "atonicality," i.e., absence of the dominating tonic. The most explicit work of Schoenberg couched in the 12-tone idiom was his *Klavierstück*, op. 33a, written in 1928–1929, which exemplifies the clearest use of the tone row in chordal combinations. Other works that present a classical use of dodecaphony are *Begleitungsmusik zu einer Lichtspielszene*, op. 34 (1929–1930); Violin Concerto (1934–1936); and Piano Concerto (1942).

Schoenberg's disciples Berg and Webern followed his 12-tone method in general outlines but with some personal deviations; thus, Berg accepted the occasional use of triadic harmonies, and Webern built tone rows in symmetric groups. As time went on, dodecaphony became a lingua franca of universal currency; even in Russia, where Schoenberg's theories were for many years unacceptable on ideological grounds, several composers, including **Shostakovich** in his last works, made use of 12-tone themes, albeit without integral development. **Ernest Bloch** used 12-tone subjects in his last string quartets, but he refrained from applying inversions and retrograde forms of his tone rows. **Stravinsky**, in his old age, turned to the 12-tone method of composition in its total form, with retrograde, inversion, and retrograde inversion; his conversion was the greatest artistic vindication for Schoenberg, who regarded Stravinsky as his most powerful antagonist, but Schoenberg was dead when Stravinsky saw the light of dodecaphony.

SCHUBERT, FRANZ (PETER), great Austrian composer, a supreme melodist and an inspired master of lieder; b. Himmelpfortgrund, Austria, Jan. 31, 1797; d. Vienna, Nov. 19, 1828. He began composing in school, writing a four-hand *Fantasie* for Piano, several chamber music works, orchestral overtures, and the unfinished singspiel *Der Spiegelritter*. His first song, *Hagars Klage*, is dated March 30, 1811. Although very young, he began writing works in large forms; between 1813 and 1816 he composed five symphonies, four masses, several string quartets, some stage music, and wrote his first opera. It was then that he wrote some of his most famous lieder. He was only 17 when he wrote *Gretchen am Spinnrade*, and 18 when he composed the overpowering dramatic song *Erlkönig*. The prodigious facility that Schubert displayed is without equal: during the year 1815 he composed about 140 songs; on a single day, Oct. 15, he wrote eight lieder. From his sketches, it is possible to follow his method of composition; he would write the melody first, indicate the harmony, and then write out the song in full; often he subjected the finished work to several revisions. He became friendly with the poets Johann Mayrhofer and Franz von Schober, and set a number of their poems to music. In 1817 he lodged with Schober and his widowed mother, arranging to pay for his keep from his meager resources. Outstanding lieder from this period include the *Three Harfenspieler, Der Wanderer, Der Tod und das Mädchen, Ganymed, An die Musik*, and *Die Forelle*. In 1820, a score of his incidental music for the play *Die Zauberharfe* was heard at the Theater an der Wien; this score contains an overture that became subsequently popular in concert performances under the name *Rosamunde Overture*, although it was not composed for the score for that play.

Although Schubert still had difficulties in earning a living, he formed a circle of influential friends in Vienna, and appeared as a pianist at private gatherings; sometimes he sang his songs, accompanying himself at the keyboard. A mystery is attached to his most famous work, begun in 1822, the Symphony in B minor, known popularly as the "Unfinished" Symphony. Only two movements are known to exist; portions of the third movement, a Scherzo, remain in sketches. What prevented him from finishing it? Speculations are as rife as they are worthless, particularly since he was usually careful in completing a work before embarking on another composition. In 1823 he completed his masterly song cycle *Die schöne Mullerin*; in 1827 he wrote another remarkable song cycle, *Die Winterreise*. On March 26, 1828, he presented in Vienna a public concert of his works. From that year, which proved to be his last, date such masterpieces as the piano sonatas in C minor, A major, and B-flat major; the String Quintet in C major; and the two books of songs collectively known as the *Schwanengesang*. His health was frail, and he moved to the lodgings of his brother Ferdinand. On the afternoon of Nov. 19, 1828, Schubert died, at the age of 31.

Schubert is often described as the creator of the genre of strophic lieder; however, Carl Friedrich Zelter wrote strophic lieder a generation before him. What Schubert truly created was an incomparably beautiful florilegium of lieder typifying the era of German Romantic sentiment and conveying deeply felt emotions, ranging from peaceful joy to enlightened melancholy, from philosophic meditation to throbbing drama.

In a sense, Schubert's *Moments musicaux, Impromptus*, and other piano works are songs without texts. On several occasions he used musical material from his songs for instrumental works, as in the great *Wanderer Fantasia* for Piano, based on his song *Der Wanderer*, and the "Forellen" Piano Quintet, in which the fourth movement is a set of variations on the song *Die Forelle*. His String Quartet in D minor includes a set of variations on his song *Der Tod und das Mädchen* in its second movement. But Schubert was not given to large theater works and oratorios. Even his extended works in sonata form are not conceived on a grand scale but, rather, are constructed according to the symmetry of recapitulations. His music captivates the listeners not by recurring variety but by the recalled felicities. Therein lies the immense difference between Schubert and **Robert Schumann**, both Romantic poets of music: where Schubert was satisfied with reminding the listener of a passage already heard, Schumann variegates. Schubert was indeed the most symmetrical composer in the era of free-flowing musical prose and poetry.

Much confusion exists in the numbering of Schubert's symphonies, the last being listed in most catalogues as No. 9; the missing uncounted symphony is No. 7, which exists as a full draft, in four movements, of which the first 110 bars are fully scored. Several "completions" exist; the third, and perhaps the most Schuberto-morphic, was constructed with artful imitation of Schubert's ways and means, by Brian Newbould, in 1977. The "Unfinished" Symphony is then No. 8. There remains the "Gmunden" or "Gastein" Symphony, so named because Schubert was supposed to have written it in Gastein, in the Tirol, in 1825. It was long regarded as irretrievably lost, but was eventually identified with No. 9, the great C major Symphony. Incredibly, as late as 1978 there came to light in a somehow overlooked pile of music in the archives of the Vienna Stadtsbibliothek a sketch of still another Schubert symphony, composed during the last months of his life. This insubstantial but magically tempting waft of Schubert's genius was completed by Brian Newbould; it is numbered as his 10th.

The recognition of Schubert's greatness was astonishingly slow. Fully 40 years elapsed before the discovery of the manuscript of the "Unfinished" Symphony. Posthumous performances were the rule for his symphonic premieres, and the publication of his symphonies was exceedingly tardy. Schumann, ever sensitive to great talent, was eager to salute the kindred genius in Schubert's symphonies, about whose "Heavenly length" he so admiringly complained. But it took half a century for Schubert to become firmly established in music history as one of the great Sch's (with Chopin phonetically counted in).

SCHUMANN, CLARA (JOSEPHINE) (née **Wieck**), famous German pianist, teacher, and composer, daughter of Friedrich Wieck and wife of **Robert (Alexander) Schumann**; b. Leipzig, Sept. 13, 1819; d. Frankfurt, May 20, 1896. She was only five when she began musical training with her father, making her debut at the Leipzig Gewandhaus, where she gave her first complete recital in 1830; her father then took her on her first major concert tour in 1831–1832, which included a visit to Paris. Robert Schumann entered Clara's life in 1830 when he became a lodger in the Wieck home; in 1837 he asked her to marry him, a request which set off a contentious battle between the couple and Clara's father. The issue was only settled after the couple went to court, and they were finally married on Sept. 12, 1840, the day before her twenty-first birthday. They went to Dresden, and then to Düsseldorf (1850). In spite of her responsibilities in rearing a large family, she continued to pursue a concert career. She also became active as a teacher, serving on the faculty of the Leipzig Conservatory and teaching privately. After her husband's death in 1856, she went to Berlin in 1857; after a sojourn in Baden-Baden (1863–1873), she lived intermittently in Berlin (1873–1878). Throughout these years, she toured widely as a pianist. In 1878 she settled in Frankfurt as a teacher at the Hoch Conservatory, a position she retained with distinction until 1892. She made her last public appearance as a pianist in 1891. As a pianist, she was a masterly and authoritative interpreter of Schumann's compositions; later she became an equally admirable interpreter of **Brahms**, her lifelong friend. She was completely free of all mannerisms, and impressed her audiences chiefly by the earnestness of her regard for the music she played. A remarkable teacher, she attracted students from many countries. As a composer, she revealed a genuine talent especially in her numerous character pieces for piano.

SCHUMANN, ROBERT (ALEXANDER), great German composer of surpassing imaginative power whose music expressed the deepest spirit of the Romantic era; b. Zwickau, June 8, 1810; d. Endenich, near Bonn, July 29, 1856. He was the fifth and youngest child of a Saxon bookseller, who encouraged his musical inclinations. At the age of 10 he began taking piano lessons, and in 1828 he enrolled at the University of Leipzig as *studiosus juris*, although he gave more attention to philosophical lectures than to law. In Leipzig he became a piano student of Friedrich Wieck, his future father-in-law. In 1829 he went to Heidelberg, where he applied himself seriously to music; in 1830 he returned to Leipzig and lodged in Wieck's home. His family life was unhappy; his father died at the age of 53 of a nervous disease not distinctly diagnosed; his sister Emily committed suicide at the age of 19. Of his three brothers, only one reached late middle age.

Schumann became absorbed in the Romantic malaise of *Weltschmerz*; his idols, the writers and poets Novalis, Kleist, Byron, Lenau, and Hölderin, all died young and in tragic circumstances. He hoped to start his music study with **Carl Maria von Weber**, but he also died unexpectedly. Schumann wrote plays and poems in the Romantic tradition and at the same time practiced his piano playing in the hope of becoming a virtuoso pianist. He never succeeded in this ambition; ironically, it was his beloved bride, Clara, who became a famous concert pianist. His own piano study was halted when he developed an ailment in the index and middle fingers of his right hand.

Schumann had a handsome appearance; he liked the company of young ladies, and enjoyed beer, wine, and strong cigars. This was in sharp contrast with his inner disquiet; as a youth, he confided to his diary a fear of madness. He had auditory hallucinations which caused insomnia; he also suffered from acrophobia. When he was 23 years old, he noted sudden onsets of inexpressible angst, momentary loss of consciousness, and difficulty in breathing. He called his sickness a pervasive melancholy, a popular malaise of the time. He thought of killing himself. What maintained his spirits then was his great love for Clara Wieck, nine years his junior. Her father must have surmised the unstable character of Schumann, and resisted any thought of allowing Clara to become engaged to him. In 1843, when Schumann and Clara already had two daughters, Wieck approached him with an offer of reconciliation. Schumann gladly accepted the offer, but the relationship remained only formal.

As Schumann's talent for music grew and he became recognized as an important composer, he continued his literary activities. In 1834 he founded, with Wieck and two other musicians, a progressive journal, *Neue Zeitschrift für Musik*, in which he militated against the vapid mannerisms of fashionable salon music and other aspects of musical stagnation. He wrote essays, signing them with the imaginary names of Florestan, Eusebius, or Meister Raro. As early as 1831, Schumann, in the guise of Eusebius, hailed the genius of **Chopin** in an article containing the famous invocation "Hut ab, ihr Herren, ein Genie!" This phrase became a favorite quotation of biographers of both Chopin and Schumann, cited as Schumann's "discovery" of Chopin's talent. Actually, Chopin was a few months older than Schumann, and had already started on a brilliant concert career, while Schumann was an unknown. One of the most fanciful inventions of Schumann was the formation of an intimate company of friends, which he named Davidsbündler to describe the sodality of David, dedicated to the mortal struggle against Philistines in art and to the passionate support of all that was new and imaginative. He immortalized this society in his brilliant piano work *Davidsbündlertänze*.

Another characteristically Romantic trait was Schumann's attachment to nocturnal moods, nature scenes, and fantasies; the titles of his piano pieces are typical: *Nachtstücke*, *Waldszenen*, and *Fantasiestücke*, the last including the poetic *Warum?* and the explosive *Aufschwung*. A child at heart himself, he created in his piano set of exquisite miniatures, *Kinderszenen*, a marvelous musical nursery, including the beautifully sentimental dream piece *Träumerei*. Parallel with his piano works, Schumann produced some of his finest lieder, including the song cycles to poems by Heine (op. 24) and Eichendorff (op. 39), *Die Frauenliebe und Leben* (op. 42), and *Dichterliebe*, to Heine's words (op. 48).

In 1841, in only four days, he sketched out his First Symphony, in B-flat major, born, as he himself said, in a single "fiery hour." He named it the *Spring* Symphony. It was followed in rapid succession by three string quartets (op. 41), the Piano Quintet (op. 44), and the Piano Quartet (op. 47). To the same period belongs also his impassioned choral work *Das Paradies und die Peri*. Three more symphonies followed the *Spring* Symphony within the next decade, and also a Piano Concerto, a masterpiece of a coalition between the percussive gaiety of the solo part and songful paragraphs in the orchestra; an arresting hocketus occurs in the finale, in which duple meters come into a striking conflict with the triple rhythm of the solo part.

In 1843 Schumann was asked by **Mendelssohn** to join him as a teacher of piano, composition, and score reading at the newly founded conservatory in Leipzig. In 1844 he and Clara undertook a concert tour to Russia; in the autumn of 1844 they moved to Dresden, remaining there until 1850. To this period belong his great C major Symphony (1846), the Piano Trio (1847), and the opera *Genoveva* (1848). In 1847 he assumed the conducting post of the Liedertafel, and in 1848 organized the Chorgesang-Verein in Dresden. In 1850 he became town music director in Düsseldorf, but his disturbed condition began to manifest itself in such alarming ways that he had to resign the post, though he continued to compose. In 1853, he hailed his latest discovery, **Johannes Brahms**, who became close to the composer in his final year, and remained a close friend of Clara's after Schumann's death.

Schumann's condition continued to deteriorate. On Feb. 27, 1854, he threw himself into the Rhine, but was rescued. On March 4, he was placed, at his own request, in a sanatorium at Endenich, near Bonn, remaining there until the end of his life. Strangely enough, he did not want to see Clara, and there were months when he did not even inquire about her and the children. But Brahms was a welcome visitor, and Schumann enjoyed his company during his not infrequent periods of lucidity. The common assumption that Schumann's illness was syphilitic in origin remains moot, but cumulative symptomology and clearly observed cyclothymic sudden changes of moods point to tertiary syphilis and final general paresis.

SCRIABIN, ALEXANDER (NIKOLAIEVICH), remarkable Russian composer whose solitary genius had no predecessors and left no disciples; b. Moscow, Jan. 6, 1872; d. there, April 27, 1915. His father was a lawyer. His mother was a talented pianist who had studied at the St. Petersburg Conservatory; she died of tuberculosis when he was an infant, and his father remarried and spent the rest of his life in the diplomatic service abroad. Scriabin was reared by an aunt, who gave him initial instruction in music, including piano. In 1885 he commenced the study of theory with Sergei Taneyev, which he continued three years later when he entered the Moscow Conservatory, also receiving instruction in piano with Vasili Safonov. Upon leaving the conservatory in 1892, he launched a career as a concert pianist. By that time he had already written several piano pieces in the manner of **Chopin**; his opp. 1, 2, 3, 5, and 7 were published in 1893. In 1894, Belaieff became his publisher and champion, financing his first European tour in 1895; on Jan. 15, 1896, Scriabin gave a concert of his own music in Paris. Returning to Russia, he completed his first major work, a Piano Concerto, and was soloist in its first performance in 1897. His first orchestral work, *Rêverie*, was conducted by Safonov in 1899; he also conducted the first performance of Scriabin's First Symphony (1901). Scriabin's Second Symphony premiered a year later.

After the death of Belaieff in 1904, Scriabin received an annual grant of 2,400 rubles from a wealthy Moscow merchant, and went to Switzerland, where he began work on his Third Symphony, *Le Poème divin*; it had its first performance in Paris in 1905. In 1906 he appeared as a soloist with Modest Altschuler and the Russian Symphony Society in New York, also giving recitals of his works there and in other U.S. music centers. Altschuler continued to champion Scriabin's music, and, in 1908, gave the world premiere of Scriabin's great work *Le poème de l'extase*.

In the spring of 1908, Scriabin met Serge Koussevitzky, who became one of his most ardent supporters, both as a conductor and as a publisher. Scriabin wrote for Koussevitzky his most ambitious work, *Promethée*, or *Poème du feu*, with an important piano part, which featured the composer as soloist at its premiere in Moscow (1911). The score also included a color keyboard (*clavier à lumière* or, in Italian, *luce*) intended to project changing colors according to the scale of the spectrum, which Scriabin devised (for at that time he was deeply immersed in the speculation about parallelism of all arts in their visual and auditory aspects). The construction of such a color organ was, however, entirely unfeasible at the time, and the premiere of the work was given without *luce*. A performance with colored lights thrown on a screen was attempted by Altschuler at Carnegie Hall in New York in 1915, but it was a total failure. The unique collaboration between Scriabin and Koussevitzky came to an unfortunate end soon after the production of *Promethée*. Scriabin regarded Koussevitzky as the chief apostle of his messianic epiphany, while Koussevitzky believed that it was due principally to his promotion that Scriabin reached the heights in musical celebrity; to this collision of two mighty egotisms was added a trivial disagreement about financial matters. His last public appearance was in a recital in Petrograd on April 15, 1915. Upon his return to Moscow, an abscess developed in his lip, leading to blood poisoning; he died after a few days' illness.

Scriabin was a genuine innovator in harmony. After an early period of strongly felt influences (Chopin, **Liszt**, and **Wagner**), he gradually evolved in his own melodic and harmonic style, marked by extreme chromaticism. In his piano piece *Désir*, op. 57 (1908), the threshold of polytonality and atonality is reached. The key signature is dispensed with in his subsequent works; chromatic alterations and compound appoggiaturas create a harmonic web of such complexity that all distinction between consonance and dissonance vanishes. Building chords by fourths rather than by thirds, Scriabin constructed his "mystic chord" of six notes (C, F-sharp, B-flat, E, A, and D), which is the harmonic foundation of *Promethée*. In his seventh Piano Sonata (1913) appears a chordal structure of 25 notes (D-flat, F-flat, G, A, and C, repeated in five octaves), which was dubbed "a five-story chord." These harmonic extensions were associated in Scriabin's mind with theosophic doctrines; he aspired to a universal art in which the impressions of the senses were to unite with religious experience. He made plans for the writing of a "Mysterium," which was to accomplish such a synthesis, but only the text of a preliminary poem (*L'Acte préalable*) was completed at his death. Scriabin dreamed of having the "Mysterium" performed as a sacred action in the Himalayas, and actually made plans for going to India; the outbreak of World War I in 1914 put an end to such a project. Scriabin's fragmentary sketches for *L'Acte préalable* were arranged in 1973 by the Russian musician Alexander Nemtin, who supplemented this material with excerpts from Scriabin's eighth Piano Sonata, *Guirlandes*, and Piano Preludes, op. 74; the resulting synthetic score was performed in Moscow under the title *Universe*. A species of color keyboard was used at the performance, projecting colors according to Scriabin's musical spectrum.

SESSIONS, ROGER (HUNTINGTON), eminent American composer and teacher; b. Brooklyn, Dec. 28, 1896; d. Princeton, N.J., March 16, 1985. He studied music at Harvard University (B.A., 1915), took a course in composition at the Yale School of Music (B.M., 1917), and then took private lessons with **Ernest Bloch** in Cleveland and New York. This association was of great importance for Sessions; his early works were strongly influenced by Bloch's rhapsodic style and rich harmonic idiom verging on polytonality. In his compositions, Sessions evolved a remarkably compact polyphonic idiom, rich in unresolvable dissonances and textural density, and yet permeated with true lyricism. In his later works, he adopted a *sui generis* method of serial composition. The music of Sessions is decidedly in advance of his time. The difficulty of his idiom, for both performers and listeners, creates a paradoxical situation in which he is recognized as one of the most important composers of the century, while actual performances of his works are exasperatingly infrequent.

SHANKAR, RAVI, famous Indian sitarist and composer; b. Benares, India, April 7, 1920. He was trained by his brother, Uday, and began his career as a musician and a dancer, and then engaged in a serious study of the Indian classical instrument, the sitar, in time becoming a great virtuoso on it. As a consequence of the growing infatuation with Oriental arts in Western countries in the 1960s, he suddenly became popular, and his concerts were greeted with reverential awe by youthful multitudes. This popularity increased a thousandfold when the Beatles went to him to receive the revelation of Eastern musical wisdom. As a composer, he distinguished himself by several film scores, including the famous *Pather Panchali* trilogy; he also wrote the film scores for *Kabulliwallah* and *Anuradha*. For the Tagore centenary he wrote a ballet, *Samanya Kshati*, based on Tagore's poem of the same name; it was produced in New Delhi in 1961. He also wrote 2 concertos for Sitar and Orchestra (1970, 1976).

SHOSTAKOVICH, DMITRI (DMITRIEVICH), preeminent Russian composer of the Soviet generation, whose style and idiom of composition largely defined the nature of new Russian music; b. St. Petersburg, Sept. 25, 1906; d. Moscow, Aug. 9, 1975. He was a member of a cultured Russian family; his father was an engineer, and his mother was a professional pianist. At the age of nine, he commenced piano lessons with his mother; in 1919 he entered the Petrograd Conservatory. As a graduation piece, he submitted his First Symphony, written at the age of 18; it was first performed by the Leningrad Philharmonic in 1926, and subsequently became one of Shostakovich's most popular works.

He pursued postgraduate work in composition until 1930. His Second Symphony, bearing the subtitle *Dedication to October* and ending with a rousing choral finale, was less successful despite its revolutionary sentiment. He then wrote a satirical opera, *The Nose*, after Gogol's whimsical story. The score featured a variety of modernistic devices and included an interlude written for percussion instruments only. It was produced in Leningrad in 1930, as was the satirical ballet, *The Golden Age*, and his Third Symphony, subtitled *May First*, with a choral finale saluting the International Workers' Day.

Shostakovich's next work was to precipitate a crisis in his career, as well as in Soviet music in general. An opera based on a short story by the 19th-century Russian writer Leskov, entitled *Lady Macbeth of the District of Mtzensk* (1934), it depicted adultery, murder, and suicide in a merchant home under the Czars. It was hailed by most Soviet musicians, but both the staging and the music ran counter to growing Soviet puritanism; a symphonic interlude portraying a scene of adultery shocked the Soviet officials present at the performance by its bold naturalism. *Pravda* published an article accusing Shostakovich of creating a "bedlam of noise." The brutality of this assault dismayed Shostakovich; he immediately declared his solemn determination to write music according to the then-emerging formula of "socialist realism." His next stage production was a ballet, *The Limpid Brook*, portraying the pastoral scenes on a Soviet collective farm. In this work he tempered his dissonant idiom, and the subject seemed eminently fitting for the Soviet theater; but it, too, was condemned in *Pravda*, this time for an insufficiently dignified treatment of Soviet life.

Having been rebuked twice for two radically different theater works, Shostakovich abandoned all attempts to write for the stage, and returned to purely instrumental composition. Although his Fourth Symphony (1935–1936) was withdrawn before its performance, Shostakovich's rehabilitation finally came with the production of his Fifth Symphony (1937), a work of rhapsodic grandeur, culminating in a powerful climax. The height of his rise to recognition was achieved in his Seventh Symphony. He began its composition during the siege of Leningrad by the Nazis in the autumn of 1941. Its symphonic development is realistic in the extreme, with the theme of the Nazis, in mechanical march time, rising to monstrous loudness, only to be overcome and reduced to a pathetic drum dribble by a victorious Russian song. The work became a musical symbol of the Russian struggle against the overwhelmingly superior Nazi war machine; it was given the subtitle *Leningrad Symphony*, and was performed during the war by virtually every orchestra in the Allied countries.

After the tremendous emotional appeal of the *Leningrad Symphony*, the Eighth Symphony, written in 1943, had a lesser impact. Seven more symphonies followed through 1972. His 13th Symphony (1962) created yet another controversy, when Soviet leader Nikita

Khrushchev criticized the content of its first movement, because its lyrics depicted the massacre of Jews by the Nazis during their occupation of the city of Kiev. Shostakovich's 15th Symphony, his last (performed in Moscow under the direction of his son Maxim in 1972), demonstrated his undying spirit of innovation; the score is set in the key of C major, but it contains a dodecaphonic passage and literal allusions to motives from **Rossini** and **Wagner**. Shostakovich's adoption, however limited, of themes built on 12 different notes, a procedure that he had himself condemned as anti-musical, is remarkable. He experimented with these techniques in several other works; his first explicit use of a 12-tone subject occurred in his 12th String Quartet (1968).

What is remarkable about Shostakovich is the unfailing consistency of his style of composition. His idiom is unmistakably of the 20th century, making free use of dissonant harmonies and intricate contrapuntal designs, yet never abandoning inherent tonality. His music is teleological, leading invariably to a tonal climax, often in a triumphal triadic declaration. Most of his works carry key signatures; his metrical structure is governed by a unifying rhythmic pulse. Shostakovich is equally eloquent in dramatic and lyric utterance. He has no fear of prolonging his slow movements in relentless dynamic rise and fall; the cumulative power of his kinetic drive in rapid movements is overwhelming. Through all the peripeties of his career, he never changed his musical language in its fundamental modalities. When the flow of his music met obstacles, whether technical or external, he obviated them without changing the main direction.

SIBELIUS, JEAN (actually, **Johan Julius Christian**), great Finnish composer whose music, infused with the deeply felt modalities of national folk songs, opened a modern era of Northern musical art; b. Hämeenlinna, Dec. 8, 1865; d. Järvenpää, Sept. 20, 1957. Sibelius was the son of an army surgeon; from early childhood, he showed a natural affinity for music. At the age of nine, he began to study piano, then took violin lessons with a local bandmaster. He learned to play violin well enough to take part in amateur performances of chamber music. In 1885 he enrolled at the University of Helsingfors (Helsinki) to study law, but abandoned it after the first semester. In the fall of 1885 he entered the Helsingfors Conservatory, where he studied violin and also took courses in composition. In 1889 his String Quartet was performed in public, and produced a sufficiently favorable impression to obtain for him a government stipend for further study in Berlin, where he took lessons in counterpoint and fugue with Albert Becker. Later he proceeded to Vienna for additional musical training, and became a student of Robert Fuchs and Karl Goldmark (1890–1891). In 1892 he married Aino Järnefelt.

From then on, his destiny as a national Finnish composer was determined; the music he wrote was inspired by native legends, with the great Finnish epic *Kalevala* as a prime source of inspiration. In 1892, his symphonic poem *Kullervo*, scored for soloists, chorus, and orchestra, was first performed in Helsingfors. There followed one of his most remarkable works, the symphonic poem entitled simply *En Saga*, that is, "a legend"; in it he displayed his genius for variation forms, based on a cumulative growth of a basic theme adorned but never encumbered with effective contrapuntal embellishments. From 1892 to 1900 he taught theory of composition at the Helsingfors Conservatory. In 1897 the Finnish Senate granted him an annual stipend of 3,000 marks. In 1899, he conducted the premiere of his First Symphony. He subsequently conducted the first performances of all of his symphonies, the Fifth excepted.

In 1900, the Helsingfors Philharmonic gave the first performance of his most celebrated and most profoundly moving patriotic work, *Finlandia*. Its melody soon became identified among Finnish patriots with the aspiration for national independence, so that the Czarist government went to the extreme of forbidding its performances during periods of political unrest. In 1901 Sibelius was invited to conduct his works at the annual festival of the Allgemeiner Deutscher Tonkunstlerverein at Heidelberg. In 1904 he settled in his country home at Järvenpää, where he remained for the rest of his life; he traveled rarely.

In 1913 he accepted a commission for an orchestral work from the American music patron Carl Stoeckel, a symphonic legend, *Aalotaret* (*Nymphs of the Ocean*; it was later revised as *The Oceanides*). He took his only sea voyage to America to conduct its premiere in 1914; on that occasion he received the honorary degree of Mus.D. from Yale University. Returning to Finland just before the outbreak of World War I, Sibelius withdrew into seclusion, but continued to

work. He made his last public appearance in Stockholm, conducting
the premiere of his Seventh Symphony in 1924. He wrote two more
works after that, including a score for Shakespeare's *The Tempest* and
a symphonic poem, *Tapiola*; he practically ceased to compose after
1927. At various times, rumors were circulated that he had completed his Eighth Symphony, but nothing was forthcoming from
Järvenpää. One persistent story was that Sibelius himself decided to
burn his incomplete works.

The music of Sibelius marked the culmination of the growth of
national Finnish art. Like his predecessors, he was schooled in the
Germanic tradition, and his early works reflect German lyricism and
dramatic thought. He opened a new era in Finnish music when he
abandoned formal conventions and began to write music that
seemed inchoate and diffuse but followed a powerful line of development by variation and repetition; a parallel with **Beethoven**'s late
works has frequently been drawn. The thematic material employed
by Sibelius is not modeled directly on known Finnish folk songs;
rather, he recreated the characteristic melodic patterns of folk music.
The prevailing mood is somber, even tragic, with a certain elemental
sweep and grandeur. His instrumentation is highly individual, with
long songful solo passages, and with protracted transitions that are
treated as integral parts of the music. His genius found its most eloquent expression in his symphonies and symphonic poems; he wrote
relatively little chamber music, and only in his earlier years.

STOCKHAUSEN, KARLHEINZ, outstanding German composer;
b. Mödrath, near Cologne, Aug. 22, 1928. He investigated the
potentialities of *musique concrète* and partly incorporated its techniques into his own empiric method of composition, which from the
very first included highly complex contrapuntal conglomerates with
uninhibited applications of noneuphonious dissonance as well as
recourse to the primal procedures of obdurate iteration of single
tones; all this set in the freest of rhythmic patterns and diversified by
constantly changing instrumental colors with obsessive percussive
effects. He further perfected a system of constructivist composition,
in which the subjective choice of the performer determines the succession of given thematic ingredients and their polyphonic simul-
taneities, ultimately leading to a totality of aleatory procedures in

which the ostensible application of a composer's commanding function is paradoxically reasserted by the inclusion of prerecorded materials and by recombinant uses of electronically altered thematic ingredients.

He evolved energetic missionary activities in behalf of new music as a lecturer and master of ceremonies at avant-garde meetings all over the world; having mastered the intricacies of the English language, he made a lecture tour of Canadian and American universities in 1958; in 1965, was a visiting professor of composition at the University of Pennsylvania, and then a visiting professor at the University of California at Davis in 1966–1967; in 1969, gave highly successful public lectures in England that were attended by hordes of musical and unmusical novitiates; and published numerous misleading guidelines for the benefit of a growing contingent of his apostles, disciples, and acolytes.

Stockhausen is a pioneer of "time-space" music, marked by a controlled improvisation, and adding the vectorial (i.e., directional) parameter to the four traditional aspects of serial music (pitch, duration, timbre, and dynamics), with performers and electronic apparatuses placed in different parts of the concert hall. Such performances, directed by himself, are often accompanied by screen projections and audience participation. He also specifies the architectural aspects of the auditoriums in which he gives his demonstrations. At the World's Fair in Osaka, Japan, in 1970, he supervised the construction of a circular auditorium in the German pavilion; these demonstrations continued for 183 days, with 20 soloists and five lantern projections in live performances of his own works, each session lasting five-and-a-half hours. The estimated live, radio, and television audience was one million listeners.

STRAUSS, (BAPTIST) JOHANN (II), greatly renowned violinist, conductor, and composer, known as "The Waltz King"; b. Vienna, Oct. 25, 1825; d. there, June 3, 1899. Johann Strauss I was a violinist, conductor, and composer of waltzes and dance music, but he was not anxious for his son to follow in his footsteps. Instead, he hoped he'd pursue a business career, but Johann II's musical talent manifested itself when he was a mere child. At six he wrote the first 36 bars of waltz music that later was published as *Erster Gedanke*. While he was still a child, his mother arranged for him to study secretly with Franz Amon, his father's concertmaster. After his father left the family in 1842, he was able to pursue violin training and theory.

He made his first public appearance as conductor of his own ensemble at Dommayer's Casino at Hietzing on Oct. 15, 1844. His success was instantaneous, and his new waltzes won wide popularity. Despite his father's objections to this rivalry in the family, Johann continued his concerts with increasing success; after his father's death in 1849, he united his father's band with his own, and subsequently made regular tours of Europe (1856–86). In 1872 he accepted an invitation to visit the U.S., and directed 14 "monster concerts" in Boston and four in New York. He then turned to the theater. His finest operetta is *Die Fledermaus* (1874), an epitome of the Viennese spirit that continues to hold the stage as one of the masterpieces of its genre. Although Strauss composed extensively for the theater, his supreme achievement remains his dance music. He wrote almost 500 pieces of it (498 opus numbers); of his waltzes the greatest popularity was achieved by *An der schönen blauen Donau* ("On the Beautiful Blue Danube"), op. 314 (1867), whose main tune became one of the best known in all music. His two brothers were also composer/conductors.

STRAUSS, RICHARD (GEORG), great German composer and distinguished conductor, one of the most inventive music masters of the modern age; b. Munich, June 11, 1864; d. Garmisch-Partenkirchen, Sept. 8, 1949. Growing up in a musical environment (his father was the horn player at Munich's Hofopera), he studied piano as a child, then took violin lessons, and later received instruction from the court conductor. According to his own account, he began to improvise songs and piano pieces at a very early age; among such incunabula was the song *Weihnachtslied*, followed by a piano dance, *Schneiderpolka*. His first orchestral work, the Symphony in D minor (1881), was premiered in Munich; this was followed by the Symphony in F minor (1884), premiered by the New York Philharmonic.

About that time Strauss became associated with the poet and musician Alexander Ritter, who introduced him to the "music of the future," as it was commonly called, represented by orchestral works of **Liszt** and operas by **Wagner**. In 1887, he conducted in Munich the first performance of his symphonic fantasy, *Aus Italien*. This was followed by the composition of his first true masterpiece, the symphonic poem *Don Juan* (1889), in which he applied the thematic ideas of Liszt; it became the first of a series of his tone poems, all of them based on literary subjects. His next tone poem was *Tod und Verklärung* (1890); Strauss conducted it for the first time on the same program with the premiere of his brilliant *Burleske* for Piano and Orchestra. Later that year the first performance of the symphonic poem *Macbeth* was given. In these works Strauss established himself as a master of program music and the most important representative of the nascent era of musical modernism. He effectively adapted Wagner's system of leading motifs (leitmotifs) to the domain of symphonic music. His tone poems were interwoven with motifs, each representing a relevant programmatic element.

In his extraordinary autobiographical tone poem *Ein Heldenleben* (1899), the hero of the title was Strauss himself, while his critics were represented in the score by a cacophonous charivari; for this exhibition of musical self-aggrandizement, he was severely chastised in the press. There followed his first successful opera, *Feuersnot* (1901). *Salome* (1907) had its American premiere at the Metropolitan Opera; the ghastly subject administered such a shock to the public and the press that it was removed from the repertoire after only two performances. Scarcely less forceful was Strauss's next opera, *Elektra*, to a libretto by the Austrian poet and dramatist Hugo von Hofmannsthal. Strauss then decided to prove to his admirers that he was quite able to write melodious operas to charm the musical ear; this he accomplished in his next production, also to a text of Hofmannsthal, *Der Rosenkavalier* (1911), a delightful opera-bouffe in an endearing popular manner. Turning once more to Greek mythology, Strauss wrote, with Hofmannsthal again as librettist, a short opera, *Ariadne auf Naxos* (1912).

When Hitler came to power in 1933, the Nazis were eager to persuade Strauss to join the official policies of the Third Reich; Strauss kept clear of formal association with the Führer and his cohorts, however. He agreed to serve as president of the newly organized Reichsmusikkammer in 1933, but resigned from it in 1935, ostensibly for reasons of poor health. He entered into open conflict with the Nazis by asking Stefan Zweig, an Austrian Jew, to provide the libretto for his opera *Die schweigsame Frau*; it was duly produced in 1935, but then taken off the boards after a few performances. His political difficulties grew even more disturbing when the Nazis found out that his daughter-in-law was Jewish. During the last weeks of the war, Strauss devoted himself to the composition of *Metamorphosen*, a symphonic work mourning the disintegration of Germany; it contained a symbolic quotation from the funeral march from **Beethoven**'s Eroica Symphony. He then completed another fine score, the Oboe Concerto. In 1947 Strauss visited London for the Strauss Festival and also appeared as a conductor of his own works. Although official suspicion continued to linger regarding his relationship with the Nazi regime, he was officially exonerated of all taint in 1948. A last flame of creative inspiration brought forth the deeply moving *Vier letzte Lieder* (1948), for Soprano and Orchestra, inspired by poems of Herman Hesse and Eichendorff.

Undeniably one of the finest master composers of modern times, Strauss never espoused extreme chromatic techniques, remaining a Romanticist at heart. His genius is unquestioned as regards such early tone poems as *Don Juan* and *Also sprach Zarathustra*; some of his operas have attained a permanent place in the repertoire, while his *Vier letzte Lieder* stand as a noble achievement of his Romantic inspiration.

STRAVINSKY, IGOR (FEODOROVICH), great Russian-born French, later American composer, one of the supreme masters of 20th-century music, whose works exercised the most profound influence on the evolution of music through the emancipation of rhythm, melody, and harmony; b. Oranienbaum, near St. Petersburg, June 17, 1882; d. New York, April 6, 1971. He was brought up in an artistic atmosphere; he often went to opera rehearsals when his father sang, and acquired an early love for the musical theater. He took piano lessons from an early age, but it was not until much later that he began to study music theory (1900–1903). His progress in composition was remarkably slow; he never entered a music school or a conservatory, and never earned an academic degree in music.

In 1901 he enrolled in the faculty of jurisprudence at St. Petersburg University, where he met Vladimir Rimsky-Korsakov, a son of the composer. In the summer of 1902 Stravinsky traveled in Germany, where he met another son of Rimsky-Korsakov, Andrei; Stravinsky befriended him, and became a regular guest at **Rimsky-**

Korsakov senior's periodic gatherings in St. Petersburg. In 1903–1904 he wrote a piano sonata for the Russian pianist Nicolai Richter, who performed it at Rimsky-Korsakov's home. In 1905 he began taking regular lessons in orchestration with Rimsky-Korsakov, who taught him free of charge. Under his tutelage Stravinsky composed a Symphony in E-flat major (1907–1908); however, there was little in this work that presaged Stravinsky's ultimate development as a master of form and orchestration. At the same concert, his *Le Faune et la bergère* for Voice and Orchestra had its first performance, revealing a certain influence of French Impressionism. To celebrate the marriage of Rimsky-Korsakov's daughter Nadezhda to the composer Maximilian Steinberg in 1908, Stravinsky wrote an orchestral fantasy entitled *Fireworks*. Rimsky-Korsakov died a few days after the wedding; Stravinsky deeply mourned his beloved teacher and wrote a funeral song for wind instruments in his memory.

A signal change in Stravinsky's fortunes came when the famous impresario Diaghilev commissioned him to write a work for the Paris season of his company, the Ballets Russes. The result was the production of his first ballet masterpiece, *The Firebird* (1910). Here he created music of extraordinary brilliance, steeped in the colors of Russian fairy tales. There are numerous striking effects in the score, such as a glissando of harmonics in the string instruments; the rhythmic drive is exhilarating, and the use of asymmetrical time signatures is extremely effective; the harmonies are opulent; the orchestration is coruscating. He drew two orchestral suites from the work. In 1919 he reorchestrated the music to conform to his new beliefs in musical economy; in effect he plucked the luminous feathers off the magical firebird, but the original scoring remained a favorite with conductors and orchestras.

Stravinsky's association with Diaghilev demanded his presence in Paris, which he made his home beginning in 1911, with frequent travels to Switzerland. His second ballet for Diaghilev was *Pétrouchka* (1911), a triumphant success. Not only was the ballet remarkably effective on the stage, but the score itself, arranged in two orchestral suites, was so new and original that it marked a turning point in 20th- century music. The spasmodically explosive rhythms, the novel instrumental sonorities, with the use of the piano as an integral part of the orchestra, the bold harmonic innovations in employing two different keys simultaneously (C major and F-sharp major, the

"Pétrouchka Chord") became a potent influence on modern European composers. **Debussy** voiced his enchantment with the score, and young Stravinsky, still in his twenties, became a Paris celebrity.

Two years later, he brought out a work of even greater revolutionary import, the ballet *Le Sacre du printemps* (Rite of Spring); its subtitle was "Scenes of Pagan Russia." It was produced by Diaghilev with his Ballets Russes, with choreography by Vaslav Nijinsky. The score marked a departure from all conventions of musical composition; while in *Pétrouchka* the harmonies, though innovative and dissonant, could still be placed in the context of modern music, the score of *Le Sacre du printemps* contained such corrosive dissonances as scales played at the intervals of major sevenths and superpositions of minor upon major triads with the common tonic, chords treated as unified blocks of sound, and rapid metrical changes that seemingly defied performance. The score still stands as one of the most daring creations of the modern musical mind. Its impact was tremendous. To some of the audience at its first performance in Paris, Stravinsky's "barbaric" music was beyond endurance; the Paris critics exercised their verbal ingenuity in indignant vituperation. In 1914, Diaghilev produced Stravinsky's lyric fairy tale *Le Rossignol*, after Hans Christian Andersen. It too abounded in corrosive discords, but here it could be explained as "Chinese" music illustrative of the exotic subject. From 1914 to 1918 he worked on his ballet *Les Noces*, evoking Russian peasant folk modalities; it was scored for an unusual ensemble of chorus, soloists, four pianos, and 17 percussion instruments.

The devastation of World War I led Stravinsky to conclude that the era of grandiose Romantic music had become obsolete, and that a new spirit of musical economy was imperative in an impoverished world. As an illustration of such economy, he wrote the musical stage play *L'Histoire du soldat*, scored for only seven players, with a narrator. About the same time he wrote a work for 11 instruments entitled *Ragtime*, inspired by the new American dance music. He continued his association with Diaghilev's Ballets Russes in writing the ballet *Pulcinella*, based on themes by **Pergolesi** and other 18th-century Italian composers. In 1922, he also wrote for Diaghilev two short operas, *Renard*, to a Russian fairy tale, and *Mavra*, after Pushkin. These two works were the last in which he used Russian subjects, with the sole exception of an orchestral *Scherzo à la russe* (1944).

Stravinsky had now entered the period usually designated as neo-Classical. The most significant works of this stage of his development were his Octet for Wind Instruments and the Piano Concerto commissioned by Serge Koussevitzky. In these works, he abandoned the luxuriant instrumentation of his ballets and their aggressively dissonant harmonies; instead, he used pandiatonic structures, firmly tonal but starkly dissonant in their superposition of tonalities within the same principal key. His reversion to old forms, however, was not an act of ascetic renunciation but, rather, a grand experiment in reviving Baroque practices, which had fallen into desuetude. The Piano Concerto (1924) provided him with an opportunity to appear as soloist; Stravinsky was never a virtuoso pianist, but he was able to acquit himself satisfactorily in works such as this. The Elizabeth Sprague Coolidge Foundation commissioned him to write a pantomime for string orchestra; the result was *Apollon Musagète* (1928), given at the Library of Congress in Washington, D.C. This score, serene and emotionally restrained, evokes the manner of **Lully**'s court ballets. He continued to explore the resources of neo-Baroque writing in his *Capriccio* for Piano and Orchestra (1929), which he performed as soloist in Paris. This score is impressed by a spirit of hedonistic entertainment, harking back to the style galant of the 18th century; yet it is unmistakably modern in its polyrhythmic collisions of pandiatonic harmonies.

Stravinsky's growing disillusionment with the external brilliance of modern music led him to seek eternal verities of music in ancient modalities. His well-nigh monastic renunciation of the grandiose edifice of glorious sound to which he himself had so abundantly contributed found expression in his opera-oratorio *Oedipus Rex* (1927). In order to emphasize its detachment from temporal aspects, he commissioned a Latin text for the work, even though the subject was derived from a Greek play; its music is deliberately hollow and its dramatic points are emphasized by ominous repetitive passages. Yet this very austerity of idiom makes *Oedipus Rex* a profoundly moving play. A turn to religious writing found its utterance in Stravinsky's *Symphony of Psalms* (1930), written for the 50th anniversary of the Boston Symphony and dedicated "to the glory of God." The work is scored for chorus and orchestra, omitting the violins and violas, thus emphasizing the lower instrumental registers and creating an austere sonority suitable to its solemn subject.

In 1931 he wrote a Violin Concerto commissioned by the violinist Samuel Dushkin, and performed by him in Berlin. On a commission from the ballerina Ida Rubinstein, he composed the ballet *Perséphone*; here again he exercised his mastery of simplicity in formal design, melodic patterns, and contrapuntal structure. For his 1937 American tour he wrote *Jeu de cartes*, a "ballet in three deals" to his own scenario depicting an imaginary game of poker (of which he was a devotee). A year later he wrote his concerto for 16 instruments entitled *Dumbarton Oaks*, named after the Washington, D.C., estate of Mr. and Mrs. Robert Woods Bliss, who commissioned the work; in Europe it was played under the noncommittal title Concerto in E-flat. Its style is hermetically neo-Baroque.

With World War II engulfing Europe, Stravinsky decided to seek permanent residence in America. He had acquired French citizenship in 1934; in 1939 he applied for American citizenship; he became an American citizen on Dec. 28, 1945. To celebrate this event he made an arrangement of the *Star-Spangled Banner*, which contained a curious modulation into the subdominant in the coda. In 1939–40 Stravinsky was named Charles Eliot Norton lecturer at Harvard University; about the same time he accepted several private students, a pedagogical role he had never exercised before. His American years form a curious panoply of subjects and manners of composition. He accepted a commission from the Ringling Bros. to write a *Circus Polka* "for a young elephant." In 1946 he wrote *Ebony Concerto* for Woody Herman's swing band. In 1951 he completed his opera *The Rake's Progress*, inspired by Hogarth's famous series of engravings, to a libretto by W. H. Auden and C. Kallman. The opera is a striking example of Stravinsky's protean capacity for adopting different styles and idioms of composition to serve his artistic purposes; *The Rake's Progress* is an ingenious conglomeration of disparate elements, ranging from 18th-century British ballads to cosmopolitan burlesque.

But whatever transmutations his music underwent during his long and productive career, he remained a man of the theater at heart. In America he became associated with the brilliant Russian choreographer George Balanchine, who produced a number of ballets to Stravinsky's music, among them his *Apollon Musagète*, Violin Concerto, Symphony in three movements, *Scherzo à la russe*, *Pulcinella*, and *Agon*. It was in his score of *Agon* that he essayed for the first time to adopt the method of composition with 12 tones as promulgated by **Schoenberg**; *Agon* (the word means "competition" in Greek) bears the subtitle "ballet for 12 tones," perhaps in allusion to the dodecaphonic technique used in the score. Yet the 12-tone method had been the very antithesis of his previous tenets. In fact, an irreconcilable polarity existed between Stravinsky and Schoenberg even in personal relations. However, after Schoenberg's death, Stravinsky became interested in examining the essence of the method of composition with 12 tones, adopting dodecaphonic writing in its aspect of canonic counterpoint as developed by **Webern**. In this manner he wrote his *Canticum sacrum ad honorem Sancti Marci nominis* (1956). Other works of the period were also written in a modified 12-tone technique, among them *The Flood*, for Narrator, Mime, Singers, and Dancers, presented in a CBS-TV broadcast in New York in 1962.

Few composers escaped the powerful impact of Stravinsky's music; ironically, it was his own country that had rejected him, partly because of the opposition of Soviet ideologues to modern music in general, and partly because of Stravinsky's open criticism of Soviet ways in art. But in 1962 he returned to Russia for a visit, and was welcomed as a prodigal son; as if by magic, his works began to appear on Russian concert programs, and Soviet music critics issued a number of laudatory studies of his works. Yet it is Stravinsky's early masterpieces, set in an attractive colorful style, that continue to enjoy favor with audiences and performers, while his more abstract and recursive scores are appreciated mainly by specialists.

SULLIVAN, SIR ARTHUR (SEYMOUR), famous English composer and conductor; b. London, May 13, 1842; d. there, Nov. 22, 1900. His father, Thomas Sullivan, was bandmaster at the Royal Military College, Sandhurst, and later professor of brass instruments at the Royal Military School of Music. His musical inclinations were encouraged by his father, and in 1854 he became a chorister in the Chapel Royal, remaining there until 1858. In 1855 his sacred song *O Israel* was published. In 1856 he received the first Mendelssohn Scholarship to the Royal Academy of Music in London, and then continued his training at the Leipzig Conservatory (1858–61). He conducted his overture *Rosenfest* in Leipzig (1860), and wrote a

String Quartet and music to *The Tempest* (Leipzig, 1861; rev. version, London, 1862). His cantata *Kenilworth* (1864) stamped him as a composer of high rank. In 1864 he visited Ireland and composed his "Irish Symphony" (1866). In 1866 he was appointed professor of composition at the Royal Academy of Music in London. About this time he formed a lifelong friendship with Sir George Grove, whom he accompanied in 1867 on a memorable journey to Vienna in search of **Schubert** manuscripts, leading to the discovery of the score of *Rosamunde*.

The year 1867 was also notable for the production of the first of those comic operas upon which Sullivan's fame chiefly rests. This was *Cox and Box* (libretto by F. C. Burnand), composed in two weeks. Less successful were *The Contrabandista* (1867) and *Thespis* (1871); but the latter is significant as inaugurating Sullivan's collaboration with Sir W. S. Gilbert, the celebrated humorist, who became the librettist of all Sullivan's most successful comic operas, beginning with *Trial by Jury* (1875). This was produced by Richard D'Oyly Carte, who in 1876 formed a company expressly for the production of the "Gilbert and Sullivan" operas. The first big success obtained by the famous team was *H.M.S. Pinafore* (1878), which had 700 consecutive performances in London, and enjoyed an enormous vogue in "pirated" productions throughout the U.S. In an endeavor to protect their interests, Gilbert and Sullivan went to New York in 1879 to give an authorized performance of *Pinafore*, and while there they also produced *The Pirates of Penzance*. In 1881, came *Patience*, a satire on exaggerated esthetic poses exemplified by Oscar Wilde, whose American lecture tour was conceived as a "publicity stunt" for this work. In 1882, *Iolanthe* began a run that lasted more than a year, followed by the comparatively unsuccessful *Princess Ida* (1884), but then came the universal favorite of all the Gilbert and Sullivan operas, *The Mikado* (1885). The list of these popular works is completed by *Ruddigore* (1887), *The Yeomen of the Guard* (1888), and *The Gondoliers* (1889). After a quarrel and a reconciliation, the pair collaborated in two further works, of less popularity: *Utopia Limited* (1893) and *The Grand Duke* (1896).

Sullivan's melodic inspiration and technical resourcefulness, united with the delicious humor of Gilbert's verses, raised the light opera to a new height of artistic achievement, and his works in this field continue to delight countless hearers. Sullivan was also active in other branches of musical life. He conducted numerous series of concerts, most notably those of the London Philharmonic Society (1885–87) and the Leeds Festivals (1880–98). He was principal of, and a professor of composition at, the National Training School for Music from 1876 to 1881. He was knighted by Queen Victoria in 1883. Parallel with his comic creations, he composed many "serious" works, including the grand opera *Ivanhoe* (1891), which enjoyed a momentary vogue. Among his cantatas the most successful was *The Golden Legend*, after Longfellow (1886); he also wrote the famous hymn "Onward, Christian Soldiers," to words by Rev. Sabine Baring-Gould (1871). His songs were highly popular in their day, and "The Lost Chord," to words by Adelaide A. Proctor (published 1877), is still a favorite. He also composed oratorios, other operas, and ballets.

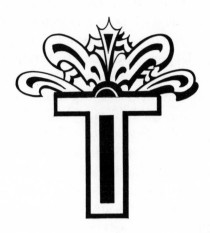

TALLIS (TALLYS, TALYS, TALLES), THOMAS, eminent English organist and composer; b. c. 1505; d. Greenwich, Nov. 23, 1585. He was organist at the Benedictine Priory in Dover (1532); was in the employ of London's Church of St. Mary-at-Hill (1537–38), most likely as organist; served as organist at Walthem Abbey (c. 1538–1540), and then was a lay clerk at Canterbury Cathedral (1541–1542). From about 1543, he served as Gentleman of the Chapel Royal during the reigns of Henry VIII, Edward VI, Mary, and Elizabeth I, and as joint organist with **William Byrd**. With Byrd, he obtained in 1575 letters patent for the exclusive privilege of printing music and ruled music paper, the first work issued by them being 34 *Cantiones quae ab argumento sacrae vocantur, 5 et 6 partium*, in 1575 (including 17 pieces by each). Tallis's most famous work is *Spem in alium non habui*, a "song of 40 parts" for eight five-part choirs. A composer of great contrapuntal skill, he was among the first to set English words to music for the rites of the Church of England.

TCHAIKOVSKY, PIOTR ILYICH, famous Russian composer; b. Votkinsk, Viatka district, May 7, 1840; d. St. Petersburg, Nov. 6, 1893. The son of a mining inspector at a plant in the Urals, he was given a good education, and had a French governess and a music teacher. When he was 10, the family moved to St. Petersburg and he was sent to a school of jurisprudence, from which he graduated at 19, becoming a government clerk. While at school he studied music, but did not display conspicuous talent as either a pianist or composer. At the age of 21 he was accepted in a musical institute, which was to become the St. Petersburg Conservatory. He graduated in 1865, winning a silver medal for his cantata to Schiller's *Hymn to Joy*. In 1866 he became professor of harmony at the Moscow Conservatory.

As if to compensate for a late beginning in his profession, he began to compose with great application. His early works reveal little individuality. With his symphonic poem *Fatum* (1868) came the first formulation of his style, highly subjective, preferring minor modes, permeated with nostalgic longing, and alive with keen rhythms. In 1869 he undertook the composition of his overture-fantasy *Romeo and Juliet*. Not content with what he had written, he profited by the advice of **Mily Balakirev**, whom he met in St. Petersburg, and revised the work in 1870; but this version proved equally unsatisfactory. Tchaikovsky laid the composition aside, and did not complete it until 1880; in its final form it became one of his most successful works.

His closest friends were members of his own family, his brothers (particularly Modest, his future biographer), and his married sister, at whose estate he spent most of his summers. The most extraordinary of his friendships was the epistolary association with Nadezhda von Meck, a wealthy widow whom he never met but who was to play an important role in his life. Through the violinist Joseph Kotek she learned about Tchaikovsky's financial difficulties, and commissioned him to write some compositions, at large fees; then arranged to pay him an annuity of 6,000 rubles. For more than 13 years they corresponded voluminously, even when they lived in the same city; on several occasions she hinted that she would not be averse to a personal meeting, but Tchaikovsky invariably declined such a suggestion, under the pretext that one should not see one's guardian angel in the flesh. On Tchaikovsky's part, this correspondence had to remain within the circumscribed domain of art, personal philosophy, and reporting of daily events, without touching on the basic problems of his existence.

In 1877, he contracted marriage with a conservatory student, Antonina Milyukova, who had declared her love for him. This was an act of defiance of his own nature; Tchaikovsky was a homosexual, and made no secret of it in the correspondence with his brother Modest, who was also a homosexual. He thought that by flaunting a wife he could prevent the already rife rumors about his sexual preference from spreading further. The result was disastrous, and Tchaikovsky fled from his wife in horror. He attempted suicide by walking into the Moskva River in order to catch pneumonia, but suffered nothing more severe than simple discomfort. His brother Anatol, a lawyer, made suitable arrangements with Tchaikovsky's wife for a separation. (They were never divorced; she died in an insane asylum in 1917.)

Von Meck, to whom Tchaikovsky wrote candidly of the hopeless failure of his marriage (without revealing the true cause of that failure), made at once an offer of further financial assistance, which he gratefully accepted. He spent several months during 1877–1878 in Italy, Switzerland, Paris, and Vienna. During these months he completed one of his greatest works, the Fourth Symphony, dedicated to von Meck. He resigned from the Moscow Conservatory in the autumn of 1878, and from that time dedicated himself entirely to composition. The continued subsidy from von Meck allowed him to forget money matters. Early in 1878 he completed his most successful opera, *Evgeny Onegin*. It was first produced in Moscow by a conservatory ensemble in 1879, but gained success only gradually; the first performance at the Imperial Opera in St. Petersburg did not take place until 1884.

A morbid depression was still Tchaikovsky's natural state of mind, but every new work sustained his faith in his destiny as a composer, despite many disheartening reversals. His Piano Concerto No. 1, rejected by Nikolai Rubinstein as unplayable, was given its world premiere in Boston in 1875, played by Hans von Bülow, and afterward was performed all over the world by famous pianists, including Rubinstein. The Violin Concerto (1881), criticized by Leopold Auer (to whom the score was originally dedicated) and attacked by critic Eduard Hanslick with sarcasm and virulence, survived all its detractors to become one of the most celebrated pieces in the violin repertoire. The Fifth Symphony (1888) was successful from the very first. Early in 1890 Tchaikovsky wrote his second important opera, *The Queen of Spades*, which was produced at the Imperial Opera in St. Petersburg. His ballets *Swan Lake* (1876) and *The Sleeping Beauty* (1889) became famous on Russian stages.

But at the peak of his career, Tchaikovsky suffered a severe psychological blow; von Meck notified him of the discontinuance of her subsidy, and with this announcement she abruptly terminated their correspondence. He could now well afford the loss of the money, but his pride was deeply hurt by the manner in which von Meck had acted. It is indicative of Tchaikovsky's inner strength that even this desertion of one whom he regarded as his staunchest friend did not affect his ability to work. In 1891 he undertook his only voyage to America. He was received with honors as a celebrated composer; he led four concerts of his works in New York and one each in Baltimore and Philadelphia. He did not linger in the U.S., however, and returned to St. Petersburg in a few weeks. Early in 1892 he made a concert tour as a conductor in Russia, and then proceeded to Warsaw and Germany. In the meantime he had purchased a house in the town of Klin, not far from Moscow, where he wrote his last symphony, the *Pathétique* (the title was suggested to him by his brother Modest). Its music is the final testament of Tchaikovsky's life, and an epitome of his philosophy of fatalism. In the first movement, the trombones are given the theme of the Russian service for the dead. Remarkably, the score of one of his gayest works, the ballet *The Nutcracker*, was composed simultaneously with the early sketches for the *Pathétique*.

Tchaikovsky was in good spirits when he went to St. Petersburg to conduct the premiere of the *Pathétique* (which was but moderately successful) on Oct. 28, 1893. A cholera epidemic was then raging in St. Petersburg, and the population was specifically warned against drinking unboiled water, but apparently he carelessly did exactly that. He showed the symptoms of cholera soon afterward, and nothing could be done to save him. Almost immediately after his death a rumor spread that he had committed suicide, and reports to that effect were published in respectable European newspapers (but not in Russian publications), and repeated even in some biographical dictionaries. In Russia, the truth of Tchaikovsky's homosexuality was totally suppressed, and any references to it in his diary and letters were expunged.

As a composer, Tchaikovsky stands apart from the militant national movement of the "Mighty Five." The Russian element is, of course, very strong in his music, and upon occasion he made use of Russian folk songs in his works, but this national spirit is instinctive rather than consciously cultivated. His personal relationship with the St. Petersburg group of nationalists was friendly without being close;

his correspondence with **Rimsky-Korsakov**, Balakirev, and others was mostly concerned with professional matters. Tchaikovsky's music was frankly sentimental; his supreme gift of melody, which none of his Russian contemporaries could match, secured for him a lasting popularity among performers and audiences. His influence was profound on the Moscow group of musicians, of whom Anton Arensky and **Sergei Rachmaninoff** were the most talented. He wrote in every genre, and was successful in each; besides his stage works, symphonies, chamber music, and piano compositions, he composed a great number of lyric songs that are the most poignant creations of his genius. Besides teaching and composing, he contributed music criticism to Moscow newspapers for several years (1868–1874), made altogether 26 trips abroad (to Paris, Berlin, Vienna, New York), and visited the first Bayreuth Festival in 1876.

TELEMANN, GEORG PHILIPP, greatly significant German composer; b. Magdeburg, March 14, 1681; d. Hamburg, June 25, 1767. He received his academic training at a local school, and also learned to play keyboard instruments and the violin. He subsequently attended the Gymnasium Andreanum in Hildesheim, where he became active in student performances of German cantatas. In 1701 he entered the University of Leipzig as a student of jurisprudence; in 1702 he organized a collegium musicum there. He later was appointed music director of the Leipzig Opera, where he used the services of his student singers and instrumentalists. In 1705 he went to Sorau as Kapellmeister to the court of Count Erdmann II of Promnitz. In 1708 he was appointed Konzertmeister to the court orchestra in Eisenach, and later he was named Kapellmeister there. In 1712 Telemann was appointed music director of the city of Frankfurt; there he wrote a quantity of sacred music as well as secular works for the public concerts given by the Frauenstein Society, of which he served as director.

    In 1721 he received the post of music director of five churches in Hamburg, which became the center of his important activities as composer and music administrator. In 1722 Telemann was appointed music director of the Hamburg Opera, a post he held until 1738. During his tenure he wrote a number of operas for production there, and also staged several works by **Handel** and Reinhard Keiser. In

1737–1738 he visited France. His eyesight began to fail as he grew older. An extraordinarily prolific composer, Telemann mastered both the German and the Italian styles of composition prevalent in his day. While he never approached the greatness of genius of **J. S. Bach** and Handel, he nevertheless became an exemplar of the German Baroque at its grandest development.

THEREMIN (real name, **Termen**), **LEON**, Russian inventor of the space-controlled electronic instrument that bears his name; b. St. Petersburg, Aug. 15, 1896; d. Moscow, Nov. 3, 1993. He studied physics and astronomy at the University of St. Petersburg, as well as cello and music theory. He continued his studies in physics at the Petrograd Physico-Technical Institute; in 1919 he became director of its Laboratory of Electrical Oscillators. In 1920, he gave a demonstration there of his Aetherophone, which was the prototype of the Thereminovox. He also gave a special demonstration of it for Lenin, who at the time was convinced that the electrification of Russia would ensure the success of communism. In 1927 he demonstrated his new instruments in Germany, France, and the U.S., where, in 1928, he obtained a patent for the Thereminovox. In 1930, at Carnegie Hall in New York, he presented a concert with an ensemble of 10 of his instruments, also introducing a space-controlled synthesis of color and music. Two years later, in the same hall, he introduced the first electrical symphony orchestra, including Theremin fingerboard and keyboard instruments. He also invented the Rhythmicon, for playing different rhythms simultaneously or separately (introduced by **Henry Cowell**), and an automatic musical instrument for playing directly from specially written musical scores (constructed for **Percy Grainger**).

With the theorist Joseph Schillinger, Theremin established an acoustical laboratory in New York. He also formed numerous scientific and artistic associations, among them Albert Einstein, who was himself an amateur violinist. Einstein was fascinated by the relationships between music, color, and geometric and stereometric figures; Theremin provided him a work space to study these geometries, but he himself took no further interest in these correlations, seeing himself "not as a theorist, but as an inventor." More to Theremin's point were experiments made by conductor Leopold Stokowski, who tried to effect an increase in sonority among certain instrumental groups in the Philadelphia Orchestra, particularly in the double basses. These experiments had to be abandoned, however, when the players complained of deleterious effects upon their abdominal muscles, which they attributed to the electronic sound waves produced by the Thereminovox.

In 1938 Theremin decided to return to Russia. He soon had difficulties with the Soviet government, which was suspicious of his foreign contacts; he was detained for a period, and speculations and rumors abounded as to his possible fate. Whatever else may have happened, he worked steadily in electronic research for the Soviet government, continuing his experiments with sound as a sideline. Upon his retirement from his work in electronics, he became a professor of acoustics at the University of Moscow (1964). With the advent of new liberal policies in the U.S.S.R., he was able to travel abroad, appearing in Paris and in Stockholm in 1989, as well as visiting the U.S. shortly before his death. Among his American students from the 1930s, he especially commended Clara Rockmore, a well-known Thereminist.

THOMSON, VIRGIL (GARNETT), many-faceted American composer of great originality and a music critic of singular brilliance; b. Kansas City, Missouri, Nov. 25, 1896; d. New York., Sept. 30, 1989. He began piano lessons at age 12 with local teachers, received instruction in organ (1909–1917; 1919), and played in local churches. He took courses at a local junior college (1915–1917; 1919), then entered Harvard University, where he studied orchestration and became assistant and accompanist to the conductor of its Glee Club; he also studied piano and organ privately in Boston. In 1921 he went with the Harvard Glee Club to Europe, where he remained on a John Knowles Paine Traveling Fellowship to study organ and counterpoint with Nadia Boulanger. Returning to Harvard in 1922, he was made organist and choirmaster at King's College; after graduating in 1923, he went to New York to study conducting and counterpoint at Juilliard. In 1925 he returned to Paris, which remained his base until 1940, establishing friendly contacts with cosmopolitan groups of musicians, writers, and painters. His association with Gertrude Stein was particularly significant in the development of his esthetic ideas.

In his music he refused to follow any set of modernistic doctrines; rather, he embraced the notion of popular universality, which allowed him to use the techniques of all ages and all degrees of simplicity or complexity, from simple triadic harmonies to dodecaphonic intricacies. In so doing he achieved an eclectic illumination of astonishing power of direct communication. Beneath the characteristic Parisian persiflage in some of his music there is a profoundly earnest intent. His most famous composition is the opera *Four Saints in Three Acts*, to the libretto by Gertrude Stein, in which the deliberate confusion wrought by the author of the play (there are actually four acts and more than a dozen saints, some of them in duplicate) and the composer's almost solemn, hymn-like treatment, create a hilarious modern opera-buffa. It was first introduced at Hartford, Connecticut, on Feb. 8, 1934, characteristically announced as being under the auspices of the "Society of Friends and Enemies of Modern Music," of which Thomson was director (1934–1937). The work became an American classic, with constant revivals staged in America and Europe. In 1940 Thomson was appointed music critic of the New York *Herald-Tribune*; far from being routine journalism, Thomson's music reviews are minor masterpieces of literary brilliance and critical acumen. He received the Pulitzer Prize in Music in 1948 for his score to the motion picture *Louisiana Story*. He resigned from the *Tribune* in 1954 to devote himself to composition and conducting. In 1983 he was awarded the Kennedy Center Honor for lifetime achievement, and he received the National Medal of Arts in 1988, among many other honors.

TOCH, ERNST, eminent Austrian-born American composer and teacher; b. Vienna, Dec. 7, 1887; d. Los Angeles, Oct. 1, 1964. Toch began playing piano without a teacher in his grandmother's pawnshop; he learned musical notation from a local violinist, and then copied **Mozart's** string quartets for practice. Using them as a model, he began to compose string quartets and other pieces of chamber music; at the age of 17 his Sixth String Quartet, op. 12 (1905), was performed by the famous Rosé Quartet in Vienna. From 1906 to

1909 he studied medicine at the University of Vienna. In 1909 he won the prestigious Mozart Prize and a scholarship to study at the Frankfurt Conservatory. In 1910 he was awarded the Mendelssohn Prize; he also won, four times in succession, the Austrian State Prize. In 1913 he was appointed instructor in piano at Zuschneid's Hochschule für Musik in Mannheim. From 1914 to 1918 he served in the Austrian army.

After the Armistice he returned to Mannheim, resumed his musical career, and became active in the modern movement, soon attaining, along with **Hindemith** and **Krenek**, a prominent position in the new German school of composition. In 1929 he went to Berlin, where he established himself as a pianist, composer, and teacher of composition. In 1932 he made an American tour as a pianist playing his own works; he returned to Berlin, but with the advent of the Nazi regime was forced to leave Germany in 1933. He went to Paris, then to London, and in 1935 emigrated to the U.S. He gave lectures on music at The New School for Social Research in New York, and then, in 1936, moved to Hollywood, where he wrote music for films. He became an American citizen on July 26, 1940; in 1940–1941, he taught composition at the University of Southern California, Los Angeles, and subsequently taught privately. Among his students were many, who, like André Previn, became well-known composers in their own right. From 1950 until his death, Toch traveled frequently and lived in Vienna, Zurich, the MacDowell Colony in New Hampshire, and Santa Monica, California.

Toch's music is rooted in the tradition of the German and Austrian Romantic movement of the 19th century, but his study of the classics made him aware of the paramount importance of formal logic in the development of thematic ideas. His early works consist mostly of chamber music and pieces for piano solo.

During his German period, he wrote several pieces for the stage in the light manner of sophisticated entertainment. He also composed effective piano works of a virtuoso quality, which enjoyed considerable popularity among pianists of the time. Toch possessed a fine wit and a sense of exploration; his *Geographical Fugue* for speaking chorus, articulating in syllabic counterpoint the names of exotic places on earth, became a classic of its genre.

It was not until 1950 that Toch wrote his first full-fledged symphony, but from that time on, until he died of stomach cancer, he composed fully seven symphonies, plus sinfoniettas for wind and string orchestra. He was greatly interested in new techniques; the theme of his last String Quartet (No. 13, 1953) is based on a 12-tone row. In the score of his Third Symphony, he introduced an optional instrument, the Hisser, a tank of carbon dioxide that produced a hissing sound through a valve.

VARÈSE, EDGARD (VICTOR ACHILLE CHARLES), remarkable French-born American composer, who introduced a totally original principle of organizing the materials and forms of sound, profoundly influencing the direction of new music; b. Paris, Dec. 22, 1883; d. New York, Nov. 6, 1965. He spent his early childhood in Paris and in Burgundy, and began to compose early in life. In 1892 his parents went to Turin, where he took private lessons in composition, and gained some performing experience by playing percussion in the school orchestra. He stayed there until 1903; then returned to Paris. In 1904 he entered the Schola Cantorum, where he studied composition, preclassical music, and conducting; he then entered the composition class of Charles-Marie Widor at the Paris Conservatoire in 1905. In 1907 he received the "bourse artistique" offered by the City of Paris; at that time he founded and conducted the chorus of the Université Populaire and organized concerts at the Château du Peuple.

He became associated with musicians and artists of the avant-garde; he also met **Debussy**, who showed interest in his career. In 1907 he married a young actress, Suzanne Bing; they had a daughter. Together they went to Berlin, at that time the center of new music that offered opportunities to Varèse. The marriage was not successful, and they separated in 1913. Romain Rolland gave to Varèse a letter of recommendation for **Richard Strauss**, who in turn showed interest in Varèse's music. He was also instrumental in arranging a performance of Varèse's symphonic poem *Bourgogne*

(1910). But the greatest experience for Varèse in Berlin was his meeting and friendship with **Ferruccio Busoni**. Varèse greatly admired Busoni's book on new music esthetics, and was profoundly influenced by Busoni's views. He composed industriously, mostly for orchestra; the most ambitious of these works was a symphonic poem, *Gargantua*, but it was never completed. Other works included various orchestral works and an incomplete opera; they were all lost, in manuscript, under somewhat mysterious circumstances.

As early as 1913, Varèse began an earnest quest for new musical resources; upon his return to Paris, he worked on related problems with the Italian musical Futurist **Luigi Russolo**, although he disapproved of the attempt to find a way to new music through the medium of instrumental noises. In 1915 he went to New York, where he met the young American writer Louise Norton. They set up a household together, and were married in 1921, after she obtained a divorce from a previous marriage. As in Paris and Berlin, Varèse had chronic financial difficulties in America. Some welcome aid came from the wealthy artist Gertrude Vanderbilt, who sent him monthly allowances for a certain length of time. Varèse also had an opportunity to appear as a conductor.

In 1922 he organized with Carlos Salzedo the International Composers' Guild, which gave its inaugural concert in New York. In 1926 he founded, in association with a few progressive musicians, the Pan American Society, dedicated to the promotion of music of the Americas. He intensified his study of the nature of sound, working with the acoustician Harvey Fletcher (1926–1936), and with the Russian electrical engineer **Leon Theremin**, then resident in the U.S. These studies led him to the formulation of the concept of "organized sound," in which the sonorous elements in themselves determined the progress of composition. This process eliminated conventional thematic development; yet the firm cohesion of musical ideas made Varèse's music all the more solid, while the distinction between consonances and dissonances became no longer of basic validity. The resulting product was unique in modern music. Characteristically, Varèse attached to his works titles from the field of mathematics or physics, such as *Intégrales, Hyperprism* (a projection of a prism into the fourth dimension), *Ionisation, Density 21.5* (the specific weight of platinum), etc., while the score of his large orchestral work *Arcana* derived its inspiration from the cosmology of Paracelsus. An important development was Varèse's application of electronic music in his *Déserts* and, much more extensively, in his *Poème électronique*, commissioned for the Brussels World Exposition in 1958. He wrote relatively few works in small forms, and none for piano solo.

The unfamiliarity of Varèse's idiom and the tremendous difficulty of his orchestral works militated against frequent performances. Among conductors, only Leopold Stokowski was bold enough to put Varèse's formidable scores *Amériques* and *Arcana* on his programs with the Philadelphia Orchestra; they evoked yelps of derision from the public and the press. Ironically, it was left to a mere beginner, Nicolas Slonimsky, to be the first to perform and record Varèse's unique masterpiece, *Ionisation*. An extraordinary reversal of attitudes toward Varèse's music, owing perhaps to the general advance of musical intelligence and the emergence of young music critics, took place within Varèse's lifetime, resulting in a spectacular increase of interest in his works and the number of their performances; also, musicians themselves learned to overcome the rhythmic difficulties presented in Varèse's scores. Thus Varèse lived to witness this long-delayed recognition of his music as a major stimulus of modern art; his name joined those of **Stravinsky, Ives, Schoenberg**, and **Webern** among the great masters of 20th-century music. Like Schoenberg, Varèse refused to regard himself as a revolutionary in music; indeed, he professed great admiration for his remote predecessors, particularly those of the Notre Dame school, representing the flowering of the Ars Antiqua.

VAUGHAN WILLIAMS, RALPH, great English composer who created the gloriously self-consistent English style of composition, deeply rooted in native folk songs, yet unmistakably participant of modern ways in harmony, counterpoint, and instrumentation; b. Down Ampney, Gloucestershire, Oct. 12, 1872; d. London, Aug. 26, 1958. Dissatisfied with his academic studies, he decided, in 1908, to seek advice in Paris from **Maurice Ravel** in order to acquire the technique of modern orchestration that emphasized color. In the meantime, he became active as a collector of English folk songs; in 1904 he joined the Folk Song Society. In 1905 he became conductor of the Leith Hill Festival in Dorking, a position that he held, off and on, until his old age. In 1906 he composed his *Three Norfolk Rhapsodies*, which reveal the ultimate techniques and manners of his national style; he discarded the second and third of the set as not satisfactory in reflecting the subject. In 1903 he began work on a choral symphony inspired by Walt Whitman's poetry and entitled *A Sea Symphony*, which he completed in 1909. *Fantasia on a Theme of Thomas Tallis* (1910) followed, scored for string quartet and double string orchestra; in it Vaughan Williams evoked the song style of an early English composer. After this brief work, he engaged in a grandiose score, entitled *A London Symphony* and intended as a musical glorification of the great capital city. However, he emphatically denied that the score was to be a representation of London life. Concurrently with *A London Symphony*, he wrote the ballad opera *Hugh the Drover*, set in England in the year 1812, and reflecting the solitary struggle of the English against Napoleon.

His Fourth Symphony, in F minor, written between 1931 and 1935, presents an extraordinary deviation from his accustomed solid style of composition. Here he experimented with dissonant harmonies in conflicting tonalities, bristling with angular rhythms. He always professed great admiration for **Sibelius**; indeed, there was a harmonious kinship between the two great contemporary nationalist composers. There was also the peculiar circumstance that in his Fourth Symphony Sibelius ventured into the domain of modernism, as did Vaughan Williams in his own Fourth Symphony, and both were taken to task by astounded critics for such musical philandering. Vaughan Williams dedicated his Fifth Symphony, in D major, composed between 1938 and 1943, to Sibelius as a token of his admiration.

In the Eighth Symphony he once more returned to the ideal of absolute music; the work is conceived in the form of a neo-Classical suite, but, faithful to the spirit of the times, he included in the score modern instruments, such as vibraphone and xylophone, as well as the sempiternal gongs and bells. His last symphony bore the fateful number "9," which had for many composers the sense of the ultimate, since it was the numeral of **Beethoven**'s last symphony. In this work Vaughan Williams, at the ancient age of 85, still asserted himself as a composer of the modern age; for the first time, he used a trio of saxophones, with a pointed caveat that they should not behave "like demented cats," but rather remain their romantic selves. Anticipating the inevitable, he added after the last bar of the score the Italian word "niente." The Ninth Symphony was first performed in London in 1958; Vaughan Williams died later in the same year.

Summarizing the esthetic and technical aspects of the style of composition of Vaughan Williams, there is a distinctly modern treatment of harmonic writing, with massive agglomeration of chordal sonorities; parallel triadic progressions are especially favored. There seems to be no intention of adopting any particular method of composition; rather, there is a great variety of procedures integrated into a distinctively personal and thoroughly English style, nationalistic but not isolationist. Vaughan Williams was particularly adept at exploring the modern ways of modal counterpoint, with tonality freely shifting between major and minor triadic entities; this procedure astutely evokes sweetly archaic usages in modern applications. Thus Vaughan Williams combines the modalities of the Tudor era with the sparkling polytonalities of the modern age.

VERDI, GIUSEPPE (FORTUNINO FRANCESCO), great Italian opera composer whose genius for dramatic, lyric, and tragic stage music has made him the perennial favorite of a multitude of opera enthusiasts; b. Le Roncole, near Busseto, Duchy of Parma, Oct. 9, 1813; d. Milan, Jan. 27, 1901. In 1838 he completed his first opera, *Oberto, conte di San Bonifacio*. In 1839 he moved to Milan. He submitted the score of *Oberto* to the directorship of La Scala; it was accepted for a performance, and had a satisfactory success. He was now under contract to write more operas for that renowned theater. His comic opera *Un giorno di regno* was performed in 1840, but it did not succeed at pleasing the public. Somewhat downhearted at this reverse, Verdi began composition of an opera, *Nabucodonosor*, on the biblical subject (the title was later abbreviated to *Nabucco*). It was staged in 1842, scoring considerable success. *Nabucco* was followed by another successful opera on a historic subject, *I Lombardi alla prima Crociata* (1843). The next opera was *Ernani* (1844), after Victor Hugo's drama on the life of a revolutionary outlaw; the subject suited the rise of national spirit, and its production in Venice won great acclaim.

In 1847, Verdi produced in Florence his first Shakespearean opera, *Macbeth*. In the same year he received a commission to write an opera for London; the result was *I Masnadieri*, based on Schiller's drama *Die Räuber*. Verdi's great triumph came in 1851 with the production of *Rigoletto*. The aria of the libidinous Duke, *La donna è mobile*, became one of the most popular operatic tunes sung, or ground on the barrel organ, throughout Europe. This success was followed by an even greater acclaim with the production in 1853 of both *Il Trovatore* and *La Traviata*.

In June 1870 he received a contract to write a new work for the opera in Cairo, Egypt, where *Rigoletto* had already been performed a year before. The terms were most advantageous, with a guarantee of 150,000 francs for the Egyptian rights alone. The opera, based on life in ancient Egypt, was *Aida*. It had its premiere in Cairo on Christmas Eve of 1871, with great éclat. A special boat was equipped to carry officials and journalists from Italy to Cairo for the occasion, but Verdi stubbornly refused to join the caravan despite persuasion by a number of influential Italian musicians and statesmen; he declared that a composer's job was to supply the music, not to attend performances. The success of *Aida* exceeded all expectations; the production was hailed as a world event, and the work itself became one of the most famous in opera history.

After **Rossini**'s death, in 1868, Verdi conceived the idea of honoring his memory by a collective composition of a Requiem, to which several Italian composers would contribute a movement each, Verdi reserving the last section, *Libera me*, for himself. He completed the score in 1869, but it was never performed in its original form. The death of the famous Italian poet Alessandro Manzoni in 1873 led him to write his great *Messa da Requiem*, which became known simply as the "Manzoni" Requiem, and he incorporated in it the section originally composed for Rossini. The *Messa da Requiem* received its premiere on the first anniversary of Manzoni's death, in Milan. There was some criticism of the Requiem as being too operatic for a religious work, but it remained in musical annals as a masterpiece. After the death of his second wife, in 1897, he founded in Milan the Casa di Riposo per Musicisti, a home for aged musicians; for its maintenance, he set aside 2,500,000 lire. On Jan. 21, 1901, Verdi suffered an apoplectic attack; he died six days later at the age of 87.

Historic evaluation of Verdi's music changed several times after his death. The musical atmosphere was heavily Wagnerian; admiration for **Wagner** produced a denigration of Verdi as a purveyor of "barrel-organ" music. Then the winds of musical opinion reversed their direction; sophisticated modern composers, music historians, and academic theoreticians discovered unexpected attractions in the flowing Verdian melodies, easily modulating harmonies, and stimulating symmetric rhythms. A theory was even advanced that the appeal of Verdi's music lies in its adaptability to modernistic elaboration and contrapuntal variegations. By natural transvaluation of opposites, Wagnerianism went into eclipse after it reached the limit of complexity. The slogan "Viva Verdi!" assumed, paradoxically, an esthetic meaning.

VILLA-LOBOS, HEITOR, remarkable Brazilian composer of great originality and unique ability to recreate native melodic and rhythmic elements in large instrumental and choral forms; b. Rio de Janeiro, March 5, 1887; d. there, Nov. 17, 1959. He studied music with his father, a writer and amateur cello player. After his father's death in 1899, Villa-Lobos earned a living by playing the cello in cafés and restaurants, and also studied cello with Benno Niederberger. From 1905 to 1912 he traveled in Brazil in order to collect authentic folk songs. In 1907 he entered the National Institute of Music in Rio de Janeiro. In 1912 he undertook an expedition into the interior of Brazil, where he gathered a rich collection of native tribal songs. In 1915, he presented in Rio de Janeiro a concert of his compositions, creating a sensation by the exuberance of his music and the radical character of his technical idiom. He met the pianist **Arthur Rubinstein**, who became his ardent admirer; for him Villa-Lobos composed a transcendentally difficult *Rudepoema*.

Villa-Lobos was one of the most original composers of the 20th century. He lacked formal academic training, but far from hampering his development, this deficiency liberated him from pedantic restrictions, so that he evolved an idiosyncratic technique of composition, curiously eclectic, but all the better suited to his musical esthetics. An ardent Brazilian nationalist, he resolved from his earliest attempts in composition to use authentic Brazilian song materials as the source of his inspiration; yet he avoided using actual quotations from popular songs. Rather, he wrote melodies which are authentic in their melodic and rhythmic content. In his desire to relate Brazilian folk resources to universal values, he composed a series of extraordinary works, *Bachianas brasileiras*, in which Brazilian melorhythms are treated in Bachian counterpoint. He also composed a number of works under the generic title *Chôros*, a popular Brazilian dance form, marked by incisive rhythm and a ballad-like melody. An experimenter by nature, Villa-Lobos devised a graphic method of composition, using geometrical contours of drawings and photographs as outlines for the melody; in this manner he wrote *The New York Skyline*, using a photograph for guidance. Villa-Lobos wrote operas, ballets, symphonies, chamber music, choruses, piano pieces, and songs; the total number of his compositions is in excess of 2,000.

VIVALDI, ANTONIO (LUCIO), greatly renowned Italian composer; b. Venice, March 4, 1678; d. Vienna, July 28, 1741. He was the son of Giovanni Battista Vivaldi, a violinist who entered the orchestra at San Marco in Venice in 1685 under the surname of Rossi, remaining there until 1729; his father was also director of instrumental music at the Mendicanti (1689–1693). The younger Vivaldi was trained for the priesthood at S. Geminiano and at S. Giovanni in Oleo, taking the tonsure in 1693, and Holy Orders ten years later. Because of his red hair he was called "il prete rosso" ("the red priest"). In 1703 he became maestro di violino at the Pio Ospedale della Pietà, where he remained until 1709; during this period, his first published works appeared. In 1711 he resumed his duties at the Pietà, and was named its maestro de' concerti in 1716. In 1711 his set of 12 concertos known as *L'estro armonico*, op. 3, appeared in print in Amsterdam; it proved to be the most important music publication of the first half of the 18th century. His first known opera, *Ottone in Villa*, was given in Vicenza in 1713, and soon thereafter he became active as a composer and impresario in Venice. From 1718 to 1720 he was active in Mantua, where the Habsburg governor made him maestro di cappella da (or di) camera, a title he retained even after leaving Mantua.

In subsequent years he traveled widely in Italy, bringing out his operas in various music centers. However, he retained his association with the Pietà. About 1725 he became associated with the contralto Anna Giraud (or Girò), one of his voice students; her sister, Paolina, also became a constant companion of the composer, leading to speculation by his contemporaries that the two sisters were his mistresses, a contention he denied. From 1735 to 1738 he once more served as maestro di cappella at the Pietà. He also was named maestro di cappella to the Duke of Lorraine (later the Emperor Francis I), in 1735. In 1738 he visited Amsterdam, where he took charge of the musical performances for the centennial celebration of the Schouwburg theater. Returning to Venice, he found little favor with the theatergoing public; as a result, he set out for Austria in 1740, arriving in Vienna in June 1741, but dying a month later. Although he had received large sums of money in his day, he died in poverty and was given a pauper's burial at the Spettaler Gottesacher (Hospital Burial Ground).

Vivaldi's greatness lies mainly in his superb instrumental works, most notably some 500 concertos, in which he displayed an extraordinary mastery of ritornello form and of orchestration. The most famous of these works are the *Four Seasons*, perhaps the most frequently recorded classical works in the entire repertoire. More than 230 of his concertos are for solo violin and strings, and another 120 or so are for other solo instrument and strings. In some 60 concerti ripieni (string concertos sans solo instrument), he honed a style akin to operatic sinfonias. He also wrote about 90 sonatas. Only 21 of his operas are extant, some missing one or more acts. He also composed various sacred vocal works.

WAGNER, (WILHELM) RICHARD, great German composer whose operas, written to his own librettos, have radically transformed the concept of stage music, postulating the inherent equality of drama and symphonic accompaniment, and establishing the uninterrupted continuity of the action; b. Leipzig, May 22, 1813; d. Venice, Feb. 13, 1883. In 1822 Wagner entered the Dresden Kreuzschule, where he remained a pupil until 1827. **Carl Maria von Weber** often visited the family home, exercising a beneficial influence on him in his formative years. In 1825 he began to take piano lessons from a local musician and also studied violin. Wagner showed strong literary inclinations, and under the spell of Shakespeare, wrote a tragedy, *Leubald*. In 1828 he was enrolled in the Nikolaischule; while in school, he had lessons in harmony with a violinist in the theater orchestra. In June 1830 he entered the Thomasschule, where he began to compose; he wrote a String Quartet and some piano music. His Overture in B-flat major was performed at the Leipzig Theater in 1830.

Now determined to dedicate himself entirely to music, he became a student of the cantor of the Thomaskirche, from whom he received a thorough training in counterpoint and composition. His first published work was a Piano Sonata in B-flat major, to which he assigned the opus number 1. It was brought out by the prestigious publishing house of Breitkopf & Härtel in 1832. In the same year, he wrote an overture to *König Enzio*, followed by an Overture in C major. Wagner's first major orchestral work, a Symphony in C major, was performed at a Prague Conservatory concert in 1832; he was 19 years old at the time.

In 1834 he obtained the position of music director with Heinrich Bethmann's theater company, based in Magdeburg; he made his debut conducting Mozart's *Don Giovanni*. In 1836, he conducted the premiere of his opera *Das Liebesverbot*, presented under the title *Die Novize von Palermo*. Bethmann's company soon went out of business; Wagner, who was by that time deeply involved with Christine Wilhelmine ("Minna") Planer, an actress with the company, followed her to Königsberg, where they were married in 1836. In Konigsberg he composed the overture *Rule Britannia*; in 1837, he was appointed music director of the town theater. His marital affairs suffered a setback when Minna left him for a rich businessman. In August, he went to Riga as music director of the theater there; coincidentally, Minna's sister was engaged as a singer at the same theater. Minna soon joined her, and became reconciled with Wagner. In Riga, Wagner worked on his new opera, *Rienzi, der letzte der Tribunen*.

In 1839 he lost his position in Riga; he and Minna, burdened by debts, left town to seek their fortune elsewhere. They made their way to London, and then set out for Boulogne; there Wagner met **Meyerbeer**, who gave him a letter of recommendation to the director of the Paris Opéra. He arrived in Paris with Minna in Sept. 1839, and remained there until 1842. In Jan. 1840 he completed his Overture to *Faust* (later revised as *Eine Faust-Ouvertüre*). Soon he found himself in dire financial straits, and on Oct. 28, 1840, he was confined in debtors' prison; he was released on Nov. 17. The conditions of his containment were light, and he was able to leave prison on certain days. In the meantime he had completed the libretto for *Der fliegende Holländer*; he submitted it to the director of the Paris Opéra, but the director had already asked Paul Foucher to prepare a libretto on the same subject. The director was willing, however, to buy Wagner's scenario for 500 francs.

In 1842 Wagner received the welcome news from Dresden that his opera *Rienzi* had been accepted for production; it was staged there with considerable success. *Der fliegende Holländer* was also accepted by Dresden, and Wagner conducted its first performance there in 1843. On Feb. 2 of that year, he was named second Hofkapellmeister in Dresden, where he conducted a large repertoire of Classical operas. He led the prestigious choral society Liedertafel, for which he wrote several works, including the "biblical scene" *Das Liebesmahl der Apostel*. He was also preoccupied during those years in working on the score and music for *Tannhäuser* (1845); he subsequently revised the score, which was staged to better advantage there in 1847. Concurrently, he began work on *Lohengrin*, which he completed in 1848. Wagner's efforts to have his works published failed, leaving him again in debt.

Without waiting for further performances of his operas that had already been presented to the public, he drew up the first prose outline of *Der Nibelungen—Mythus als Entwurf zu einem Drama*, the prototype of the epic *Ring* cycle; in 1848 he began work on the poem for *Siegfrieds Tod*. At that time he joined the revolutionary Vaterlandsverein, and was drawn into active participation in the movement, culminating in an open uprising in May 1849. An order was issued for his arrest, and he had to leave Dresden. He made his way to Weimar, where he found a cordial reception from **Liszt**; he then proceeded to Vienna, where he made his home in July; Minna joined him there a few months later. In Zurich he wrote a number of essays expounding his philosophy of art. The ideas expressed in *Das Kunstwerk der Zukunft* (1849) gave rise to the description of Wagner's operas as "music of the future" by his opponents; they were also described as *Gesamtkunstwerk*, "total artwork," by his admirers. In 1850, Liszt conducted the successful premiere of *Lohengrin* in Weimar.

In 1851 Wagner wrote the verse text of *Der junge Siegfried*, and prose sketches for *Das Rheingold* and *Die Walküre*. In June 1852 he finished the text of *Die Walküre* and of *Das Rheingold*; he completed the entire libretto of *Der Ring des Nibelungen* on Dec. 15, and it was privately printed in 1853. In Nov. 1853 he began composition of the music for *Das Rheingold*, completing the full score in 1854. In June 1854 he commenced work on the music of *Die Walküre*, which he finished on March 20, 1856. In June 1856 he made substantial revisions in the last dramas of *Der Ring des Nibelungen*, changing their titles to *Siegfried* and *Götterdämmerung*. Throughout these years he was preoccupied with writing a new opera, *Tristan und Isolde*, permeated with the dual feelings of love and death. In April 1857 he prepared the first sketch of *Parzival* (later titled *Parsifal*). In 1858 he moved to Venice, where he completed the full score of the second act of *Tristan und Isolde*. The Dresden authorities, acting through their

Austrian confederates and still determined to bring Wagner to trial as a revolutionary, pressured Venice to expel him from its territory. Once more Wagner took refuge in Switzerland. He decided to stay in Lucerne, where he completed the score of *Tristan und Isolde* in 1859.

In Sept. 1859 he moved to Paris, where Minna joined him. In 1860 he conducted three concerts of his music at the Théâtre-Italien. Napoleon III became interested in his work, and in 1860 ordered the director of the Paris Opéra to produce Wagner's opera *Tannhäuser*; after considerable work, revisions, and translation into French, it was given at the Opéra in 1861. It proved to be a fiasco, and Wagner withdrew the opera after three performances. For some reason the Jockey Club of Paris led a vehement protest against him; the critics also joined in this opposition, mainly because the French audiences were not accustomed to the mystically romantic, heavily Germanic operatic music.

Politically, Wagner's prospects began to improve; on July 22, 1860, he was informed of a partial amnesty by the Saxon authorities. In Aug. 1860 he visited Baden-Baden, in his first visit to Germany in 11 years. Finally, in March 1862, he was granted a total amnesty, which allowed him access to Saxony. Minna, after a brief period of reconciliation with Wagner, left him, settling in Dresden, where she died in 1866. In order to repair his financial situation, he accepted a number of concert appearances, traveling as an orchestra conductor to Vienna, Prague, St. Petersburg, Moscow, and other cities (1862–1863).

Wagner's fortunes changed spectacularly in 1864 when young King Ludwig II of Bavaria ascended the throne and invited him to Munich with the promise of unlimited help in carrying out his various projects. Still, difficulties soon developed when the Bavarian Cabinet told Ludwig that his lavish support of Wagner's projects threatened the Bavarian economy. Ludwig was forced to advise him to leave Munich. Wagner took this advice as an order, and late in 1865 he went to Switzerland. A very serious difficulty arose also in Wagner's emotional life, when he became intimately involved with Liszt's daughter Cosima, wife of Hans von Bülow, the famous conductor and an impassioned proponent of Wagner's music. On April 10, 1865, Cosima Bülow gave birth to Wagner's daughter, whom he named Isolde after the heroine of his opera that Bülow was preparing for performance in Munich. Its premiere took place with great acclaim two months after the birth of Isolde, with Bülow conducting. During the summer of 1865 he prepared the prose sketch of *Parzival*, and began to dictate his autobiography, *Mein Leben*, to Cosima. In Jan. 1866 he resumed the composition of *Die Meistersinger*; he settled in a villa in Tribschen, on Lake Lucerne, where Cosima joined him permanently in Nov. 1868. He completed the full score of *Die Meistersinger* in 1867. In 1868, Bülow conducted its premiere in Munich in the presence of King Ludwig, who sat in the royal box with Wagner; a year later *Das Rheingold* was produced, followed in the next year by *Die Walküre*. On July 18, 1870, Cosima and Bülow were divorced, and on Aug. 25, Wagner and Cosima were married in Lucerne.

In 1871, while in Leipzig, Wagner made public his plans for realizing his cherished dream of building his own theater in Bayreuth for the production of the entire cycle of *Der Ring des Nibelungen*. In December the Bayreuth town council offered him a site for a proposed Festspielhaus, and on May 22, 1872, the cornerstone was laid; Wagner commemorated the event by conducting a performance of **Beethoven**'s Ninth Symphony (this was his 59th birthday). In 1873 Wagner began to build his own home in Bayreuth, which he called "Wahnfried," i.e., "Free from Delusion." In order to complete the building of the Festspielhaus, he appealed to King Ludwig for additional funds. Ludwig gave him 100,000 talers for this purpose. Now the dream of Wagner's life was realized. Between June and Aug. 1876 *Der Ring des Nibelungen* went through three rehearsals. The official premiere of the cycle took place on Aug. 13, 14, 16, and 17, 1876, under the direction of Hans Richter. In all, three complete productions of the *Ring* cycle were given between Aug. 13 and 30.

The spectacles in Bayreuth attracted music-lovers and notables from all over the world. Even those who were not partial to Wagner's ideas or appreciative of his music went to Bayreuth out of curiosity. **Tchaikovsky** was one such skeptical visitor. Despite world success and fame, Wagner still labored under financial difficulties. He completed the full score of *Parsifal* (as it was now called) in 1882, in Palermo; it was performed for the first time at the Bayreuth Festival on July 26, followed by 15 subsequent performances. At the final performance, Wagner stepped to the podium in the last act and conducted the work to its close; this was his last appearance as a conductor. Early in the afternoon of Feb. 13, 1883, he suffered a massive heart attack, and died in Cosima's presence. His body was interred in a vault in the garden of his Wahnfried villa in Bayreuth.

Wagner's role in music history is immense. Not only did he create works of great beauty and tremendous brilliance, but he generated an entirely new concept of the art of music, exercising an influence on generations of composers all over the globe. **Richard Strauss** extended Wagner's grandiose vision to symphonic music, fashioning the form of a tone poem that uses leading motifs and vivid programmatic description of the scenes portrayed in his music. Even **Rimsky-Korsakov**, far as he stood from Wagner's ideas of musical composition, reflected the spirit of *Parsifal* in his own religious opera, *The Legend of the City of Kitezh*. **Schoenberg**'s first significant work, *Verklärte Nacht*, is Wagnerian in its color. Wagner's reform of opera was incomparably more far-reaching in aim, import, and effect than that of **Gluck**, whose main purpose was to counteract the arbitrary predominance of the singers; this goal Wagner accomplished through insistence upon the dramatic truth of his music. When he rejected traditional opera, he did so in the conviction that such an artificial form could not serve as a basis for true dramatic expression. In its place he gave the world a new form and new techniques. So revolutionary was Wagner's art that conductors and singers had to undergo special training in the new style of interpretation in order to perform his works. Thus he became the founder of interpretative conducting and of a new school of dramatic singing.

In his many essays and declarations Wagner condemns the illogical plan of Italian opera and French grand opera. The new artwork creates its own artistic form; continuous thematic development of basic motifs becomes a fundamental procedure for the logical cohesion of the drama. These highly individualized generating motifs, appearing singly, in bold relief, or subtly varied and intertwined with other motifs, present the ever-changing soul states of the characters of the drama, and form the connecting links for the dramatic situations of the total artwork, in a form of musical declamation that Wagner described as "Sprechsingen." Characters in Wagner's stage works become themselves symbols of such soul states, so that even mythical gods, magic- workers, heroic horses, and speaking birds become expressions of eternal verities, illuminating the human behavior. It is for this reason that Wagner selected in most of his operas figures that reflect philosophical ideas. Yet, this very solemnity of Wagner's great images on the stage bore the seeds of their own destruction in a world governed by different esthetic principles. Thus it came to pass that the Wagnerian domination of the musical stage suddenly lost its power with changes in human society and esthetic codes. Spectators and listeners were no longer interested in solving artistic puzzles on the stage. A demand for human simplicity arose against Wagnerian heroic complexity. The public at large found greater enjoyment in the realistic nonsense of **Verdi**'s romantic operas than in the unreality of symbolic truth in Wagner's operas. By the second quarter of the 20th century, few if any composers tried to imitate Wagner; all at once his grandeur and animation became an unnatural and asphyxiating constraint.

In the domain of melody, harmony, and orchestration, Wagner's art was as revolutionary as was his total artwork on the stage. He introduced the idea of an endless melody, a continuous flow of diatonic and chromatic tones; the tonality became fluid and uncertain, producing an impression of unattainability, so that the listener accustomed to Classical modulatory schemes could not easily feel the direction toward the tonic. The Prelude to *Tristan und Isolde* is a classic example of such fluidity of harmonic elements. The use of long unresolved dominant ninth chords and the dramatic tremolos of diminished seventh chords contributed to this state of musical uncertainty, which disturbed the critics and the audiences alike. But Wagnerian harmony also became the foundation of the new method of composition that adopted a free flow of modulatory progressions. Without Wagner the chromatic idioms of the 20th century could not exist. In orchestration, too, Wagner introduced great innovations. He created new instruments, and he increased his demands on the virtuosity of individual orchestra players. The vertiginous flight of the bassoon to the high E in the Overture to *Tannhäuser* could not have been attempted before the advent of Wagner.

WEBER, CARL MARIA (FRIEDRICH ERNST) VON, celebrated German composer, pianist, and conductor; b. Eutin, Oldenburg, Nov. 18, 1786; d. London, June 5, 1826. His father, Franz Anton, led a wandering life as music director of his own theater company, taking his family with him on his tours. Although this mode of life interfered with his son's regular education, it gave him practical knowledge of the stage, and stimulated his imagination as a dramatic composer. At the age of 12, he wrote an opera, *Die Macht der Liebe und des Weins*; it was never performed and the manuscript has not survived. He composed a two-act comic opera, *Das Waldmädchen*, in 1800. It was premiered in Freiberg six days after his 14th birthday; performances followed in Chemnitz and Vienna (1804). He gave a concert in Hamburg in 1802, and the family then proceeded to Augsburg; they remained there from Dec. 1802 until settling in Vienna in Sept. 1803. Weber continued his studies there with Abbé Vogler, at whose recommendation he secured the post of conductor of the Breslau Opera in 1804. He resigned this post in 1806 after his attempts at operatic reform caused dissension. In 1806 he became honorary Intendant to Duke Eugen of Württemberg-Öls in Upper Silesia; much of his time was devoted to composition there. In 1807 he was engaged as private secretary to Duke Ludwig in Stuttgart, and also gave music lessons to his children. He then went to Mannheim, where he made appearances as a pianist. He next went to Darmstadt, where he rejoined his former teacher, Vogler.

In 1810, Weber's opera *Silvana* was successfully premiered in Frankfurt. The title role was sung by Caroline Brandt, who later became a member of the Prague Opera; Weber and Brandt were married in Prague in 1817. Weber left Darmstadt in 1811 for Munich, where he composed several important orchestral works, including the Clarinet Concertino, the two clarinet concertos, and the Bassoon Concerto. Weber's one-act singspiel, *Abu Hassan*, was also successfully given in Munich. Upon his return to Prague in 1813, he was informed that he was to be the director of the German Opera there. During his tenure, Weber presented a distinguished repertoire, which included Beethoven's *Fidelio*; however, when his reforms encountered determined opposition, he submitted his resignation (1816).

On Dec. 14, 1816, he was appointed Musikdirektor of the German Opera in Dresden by King Friedrich August III. He opened his first season on Jan. 30, 1817; that same year he was named Königlich Kapellmeister, and began to make sweeping reforms. About this time he approached Friedrich Kind, a Dresden lawyer and writer, and suggested to him the idea of preparing a libretto on a Romantic German subject for his next opera. They agreed on *Der*

Freischütz, a fairy tale from the *Gespensterbuch*, a collection of ghost stories. The composition of this work, which was to prove his masterpiece, occupied him for three years; the score was completed in 1820. Two weeks later Weber began work on the incidental music to Wolff's *Preciosa*, a play in four acts with spoken dialogue; it was produced in Berlin on March 14, 1821. After some revisions, *Der Freischütz* was accepted for performance at the opening of Berlin's Neues Schauspielhaus; Weber conducted its triumphant premiere on June 18, 1821. Its success surpassed all expectations and the cause of new Romantic art was won; *Der Freischütz* was soon staged by all the major opera houses of Europe.

Weber's next opera was *Euryanthe*, produced in Vienna in 1823, with only moderate success. Meanwhile, Weber's health was affected by incipient tuberculosis and he was compelled to spend part of 1824 in Marienbad for a cure. He recovered sufficiently to begin the composition of *Oberon*, a commission from London's Covent Garden. Once more illness interrupted Weber's progress on his work; he spent part of the summer of 1825 in Ems to prepare himself for the journey to England. He set out for London in Feb. 1826, a dying man. Weber threw himself into his work, presiding over 16 rehearsals for *Oberon*. On April 12, 1826, he conducted its premiere at Covent Garden, obtaining a tremendous success. Despite his greatly weakened condition, he conducted 11 more performances of the score, and also participated in various London concerts, playing for the last time a week before his death. He was found dead in his room on the morning of June 5, 1826.

Weber's role in music history is epoch-making; in his operas, particularly in *Der Freischütz*, he opened the era of musical Romanticism, in decisive opposition to the established Italianate style. The highly dramatic and poetic portrayal of a German fairy tale, with its aura of supernatural mystery, appealed to the public, whose imagination had been stirred by the emergent Romantic literature of the period. Weber's melodic genius and mastery of the craft of composition made it possible for him to break with tradition and to start on a new path, at a critical time when individualism and nationalism began to emerge as sources of creative artistry. His instrumental works, too, possessed a new quality that signalized the transition from Classical to Romantic music. For piano he wrote pieces of extraordinary brilliance, introducing some novel elements in chord writing and passage work. He was himself an excellent pianist; his large hands gave him an unusual command of the keyboard (he could stretch the interval of a twelfth). Weber's influence on the development of German music was very great. The evolutionary link to **Wagner**'s music drama is evident in the coloring of the orchestral parts in Weber's operas and in the adumbration of the principle of leading motifs. Finally, he was one of the first outstanding interpretative conductors.

WEBERN, ANTON (FRIEDRICH WILHELM) VON, remarkable Austrian composer; b. Vienna, Dec. 3, 1883; d. Mittersill, Sept. 15, 1945. He received his first instruction in music from his mother, an amateur pianist; then studied piano, cello, and theory in Klagenfurt, and also played cello in the orchestra there. In 1902 he entered the University of Vienna, where he studied harmony and counterpoint, and also attended classes in musicology. He received his Ph.D. in 1906. In 1904 he began private studies in composition with **Arnold Schoenberg**, whose ardent disciple he became; **Alban Berg** also studied with Schoenberg. Together, Schoenberg, Berg, and Webern laid the foundations of what became known as the Second Viennese School of composition. The unifying element was the adoption of Schoenberg's method of composition with 12 tones related only to one another. Malevolent opponents referred to Schoenberg, Berg, and Webern as a Vienna Trinity, with Schoenberg as God the Father, Berg as God the Son, and Webern as the Holy Ghost; the last appellation was supposed to describe the phantomlike substance of some of Webern's works.

From 1908 to 1914 Webern was active as a conductor in Vienna and in Germany; in 1915–1916 he served in the army; in 1917–18, he was conductor at the Deutsches Theater in Prague. In 1918 he settled in Mödling, near Vienna, where he taught composition privately; from 1918 to 1922 he supervised the programs of the Society for Private Musical Performances, organized in Vienna by Schoenberg with the intention of promoting modern music without being exposed to reactionary opposition (music critics were not admitted to these performances). Webern was conductor of the Schubertbund (1921–1922) and the Mödling Male Chorus (1921–1926); he also led the Vienna Workers' Symphony concerts (1922–1934) and the

Vienna Workers' Chorus (1923–1934), both sponsored by the Social Democratic Party. From 1927 to 1938 he was a conductor on Austrian Radio; furthermore, he conducted guest engagements in Germany, Switzerland, and Spain. From 1929, he made several visits to England, where he was a guest conductor with the BBC Symphony Orchestra. For the most part, however, he devoted himself to composition, private teaching, and lecturing.

After Hitler came to power in Germany in 1933, Webern's music was banned as a manifestation of "cultural Bolshevism" and "degenerate art." His position became more difficult after the Anschluss in 1938, for his works could no longer be published; he eked out an existence by teaching a few private pupils and making piano arrangements of musical scores by others. After his son was killed in an air bombardment of a train in Feb. 1945, he and his wife fled from Vienna to Mittersill, near Salzburg, to stay with his married daughters and grandchildren. His life ended tragically on the evening of Sept. 15, 1945, when he was accidentally shot and killed by an American soldier after stepping outside his son-in-law's residence.

Webern left relatively few works, and most of them are of short duration (the fourth of his five Pieces for Orchestra, op. 10, takes only 19 seconds to play), but in his music he achieves the utmost subtilization of expressive means. He adopted the 12-tone method of composition almost immediately after its definitive formulation by Schoenberg (1924), and extended the principle of nonrepetition of notes to tone colors, so that in some of his works (e.g., Symphony, op. 21) solo instruments are rarely allowed to play two successive thematic notes. Dynamic marks are similarly diversified. Typically, each 12-tone row is divided into symmetric sections of two, four, or six members, which enter mutually into intricate but invariably logical canonic imitations. Inversions and augmentations are inherent features; melodically and harmonically, the intervals of the major seventh and minor ninth are stressed. Single motifs are brief, and stand out as individual particles or lyric ejaculations. The impact of these works on the general public and on the critics was disconcerting, and upon occasion led to violent demonstrations. However, the extraordinary skill and novelty of technique made this music endure beyond the fashions of the times; performances of Webern's works multiplied after his death, and began to influence increasingly larger groups of modern musicians. **Stravinsky** acknowledged the use of

Webern's methods in his latest works, and jazz composers have professed to follow Webern's ideas of tone color.

WEILL, KURT (JULIAN), remarkable German-born American composer; b. Dessau, March 2, 1900; d. New York, April 3, 1950. His first major work, the Symphony No. 1, *Berliner Sinfonie*, was composed in 1921. However, it was not performed in his lifetime; indeed, its manuscript was not recovered until 1955, and it was finally premiered in 1958. Under the impact of new trends in the musical theater, Weill wrote short satirical operas in a sharp modernistic manner: *Der Protagonist* (1924–1925) and *Royal Palace* (1925–1926). There followed a striking "songspiel" (a hybrid term of English and German words), *Mahagonny*, to a libretto by Bertolt Brecht, savagely satirizing the American primacy of money (1927); it was remodeled and was presented as the three-act opera *Aufstieg und Fall der Stadt Mahagonny* (1929). Weill's greatest hit in this genre came with a modernistic version of Gay's *The Beggar's Opera*, to a pungent libretto by Brecht; under the title *Die Dreigroschenoper* (1928), it was staged all over Germany, and was also produced in translation throughout Europe. Marc Blitzstein later made a new libretto for the opera, versified in a modern American style, which was produced as *The Threepenny Opera*, the exact translation of the German title. Its hit number, "Mack the Knife," became tremendously successful.

After the Nazi ascent to power in Germany, Weill and his wife, the actress and singer Lotte Lenya, who appeared in many of his musical plays, went to Paris in 1934. They settled in the U.S. in 1935; Weill became a naturalized American citizen in 1943. Quickly absorbing the modes and fashions of American popular music, he recreated, with astonishing facility, and felicity, the typical form and content of American musicals; this stylistic transition was facilitated by the fact that in his European productions he had already absorbed elements of American popular songs and jazz rhythms. His highly developed assimilative faculty enabled him to combine this Americanized idiom with the advanced techniques of modern music (atonality, polytonality, polyrhythms) and present the product in a pleasing, and yet sophisticated and challenging, manner. But for all his success in American-produced scores, the great majority of his European works remained to be produced in America only posthumously.

XENAKIS, IANNIS, eminent Greek-born French composer and music theorist; b. Braila, Romania (of Greek parents), May 29, 1922. At the age of 10 he was taken by his family to Greece, where he began to study engineering, but he became involved in the Greek resistance movement against the Nazi occupation forces. He was wounded in a skirmish in 1945, and lost sight in one eye. Shortly after he was captured, but managed to escape to the U.S. In 1947 he went to Paris and later became a naturalized French citizen; he studied architecture with Le Corbusier and became his assistant (1948–1960). During the same period, he took lessons in composition with **Arthur Honegger** and **Darius Milhaud** at the École Normale de Musique in Paris and with **Olivier Messiaen** at the Paris Conservatoire (1950–1953). He aided Le Corbusier in the design of the Philips Pavillion at the 1958 World's Fair in Brussels, where he met **Edgard Varèse**, who was then working on his *Poème électronique* for the exhibit, and received from him some stimulating advice on the creative potentialities of the electronic medium.

During his entire career, Xenakis strove to connect mathematical concepts with the organization of a musical composition, using the theory of sets, symbolic logic, and probabilistic calculus. He promulgated the stochastic method, which is teleologically directed and deterministic, as distinct from a purely aleatory handling of data. He was founder and director of the Centre d'Études Mathématiques et Automatiques Musicales in Paris in 1966, and founder and director of the Center for Mathematical and Automated Music at Indiana

University in the U.S., where he served on the faculty from 1967 to 1972. His influence on the development of advanced composition in Europe and America is considerable. Several composers adopted his theories and imitated the scientific-sounding titles of some of his compositions. Xenakis uses Greek words for the titles of virtually all of his works to stress the philosophical derivation of modern science and modern arts from classical Greek concepts; in some cases he uses computer symbols for titles.

ZAPPA, FRANK (FRANCIS VINCENT), seeded American rock artist; b. Baltimore, Dec. 21, 1940, of Italian descent (Zappa means "hoe" in Italian); d. Los Angeles, California, Dec. 4, 1993. Early in Zappa's life, the family moved to California. From his school days he played guitar and organized groups with weird names such as The Omens and Captain Glasspack and His Magic Mufflers. In 1960 he composed the sound track for the film *The World's Greatest Sinner*, and in 1963 he wrote another sound track, *Run Home Slow*. In 1965 he joined the rhythm-and-blues band The Soul Giants; he soon took it under his own aegis and thought up for it the surrealist logo The Mothers of Invention. Their self-named debut album and their second record, *Freak Out!*, became underground hits; along with *We're Only in It for the Money* and *Cruising with Ruben and The Jets*, these works constituted the earliest "concept" albums, touching every nerve in a gradually decivilized California life-style—rebellious, anarchistic, incomprehensible, and yet tantalizing. The band became a mixed-media celebration of total artistic, political, and social opposition to the Establishment, the ingredients of their final album, *Mothermania*.

Moving farther afield, Zappa produced a video-movie, *200 Motels*, glorifying itinerant sex activities. He became a cult figure, and as such suffered the penalty of violent adulation. Playing in London in 1971, he was painfully injured when a besotted fan pushed him off the stage. Similar assaults forced Zappa to hire an athletic bodyguard for protection. In 1982 his planned appearance in Palermo, Sicily, the birthplace of his parents, had to be cancelled because the mob rioted in anticipation of the event. He deliberately confronted the most cherished social and emotional sentiments by writing such songs as "Broken Hearts Are for Assholes." His release "Jewish Princess" offended, mistakenly, the sensitivity of American Jews; he managed to upset the members of his own faith in the number titled "Catholic Girls." His production *Joe's Garage* contained Zappa's favorite scatological materials, and he went on analyzing and ridiculing urinary functions in such numbers as "Why Does It Hurt When I Pee?" His *Hot Rats*, a jazz-rock release, included the famous "Willie the Pimp," and exploited the natural revulsion to unclean animals. In 1980 he produced the film *Baby Snakes*, which shocked even the most impervious senses.

He declared in an interview that classical music is only "for old ladies and faggots." But he astounded the musical community when he proclaimed his total adoration of the music of **Edgard Varèse** and gave a lecture on Varèse in New York. Somehow, without formal study, he managed to absorb the essence of Varèse's difficult music. This process led Zappa to produce truly astonishing full orchestral scores reveling in artful dissonant counterpoint, *Bob in Dacron and Sad Jane* and *Mo' 'n Herb's Vacation*, and the cataclysmic *Penis Dimension* for chorus, soloists, and orchestra, with a text so anatomically precise that it could not be performed for any English-speaking audience. True to his ecclectic tastes, he also revived the Baroque compositions of a forgotten 18th-century Italian composer who happened to be named Francesco Zappa. Late in his career, Zappa composed complex compositions for synthesizer. He died of prostate cancer in 1993.

About the Authors

The following biographies are abbreviated from those that appear in *Baker's Biographical Dictionary of Music, 8th Edition*.

Baker, Theodore, American writer on music, and the compiler of the original edition of the present dictionary bearing his name; b. New York, June 3, 1851; d. Dresden, Oct. 13, 1934. As a young man, he was trained for business pursuits. In 1874 he decided to devote himself to musical studies. He went to Leipzig, where he took courses with Oskar Paul; he received his Ph.D. there in 1882 for his dissertation, the first serious study of Native American music. He lived in Germany until 1890; then returned to the U.S., and became literary editor and translator for the publishing house of G. Schirmer, Inc. (1892); he retired in 1926 and returned to Germany. In 1895, he published *A Dictionary of Musical Terms*, which went through more than 25 printings and sold over a million copies; another valuable work was *A Pronouncing Pocket Manual of Musical Terms* (1905), still in print in its fifth edition. He also issued *The Musician's Calendar and*

Birthday Book (1915–17). In 1900, G. Schirmer, Inc., published *Baker's Biographical Dictionary of Musicians,* which became Baker's imperishable monument. The original edition was a landmark work for representing American as well as European musicians; the book remains in print in its most recent revision by master musicologist **Nicolas Slonimsky**.

Slonimsky, Nicolas (actually, **Nikolai Leonidovich**), legendary Russian-born American musicologist of manifold endeavors; b. St. Petersburg, April 27, 1894. A self-described failed wunderkind, he was given his first piano lesson by his illustrious maternal aunt Isabelle Vengerova. He enrolled in the St. Petersburg Conservatory and studied harmony and orchestration with two pupils of **Rimsky-Korsakov**. After the Revolution he made his way south; he was a rehearsal pianist at the Kiev Opera, where he took some composition lessons, and then was in Yalta where he earned his living as a piano accompanist to displaced Russian singers, and as an instructor at a dilapidated Yalta conservatory. He thence proceeded to Turkey, Bulgaria, and Paris, where he became secretary and piano-pounder to Serge Koussevitzky. In 1923 he went to the U.S., becoming coach in the opera department of the Eastman School of Music in Rochester, New York, where he took an opportunity to study some more composition and conducting. In 1925, he was again with Koussevitzky in Paris and Boston, but was fired for insubordination in 1927. He learned to speak polysyllabic English and began writing music articles for the *Boston Evening Transcript* and the *Christian Science Monitor,* and ran a monthly column of musical anecdotes of questionable authenticity in *Étude* magazine. In 1927 he organized the Chamber Orchestra of Boston with the purpose of presenting modern works; with it he gave first performances of works by **Charles Ives, Edgar Varèse, Henry Cowell,** and others. He became a naturalized U.S. citizen in 1931. In 1931–32 he conducted special concerts of modern American, Cuban, and Mexican music in Paris, Berlin, and Budapest under the auspices of the Pan-American Association of Composers, producing a ripple of excitement. He repeated these programs at his engagements with the Los Angeles Philharmonic (1932) and at the Hollywood Bowl (1933), which created such consternation that his conducting career came to a jarring halt. From 1945 to 1947 he was, by accident (the head of the department had died of a heart attack), lecturer in Slavonic languages and literatures at Harvard University. In 1962–63 he traveled in Russia, Poland, Yugoslavia, Bulgaria, Romania, Greece, and Israel under the auspices of the Office of Cultural Exchange at the U.S. State Department, as lecturer in native Russian, ersatz Polish, synthetic Serbo-Croatian, Russianized Bulgarian, Latinized Romanian, archaic Greek, passable French, and tolerable German. Returning from his multinational travels, he taught variegated musical subjects at the University of California, Los Angeles; and was irretrievably retired after a triennial service (1964–67), ostensibly owing to irreversible obsolescence and recessive infantiloquy. But, disdaining the inexorable statistics of the actuarial tables, he continued to agitate and gave long-winded lecture-recitals in institutions of dubious learning.

As a composer, he cultivated miniature forms, usually with a gimmick, e.g., *Studies in Black and White* for piano (1928) in "mutually exclusive consonant counterpoint," a song cycle, *Gravestones*, to texts from tombstones in an old cemetery in Hancock, New Hampshire (1945), and *Minitudes*, a collection of 50 quaquaversal piano pieces (1971–77). His only decent orchestral work is *My Toy Balloon* (1942), a set of variations on a Brazilian song, which includes in the score 100 colored balloons to be exploded multi-fortissimo at the climax. He also conjured up a *Möbius Strip-Tease*, a perpetual vocal canon notated on a Möbius band to be revolved around the singer's head. A priority must be conceded to him for writing the earliest singing commercials to authentic texts from the *Saturday Evening Post* advertisements, among them *Make This a Day of Pepsodent, No More Shiny Nose*, and *Children Cry for Castoria* (1925).

More "scholarly," though no less defiant of academic conventions, is his *Thesaurus of Scales and Melodic Patterns* (1947), an inventory of all conceivable and inconceivable tonal combinations, culminating in a mind-boggling "Grandmother Chord" containing 12 different tones and 11 different intervals. Beset by a chronic itch for novelty, he coined the term "pandiatonicism" (1937), which *mirabile dictu*, took root. In his quest for trivial but not readily accessible information, he blundered into the muddy field of musical lexicography, publishing *Music Since 1900*, a chronology of musical events, which actually contains some beguiling serendipities (New York, 1937; 5th ed., 1994); took over the vacated editorship (because of the predecessor's sudden death during sleep) of Thompson's *International Cyclopedia of Music and Musicians* (4th to 8th editions, 1946–58); and accepted the editorship of the 5th to 8th editions of the prestigious *Baker's Biographical Dictionary of Musicians* (1958–1991). He also abridged this venerable volume into *The Concise Baker's Biographical Dictionary of Musicians* (1988, 1993). In 1978 he mobilized his powers of retrospection in preparing an autobiography, *Perfect Pitch* (1988), which was followed by his *Lectionary of Music*, a compendium of articles on music. His other works include *Lexicon of Musical Invective*, a random collection of pejorative reviews of musical masterpieces (1952); numerous articles for encyclopedias; also a learned paper, *Sex and the Music Librarian*, valuable for its painstaking research. *Nicolas Slonimsky: The First Hundred Years* (1994), is Richard Kostelanetz's anniversary celebration of his writings.

About the Editor

Kostelanetz, Richard, versatile American music critic, writer on contemporary music and the arts, and composer, nephew of André Kostelanetz; b. New York, May 14, 1940. He studied American civilization and history at Brown University (A.B., 1962) and Columbia University (M.A., 1966), and was a Fulbright scholar at King's College, University of London (1964–65), and also attended classes at London's Morely College and The New School in New York. His extensive list of publications includes articles, books, poetry, fiction, plays, and experimental prose; among his numerous anthologies on contemporary American arts are several with emphasis on music. Included in his compositional output are audiotapes and videotapes as well as a number of films and holograms, many of which have been exhibited and broadcast around the world. He has written numerous theatrical performance texts (*Epiphanies*, 1980), composers' libretti (*Central Park*, 1980), and also has composed choreographic works. He has prepared extended features for radio, and his visual art has appeared in both solo and group exhibitions. Among his awards are a Pulitzer fellowship for critical writing (1965), a Guggenheim fellowship (1967), and annual ASCAP stipends (from 1983). His compositions included audiocassette editions and horspiels, many of which were commissioned by the West German Radio. He has also produced videotapes, for which he customarily provides the visuals. He describes his critical writings and his art as both "avant-garde" and "anarchist libertarian."

INDEX OF PROPER NAMES